THE DEBRIS OF HAM

Ethnicity, Regionalism,
and the 1994 Rwandan Genocide

L   xford

Copyright © 2003 by
University Press of America,® Inc.
4501 Forbes Boulevard
Suite 200
Lanham, Maryland 20706
UPA Acquisitions Department (301) 459-3366

PO Box 317
Oxford
OX2 9RU, UK

ISBN 0-7618-2585-1 (paperback : alk. ppr.)

In memory of my father, Louis Mudugu,
1914-1994

Map of Rwanda

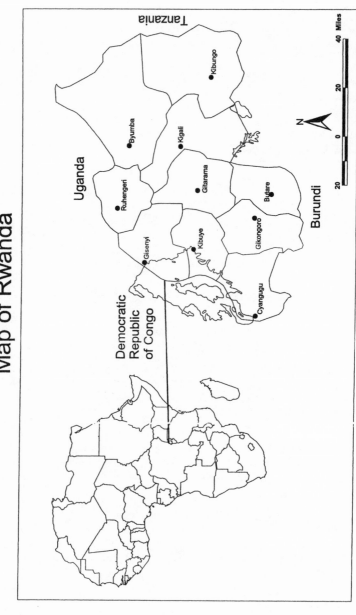

Contents

List of Abbreviations

CDR   Coalition pour la Défense de la République (Coalition for the Defense of the Republic): an extremist Hutu party with strong following in Gisenyi and Ruhengeri. It organized, with the MRNDD, the 1994 genocide.

FRODEBU   Front pour la Démocratie au Burundi (Front for Democracy in Burundi)

MDR   Mouvement Démocratique Républicain (Democratic Republican Movement): main opposition party in Rwanda, 1991-1994.

MRND(D)   Mouvement Révolutionnaire National pour le Développement (et la Démocratie) : Habyarimana's single party founded in 1975, revamped in 1991 by the addition of a second D standing for "Démocratie." While it was implanted in the whole country, it was strongest in the northern prefectures. It organized, with the CDR, the 1994 genocide.

PDC   Parti Démocrate Chrétien (Christian Democratic Party) : a small opposition party.

PDI   Parti Démocrate Islamique (Islamic Democratic Party): a party that represented the small Muslim community in Rwanda.

PL   Parti Libéral (Liberal Party): the third largest opposition party. It probably had more Tutsi members than any other opposition party. It was dubbed the party of the Tutsi by the extremist Hutu ideologues and was often accused of close collaboration with the Rwandan Patriotic Front.

PSD   Parti Social Démocrate (Social Democratic Party): the second largest opposition party, with strong following in the south (Kigali city, Butare, Gikongoro, and parts of Kibuye, Kibungo, Gitarama, and Cyangugu).

RPF   Rwandan Patriotic Front: a guerilla force formed in Uganda by Rwandan refugees in the late 1980s. It invaded Rwanda on October 1, 1990.

RTLM   Radio Télévision Libre des Mille Collines: a "private" radio station set up by MRND and CDR ideologues as the voice of Hutu extremism. It was instrumental in the anti-Tutsi propaganda and in the implementation of the genocide.

UNAMIR   United Nations Assistance Mission to Rwanda: the UN military force that was supposed to help with the implementation of the August 1993 Arusha Power-sharing Agreement but later watched the genocide unfold without being given neither the authority nor the manpower to stop it.

Preface and Acknowledgments

> Silence is the only adequate response, but the pressure of the
> scream persists.
> —Terence Des Pres, *The Survivor: An Anatomy of Life in the
> Death Camps*.

Genocide epitomizes extreme evil, the most heinous of all crimes against humanity because it negates the very idea of our human essence. Thus is it not surprising that, at first glance, the terror, brutality, and annihilation that accompany it defy human understanding and induce silence. Yet the history of humanity, particularly in the twentieth century, has taught us that, as unleashed by the Turks on the Armenians in 1915, the Nazis on the Jews in 1933-1945, the Tutsi government of Burundi on Hutu (especially the educated) in 1972, Pol Pot and the Kmers Rouges on Cambodians in the 1970s, and the extremist Hutu on the Tutsi and moderate Hutu of Rwanda in 1994, evil involves rational, calculated (not necessarily pathological) processes that can be explained, though not fully understood. Explaining these processes defeats silence and gives voice to the dead.

Since 1994, dozens of books and reports have been published about the Rwandan genocide, trying to explain the historical, political, and anthropological dimensions of the ultimate evil that we call "genocide." Among the magisterial ones are *Rwanda: Death, Despair and Defiance* (African Rights report, 1995); Gérard Prunier's *The Rwanda Crisis: History of a Genocide* (Columbia University Press, 1995); Philip Gourevitch's *We Wish to Inform You that Tomorrow We Will Be Killed with our Families. Stories from Rwanda* (Farrar Strauss and Giroux, 1998); *Leave None to Tell the Story: Genocide in Rwanda* (written by Alison Des Forges for Human Rights Watch and Fédération Internationale des Droits de l'Homme) (Human Rights Watch, 1999); Filip Reyntjens' *Rwanda: Trois jours qui ont fait basculer l'histoire;* and Jean-Pierre Chrétien at al.'s *Rwanda: les médias du génocide (Rwanda: Media of Genocide)* (Paris: Editions Karthala, 1995) (a study of the role played by the extremist media before and during the genocide).

Probably because of the predominance of ethnic strife in international affairs since 1945, in Rwanda and Burundi in particular, books written about the Rwandan genocide have focused almost exclusively on ethnicity at the expense of other factors. My book argues that while ethnic ideology provided the materials for the relentless propaganda against the Tutsi and the Hutu of the political opposition in 1990-1994, in a parallel but more powerful mode, regional politics provided the sine qua non that made the 1994 Rwandan genocide possible. Failure to account fully for the interaction between the two forces has only yielded partial explanations of the Tutsi genocide and the murder of thousands of Hutu politicians, professionals, and ordinary men who opposed it. This book investigates the dreadful juxtaposition of ethnicity and regionalism in Rwandan politics in the unfolding of the worst mass murder of the end of the twentieth century. While there is little doubt about the centrality of the anti-Tutsi ideology in the worldview of the two Republics (1961-1973 and 1973-1994) and of those who planned the 1994 genocide, ethnic extremism was only a necessary (not a sufficient) condition for mass murder. The leaders of the two republics consistently defined the Tutsi, at least in practices, as the enemy of the Republic, but the Second Republic developed an obsession with ethnic purity with the myth of the "Hutu pur et dur" (unsullied and rough Hutu) that necessarily made the Hutu of the south suspicious in the eyes of those from Gisenyi and Ruhengeri. If Rwanda was a Hutu nation, then it followed that the unsullied and rough Hutu were the rightful owners of the Republic and were thus entitled to disproportionate access to national resources. For competition reasons, checking on the Tutsi and the Hutu of the south (especially the outspoken ones) became a leitmotif in Rwandan politics since 1973. From 1990 to 1994, it was the calculation to keep power in the hands of the political and military elite of Gisenyi and Ruhengeri that created the manifold dynamics necessary and sufficient for genocide.

A native of Rwanda, where I lived for 29 years, I bring to the discussion knowledge of the subtlety of the Rwandan and African cultures. The vast majority of scholars who have written about the 1994 genocide are European and American. Positioning myself as a critical witness of history, I add a native voice to the scholarship on the Rwandan genocide. My knowledge of Kinyarwanda (the mother tongue of Rwandans) and French (a language I have used since the age of 8) has also allowed me to exploit ideas and documents that European and American scholars did not explore because of linguistic barriers. In 1991/1992, I was a member of ADL (Association Rwandaise pour la Défense des Droits de la Personne et des Libertés Publiques) (Rwandan Association for the Defense of Human Rights and Public Freedom), a human rights organization that monitored human rights violations by the Rwandan government since 1991. In this capacity, I had access to first hand reports of events discussed in Chapter Four. On the political side, I was a founding member of the Social Democratic Party (PSD) on June 30 and July 1, 1991. On that occasion I served on the committee in charge of the statutes of the party. The initial text, like the initial texts of the other major opposition parties, repeatedly justified the launching of the party by the urgency to put an end to what they characterized as the hegemony of one region--Gisenyi and Ruhengeri.

After I moved to the United States in July 1992, I continued to follow closely the events unfolding in Rwanda, especially in the domain of human rights. Also, it was with a sense of urgency that I felt compelled to dramatize what I had witnessed in Rwanda between 1990 and 1992 in a novel titled *Manifold Annihilation* (Rivercross: New York and Orlando, 1996). Even though the novel was published in 1996, I had finished writing it in August 1993. The title was inspired by a verse from *The Book of Urizen* by William Blake, but I was actually thinking about what I had experienced, seen, and heard in the northern part of Rwanda between October 1990 and July 1992. Having lived in Ruhengeri between 1981 and 1992, I had acquired a good understanding of northern ethnic and regional sensitivities. By July 1992, the drawing of lists of people to kill, the definition of the enemy, the techniques of rounding up victims (using hunting vocabulary and techniques, among other strategies), the manipulation of the masses, and the metaphors of the 1994 genocide--for example, *gukora* (to work), *umuganda* (community work), *guhiga* and *gutangatanga* (to hunt and to circle)--had already been experimented with in Ruhengeri and Gisenyi.

Acknowledgments

I would like to thank the people and organizations that made possible the writing of this book. Special consideration goes to the National Endowment for the Humanities for funding the NEH Summer Institute on "History, Memory, and Dictatorship: The Legacy of World War II in France, Germany, and Italy" (Paris and Caen, France, June 21-July 30, 1999) and to the Institute directors, Professors Joseph Golsan and Nathan Bracher of Texas A & M University, for making me part of a fine and engaging group of college and university professors and scholars. The scholarship on the memory of World War II and the Holocaust equipped me with the critical vocabulary to talk about the 1994 Rwandan genocide and its aftermath and particularly shaped the writing of Chapter Five and the conclusion of this book.

My thanks also go to Irving J. Massey, Professor Emeritus, State University of New York at Buffalo, who introduced me to ethnic studies and published versions of the first and second chapters of this book in *Occasional Papers V and Occasional Papers VI in* 1995 and 1996 respectively. I am grateful to him for allowing me to use expanded versions of the two texts.

Excerpt from NIGHT by Elie Wiesel, translated by Stella Bodway. Copyright © 1960 by MacGibbon & Kee. Copyright renewed © 1988 by The Collins Publishing Group. Reprinted by permission of Hill and Wang, a division of Farrar, Strauss and Giroux, LLC.

I am indebted to Alison Des Forges for useful comments on early versions of Chapters One and Two and for her help with documentation.

I am also grateful for the support of my institution (the State University of New York College at Buffalo, locally more known as Buffalo State College) for funding a few trips to conferences to present parts of my work and granting me a sabbatical leave in the fall of 2001, part of which I used to finish writing this book.

Jenifer Stelmach and Marc Ruppel graciously took on the painstaking task of proofreading the manuscript. I thank them for their professional touch and their attention to details.

My thanks also go to my anonymous informants who witnessed the unfolding of the events of April-July 1994 and were willing to share with me their experiences and views.

Last by not least, I would like to express my appreciation to my family for their encouragement. I hope that one day our children, Leandre and Raissa, will be able to read the book and have some understanding of the darkest period of the history of their native land.

Introduction

From Auschwitz to Rwanda

> We are often asked, as if our past conferred a prophetic ability upon us, whether Auschwitz will return: whether, that is, other slaughters will take place, unilateral, systematic, mechanized, willed, at a governmental level, perpetrated upon innocent and defenseless populations and legitimized by the doctrine of contempt.
> --Primo Levi, *The Drowned and the Saved*

Auschwitz has entered the human collective consciousness as the metaphor of man's inhumanity to man. It encompasses extreme physical and psychological suffering, humiliation, annihilation, darkness, and silence—in short, absolute negation of what it is to be human. As a metaphor, Auschwitz simultaneously expresses and conceals these extremes. Uttering Auschwitz has thus become a safe way for us as contemporary witnesses of history not to say the unspeakable atrocities while naming them. Metaphors have that rhetorical power to condense and silence multiple signifieds, wrapping them and offering them in a semantic box, thus putting a sense of order, coherence, and understanding to an otherwise violent, chaotic, threatening, and incomprehensible universe.

Memory in the form of documentaries, survivors' testimonies, memorials, scholarship, and other vectors unwrap the evil inside the metaphorical box. I remember watching Alain Resnais's *Night and Fog* one afternoon of July 1999 with a group of colleagues from universities around the United States. We were attending a six-week summer institute funded by the National Endowment for the Humanities on the topic of "History, Memory and Dictatorship: The Legacy of World War II in France, Germany and Italy." The screening was taking place in a room at the "Mémorial de Caen" in Normandy, France, on a hot afternoon. We were supposed to discuss the thirty-four minute documentary after the screening, but we all found our way to our apartments, speechless. Some of us had seen the tape more than once before, yet the response was not the inclination to discuss it, but the submission to silence because the words to say, let alone understand, extreme evil were not readily available to this otherwise enthusiastic group.

Ten years after his liberation from the "univers concentrationnaire," Elie Wiesel plunged back into the depths of that inhospitable universe of the total erasure of humanity when he wrote about the first night at Auschwitz:

> Never shall I forget that night, the first night in camp, which has turned my life into one long night, seven times cursed and seven times sealed. Never shall I forget the little faces of the children, whose bodies I saw turned into wreaths of smoke beneath a silent blue sky.
> Never shall I forget those flames which consumed my faith forever.
> Never shall I forget that nocturnal silence which deprived me, for all eternity, to the desire to live. Never shall I forget those moments which murdered my God and my soul and turned my dreams to dust. Never shall I forget these things, even if I am condemned to live as long as God himself. Never.[1]

Night or the absence of light also encompasses evil, death, fire, consumption, fatigue, shame, defeat, transformation, and, above all, silence as the expression of the unspeakable that desensitizes normal psychosomatic and linguistic functions to make extreme evil unspoken.

Beyond the Nazi years, Auschwitz has become a metalepsis, a meta-metaphor, so to speak, that is, a metaphor that hides another. After the Nazi *univers concentrationnaire* and after that "Never Again!" in 1945 emptied of its force by the killing fields of Cambodia in the 1970s and Rwanda in 1994, Auschwitz today, to my mind, signifies beyond its own name, space, and annihilation. Whoever says Auschwitz also invokes Bergen-Belsen, Birkenau, Buchenwald, Dachau, Maidanek, Mauthausen, Ravensbruck, Schwerin, and Treblinka. Beyond the signifying capability of the other names, Auschwitz has come to signify beyond the others, for the others. Because of its uniqueness and the extreme evil involved, it is invested with the power to represent the others on a discursive level. The other genocides are also unique in their own circumstances, but speaking "Auschwitz" makes the uttering of other concentration camps and post-Shoah genocides speakable. Auschwitz is, to play on Roland Barthes' expression "le degré zéro de l'écriture," the degree zero, the rhetorical reference par excellence of any discourse on the Shoah and other genocides that followed it, in different cultural and geo-political contexts

Any academic investigation of mass murder, such as the Shoah or the Tutsi genocide in Rwanda, is doomed to be uncomfortable for several reasons. Wherever it occurs, mass murder is a gruesome moment in the history of humanity and a harrowing story to tell. Because of the gravity of the subject matter, there is fear of trivializing the horror of mass murder in the process of naming and dissecting it. As a Rwandan, trying to understand the Rwandan genocide has been a quest since 1994, as well as a matter of immeasurable embarrassment since the murders were committed by my people on my people. People I knew personally were victims and others killers. Writing about the motivations of the latter is my personal contribution to the memory of their victims and to the defeat of silence and indifference in the face of extreme human tragedy.

When I left Rwanda in July 1992, I was very familiar with the circumstances surrounding the killings of several hundreds of Tutsi in Kibilira in October 1990, the slaughter of the Bagogwe (1991), and the massacres in Bugesera (March 1992) (all discussed in Chapter Four). I knew from my knowledge of the regime in place that the Habyarimana government would continue to kill political opponents, but I would not have imagined the enormity, barbarity, and speed of the mass murder that engulfed Rwanda in April-July 1994. Never would I have imagined that as the world was celebrating the end of Apartheid in South Africa, the fiftieth anniversary of the Allies' invasion of Normandy, and the "Never Again!" promise after the liberation of concentration camps in 1945, there would be another genocide. The international community betrayed the memory of the Holocaust by letting a long-announced genocide exterminate about one million Tutsi and Hutu who opposed it--in a record period of three months. Since 1994, I have had great difficulty rethinking myself into the Rwandan collective consciousness:

Rwanda 1994 has shattered my identity and altered many of the views that had shaped my previous life. The biggest disappointment was the silence and complicity of the ubiquitous and very powerful Catholic Church and other Christian churches. Had the Church used its moral authority to uphold its teachings, the genocide in Rwanda could have failed, no matter how determined the army and the interahamwe militia proved to be. The priests' moral authority was so huge that any opposition to the kind of social engineering that the implementation of genocide demanded would have thwarted it. Instead, the indifference, silence, and participation of religious people in the attacks eroded that moral authority and encouraged, along with other factors (discussed in Chapter Five), the participation of many ordinary citizens and Christians.

It is the duty of human beings to make sense of catastrophes, using the modes and paradigms tested in social sciences, no matter how challenging it is to grasp the magnitude of the Holocaust, the Rwandan genocide, and more recently the terrorist attacks on the World Trade Towers in New York City and the Pentagon in Washington, D.C.--what these mass murders have in common is that the victims were innocent civilians, not real or declared enemies of their killers.

Explanations--and many books and programs have succeeded in doing the explaining--do not necessarily yield understanding, but they defeat silence. Then comes the next duty, the duty to remember, never to forget. Elie Wiesel, a concentration camp survivor and one of the relentless voices that spoke the unspeakable evil of the *univers concentrationnaire*, wrote, "Auschwitz defies imagination and perception; it submits only to memory.... Between the dead and the rest of us there exists an abyss that no talent can understand."[2] Yet, we cannot surrender to the silence of that abyss; we must conquer silence. Any contribution to this endeavor is a welcome addition to the already rich repertoire of scholarship on genocide studies. I want my own book to contribute to this human duty to remember.

Historians and other social scientists probe the motivation of mass murder ideologues, organizers, and executioners, and touch on the suffering of the victims only tangentially. As a result, there is much more understanding of the butchers and little of the victims. In addition, scholarly investigation of mass murder can easily drift into inadequate interpretations and even be the occasion for revisionism and negationism, which, in the case of the Rwandan genocide, has given rise to the claim of a double genocide from Hutu extremists, especially in the Rwandan refugee communities in Africa, Europe, and North America. Given the imperfection and inadequacy that are necessarily associated with explaining extreme evil, we, as scholars, must always approach the subject with a strong sense of humility.

For more than fifty years now, numerous attempts have been made to find the words to say it, to conquer the silence, to speak the unspeakable, to explain evil. Yet the ghost will continue to walk the earth as long as mankind exists. The "ghastly tale" needs retelling over and over again, because the Holocaust and other genocides represent humanity's ultimate agony.[3] This harrowing tale continues today and will continue in the future to call upon the children of the survivors and upon us humans as contemporary witnesses of history to tell it, to interpret it for ourselves and for future generations. Any addition to this attempt to name the ultimate evil is a welcome contribution.

Primo Levi, another survivor of the *univers concentration-naire*, prophetically surmised in *The Drowned and the Saved*:

> Prophets, to our good fortune, we are not, but something can be said. That a similar tragedy, almost ignored in the West, did take place, in Cambodia, in about 1975. That the German slaughter could be set off—and after that feed on itself—out of a desire for servitude and smallness of soul, thanks to the concurrence of a number of factors (the state of war, German technological and organizational perfectionism, Hitler's will and inverted charisma, the lack in Germany of solid democratic roots), not very numerous, each of them indispensable but insufficient if taken singly. These factors can occur again and are already recurring in various parts of the world. The convergence again of all of them within ten or twenty years (there is no sense in speaking of a more remote future) is not very likely but also not impossible. In my opinion, a mass slaughter is particularly unlikely in the Western world, Japan, and also the Soviet Union.... As to what might happen in other parts of the world, or later on, it is prudent to suspend judgment.[4]

Eight years after the publication of Levi's book, it happened again, in Rwanda, and it encumbers upon us to once again make sense of the ultimate evil. The 1994 genocide of Tutsi in Rwanda was indeed the result of a deliberate policy carefully conceived by a regional elite that encouraged hatred, fear, and extermination of a part of the population so as to maintain itself in power. Without being able to pinpoint the exact date of the dreadful decision, I contend that a small group of people from the Gisenyi-Ruhengeri axis, in power since July 5, 1973, created a plan grounded in the flawed Rwandan historiography to set the majority Hutu against the minority Tutsi (and the Hutu who opposed the scheme). As it became increasingly clear that the government army was losing on the battlefield against the invading Rwandan Patriotic Front, a force made up of refugees produced by the same historiography of exclusion, and also that the Hutu solidarity it counted on was not materializing, the group resorted to select and increasing violence and then to genocide. Even though it is difficult to understand, at least in military terms, how they hoped to win the war by concentrating on killing the non-combatant civilian Tutsi and moderate Hutu, it is generally assumed that they hoped that a total campaign of Tutsi extermination would restore Hutu solidarity, which would then win them the war with the external enemy. While thousands of Hutu throughout the country eventually chose to join the killing frenzy because of a careful combination of propaganda repeated over and over for three years in the media, outright hatred of the Tutsi, the violence and pressure of a totalitarian regime, public criticism of those reluctant to kill, unjustified fines, death threats, property destruction, injury, and harassment, fear, terror, opportunism, cowardice, apathy, unquestioning obedience to authority, poverty, and incentives of all kinds, we need to posit a necessary and sufficient condition without which all these elements would not have come into play. That sine qua non was not only an ethnic one, as it is generally assumed, but a careful combination of ethnic and regional politics in Rwanda. One needs only to look at history to grasp the centrality of this proposition. It follows from this thesis that July 5, 1973 occupies a date of paramount importance in understanding the events leading up to and accompanying the genocide. I contend that any explanation of the Rwandan genocide that discusses only its history and the accompanying elements of ethnicity, the 1959 Hutu revolution, the economic crisis of the late 1980s, the October 1990 RPF attack, the emergence of Hutu extreme ideology epitomized by CDR, MRND, and the Hutu Power movement, without positing the existence and necessity of a core group of the Gisenyi-Ruhengeri axis and what the 1973 military coup meant for that reason historically, politically, and economically, cannot possibly fully grasp the development towards genocide in Rwanda.

This book argues that the 1994 Rwandan genocide is a ghastly tale of two forces: one ethnic and the other regional, both grounded in the Hamitic Hypothesis, a flawed and racist myth that the German and Belgian colonial administrations used to make sense of Rwanda and recreate its institutions. The Tutsi elite and later the 1959 Revolution and post-independence Hutu leaders appropriated the debris of that old Biblical myth, the former to justify their European inspired supremacy and the latter to destroy it even as they adopted it as their ideology.

Books written about the Rwandan genocide since 1994 have favored ethnicity in the attempt to explain the mass killings of the Tutsi of Rwanda in April-July 1994. Yet, July 5, 1973, the day when the northerner Major General Juvénal Habyarimana overthrew the civilian government of Grégoire Kayibanda, who was from the central/south prefecture of Gitarama, reversed centuries of Rwandan history in very tremendous ways and concentrated power in the hands of the Gisenyi-Ruhengeri axis, thus adding another explosive element to Rwandan politics: regionalism. The birth of the Second Republic under the banner of a "moral revolution" claimed to defend the 1959 Hutu social Revolution, but it also marked a new historical moment in Rwandan politics. As a matter of fact, for the first time in the existence of Rwanda, northerners became the powerbrokers of a unified Rwanda. The elites from the prefectures of Gisenyi and Ruhengeri, which many Rwandans commonly called the "sacred region" (région sacrée) in the 1970s and 1980s, tacitly juxtaposed Kayibanda's 1960 pronouncement that "Rwanda is a Hutu nation" with their own, "the country is ours" (igihugu ni icacu), an idea carried among other things by a new northern myth of a "Hutu pur and dur" (unsullied and rough Hutu). As a consequence, they were ready to do anything at their disposal to derail any political arrangement that would make them share power with the Tutsi and the southerners, after only two decades of their exercising it. When the Rwandan Patriotic Front attacked from Uganda in October 1990, the Habyarimana government presented the invasion as a threat to the "Hutu nation" as conceived in the 1959 Revolution but rounded up around ten thousand Tutsi and Hutu, mostly from the south. Under internal and international pressure, Habyarimana's former single party opened the door to a power-sharing arrangement with four opposition parties—the MDR, PL, PSD, and PDC, whose memberships drew overwhelmingly from regions other than Gisenyi and Ruhengeri, that is, from the "political" south. More significantly, the protocols of the August 1993 Arusha Agreement with the RPF literally put an end to the hegemony of the Gisenyi-Ruhengeri bloc politically and militarily. The terms of the accords highly favored the RPF and the opposition parties at the expense of the Gisenyi-Ruhengeri axis. Only from this perspective can one better grasp the significance of the unfolding of events from August 1993 to April 1994, when all kinds of tactics (including the use of violence as a political tool) were put in place to prevent the implementation of the accords despite intense domestic and international pressure.

The refusal of, and resistance to, the new political and military arrangement were embodied first in the reformed former single party MRND and more forcefully by the extremist party CDR (Coalition for the Defense of the Republic), in reality the extreme and uncompromising wing of the axis, the military (especially the elite troops), and the extremist media, the journal *Kangura* and the Radio et Télévision Libre des Mille Collines (RTLM). What these entities have in common is their regional basis—Gisenyi and Ruhengeri—and their leadership and financing, which came from a select group of people around Habyarimana and his wife. In Rwandan politics, this group was known as "akazu" or little house.

The temptation among scholars has been to limit their explanation of the Rwandan genocide to obvious issues without seriously considering what single element in contemporary Rwandan politics needed to be present for the genocide to unfold. This cannot be done without a judicious analysis of the historical, political, and economic consequences of July 5, 1973, the day on which the northerner Major General Juvénal Habyarimana overthrew his mentor Kayibanda. He inherited and indeed solidified the ethnic ideology that came out of the 1959 revolution that shaped the policies of the First Republic. For the northerners, however, July 5, 1973 represented more than the 1959 revolution even as it reaffirmed it. For centuries, power was in the south, under the monarchy and the First Republic. Tutsi Kings had their palaces in the South, and when Rwanda recovered its independence, it was under the control of a man from Gitarama, which was part of a region that northerners generally associated with the hegemony of the south. It was early in the twentieth century that the North of Rwanda was completely incorporated in the Kingdom of Rwanda with the help of the Germans and Belgians, putting an end to the independent Hutu small kingdoms in the north. This was felt as historical humiliation that translated in strong anti-Tutsi sentiments in the regions of Gisenyi, Ruhengeri, and immediately surrounding areas (especially in the Byumba prefecture). Hutu leaders from the two provinces were very instrumental, in fact central to the ethnic mobilization of the 1950s that eventually culminated in the Hutu revolution, but under the First Republic (1962-1973), Kayibanda played the Ruhengeri/Gisenyi Hutu leaders against the Butare intellectuals only to increase the power of the Hutu leaders from Gitarama. At the end of the 1960s, Kayibanda was surrounded by a restricted inner group from Gitarama that controlled the Hutu movement, which irked the northerners.[5] It is thus important to understand the coup of July 1973 from these two historical and political premises: it was historical payback (the northerners' turn to conquer the south, Tutsi and Hutu combined) and a political victory over the Gitarama clique. It is revealing that eight of the eleven officers who staged the 1973 Coup were from the North; of the remaining three, two were Hutu from the South, and one was a Tutsi, the only Tutsi officer in the Rwandan army (it was then called the National Guard). As Chapter Five of this book will show, any explanation of the 1994 Rwandan genocide that fails to figure in this central historical moment and its significance is likely to miss the prime motivation of the clique that planned the genocide. To my knowledge, no book has given this historical reversal the necessary weight it deserves in explaining the Rwandan genocide.

The consequences of this hypothesis are enormous in terms of the other elements usually discussed in the interpretation of the Rwandan genocide, including race, ethnicity, the Hamitic Hypothesis, the 1959 (Hutu) social revolution, human rights issues, and more. All these elements were tools carefully used by the genocide planners in the three-year propaganda that coalesced with the totalitarian regime and a host of other individual motivations to make the genocide possible. These other elements helped to gain the consent, support, and participation of the Hutu population all over the country through coordinated strategies. These postulates will be discussed in Chapter Five.

No doubt, we also need to account for the executioners' capacity to make their own decisions to kill and to have a moral sense of their values and actions as well as the significance of such mobilizing ideas as ethnicity, the 1959 Hutu revolution, and the ideology that came from it (Hutu solidarity, Hutu majority, Rwanda as a Hutu country, and Hutu Power), since these became the rallying forces of killers in April-July 1994. We also need to explain why, once they chose to kill, they did so to the end without showing any sign of remorse, with "useless violence"[6] and sadistically inflicting horrendous tortures and death. The Hutu who participated in the numerous attacks against the Tutsi could have carried their attacks in a lax manner, but many preferred horror, brutality, and gruesomeness: does this tell us anything about their motivation? In elaborating any theory, however, we must keep in mind that we are dealing with an extraordinary and complex event that led to the killing of nearly one million Tutsi and moderate Hutu. In Gisenyi and Ruhengeri, where the government of Habyarimana had the strongest support, the killing of the Tutsi already started in October 1990 and by the time of the genocide proper, there were only a few Tutsi left to kill. We need to make clear, however, that there were also thousands of Hutu who participated only reluctantly and calculatingly in order to save their lives as well as thousands of others who chose to resist or who helped their Tutsi neighbors in many ways.

It would be unconscionable to suggest that the Rwandans who

killed were somehow automatons who killed without any conscience of what they were doing. This book assumes full agency, that is, the killers, for whatever motivation, retained their ability to understand the significance of what they were doing. They knew it was morally wrong to kill, yet they still chose to kill and often inflicted unnecessarily suffering on their victims.

Of course, any scholar of the Rwandan genocide will need to discuss the colonial construction of identity in Rwanda, the 1959 revolution and the resulting ideology that guided the two Republics (1962-1973 and 1973-1994), the RPF invasion from Uganda on October 1, 1990, the role of multiparty democracy since 1991, the role of the media, ethnic politics and poetics, but these elements must be dealt with in the framework provided by ethnic and regional politics.

The colonial construction of ethnicity and its appropriation by both the Tutsi and the Hutu elites is one of the regularly discussed issues in Rwandan historiography and its predominance in the discourse on genocide. Chapter One of this book revisits the issue to suggest that looking at ethnicity in a period of open conflict (for example, war and elections in an ethnically divided country) offers the best chance to capture all its dimensions. One of the possible ways of looking at the Rwandan case is to compare it with the many ethnic and nationalist conflicts going on in the world today. These are today's but also tomorrow's conflicts. Since the end of World War II, ethnic and nationalist conflicts have raised intractable problems in international affairs. From that time up to the present, ethnic, nationalist, and religious conflicts have claimed at least ten million lives worldwide. The bad news about these upheavals is that as major world conflicts such as the West versus the East, the Northern Ireland conflict, and the problem of apartheid in South Africa have found some solutions or are in a promising process of finding one, ethnic, nationalist, and religious violence tends to localize so that the world has to deal less with international conflicts than with intra-national conflicts.

The conflicts of the 1990s such as the Balkan war, the Ireland conflict, the Somali unrest, the continuing violence in the Israeli-Palestinian conflict (despite the promise of an agreement in the last few years), the ethnic butchery that took place in Burundi in October-December 1993 (that continues in different forms despite the peace agreement brokered with help of former South African President Nelson Mandela), the Indian peasants' rebellion in Mexico that started on January 1, 1994, Islamic fundamentalism in the Maghreb countries (especially in Algeria, Egypt and Sudan) and in the Middle East in general, all share the same pattern of internal wars. Of course, being religion-based, Islamic fundamentalism easily exports to other countries of the world, where it has established terrorist networks, as investigations in the aftermath of the September 11, 2001 attacks on the Twin Towers of the World Trade Center in New York City and on the Pentagon in Washington, D. C. have shown.

One may argue that most of the conflicts have been there for a long time and may have been repressed by more international concern and resurged after the Cold War--one good example is that of Bosnia-Herzegovina, which suddenly exploded in one of the most difficult conflicts of post-Cold War era and nourished the ambition of a greater Serbia sustained by Serbia and the Bosnian Serbs—and astonishingly in the very backyard of western Europe, and after the fall of the Berlin Wall, the collapse of the Soviet Union and of the Communist regimes, which were the nightmares and the strategic focus of the West as a whole.

It is now a political truism that ethnic and nationalist conflicts constitute a frustrating problem in world affairs. We tend to be aware of the big wars, such as the war against terrorism that the United States and its allies are now waging in Afghanistan and around the world, as well as the Israeli-Palestinian conflict, because we see both on our television sets and read about them in major dailies. Yet, there are dozens of ethnic conflicts that have been going on for decades that do not benefit from what is now commonly known as the CNN effect. A consistent and sustained effort of research is needed to circumscribe fully the problem in all its dimensions, and, most importantly, effective and fast ways of dealing with it, if carnages of the scale witnessed in Rwanda in 1994 are to be avoided. A comprehensive internal strategy to deal with it will come, I believe, from very informed local case studies that go beyond the issue of ethnicity. To prevent further human catastrophes, comprehensive global and local strategies will have to be adopted and should include democracy and good governance, respect for human rights, and, perhaps most importantly, real and sustained poverty reduction strategies.

In looking at ethnicity in Rwanda, I consider historical, political, and economic factors behind the ethnic and regional relations in Rwanda and their changing dynamics since the colonial times through the 1994 genocide. I make frequent references to Burundi, the southern neighbor of Rwanda, in hopes that national and international efforts which are being put into helping the two nations come to grips with the ethnic problems since their independence be better alert and informed about the complex nature of the enterprise.

Chapter Two looks at the myths and narratives that sustained the different ideologies in contention in Rwanda, from the colonial stereotypes and myths that were used to imagine and interpret a social situation that European explorers and colonialists did not understand. The most important of these myths is the "Hamitic Hypothesis," a divisive myth that became the cornerstone of Rwandan historiography. When Europeans reached Rwanda at the end of the nineteenth century, they found a very centralized state and a rich culture. Because of their biases and stereotypes, they projected their racist ethnology on the Kingdom of Rwanda to justify its social, cultural, and political sophistication. Something this good could only be the work of people related to Europeans--European cousins! Chief among the European ethnologists was John Speke, who put forward the Hamitic Hypothesis to explain Hima/Tutsi domination in the kingdoms of the Great Lakes of Africa. German and later Belgian colonialists appropriated this ethnology and made it the foundation of the indirect rule, favoring the Tutsi over the Hutu and the Twa. According to this narrative of origin, the shrewd and tall Tutsi had come from the northeast of Africa and had conquered the Hutu and the Twa because of their superior civilization akin to Europe's. As for the Hutu, they were short, base, servile, and lacking in tact. The Tutsi were cattle breeders, the Hutu were cultivators, and the Twa were game hunters. Another reality the colonialist imposed on people in his theory was that the Tutsi was to reign over the Hutu vassals. We observe here a process of appropriation whereby John Speke and other European explorers recuperated the Biblical myth of Noah cursing the sons of Ham. The German and Belgian colonial administrators and the Catholic Church embraced the same ethnology to focus their "civilizing" mission on the Tutsi and entrust power to them until the 1950s. Paradoxically, the Tutsi elite appropriated this myth and convinced themselves of the superiority of their ethnicity. In the 1950s, the Hutu elite recuperated the same debris of an erroneous Hamitic Hypothesis and used it as the foundation of their struggle for liberation. At the helms of power in the new independent state, the Hutu leaders transformed the debris into political practices. In the years preceding 1994 and during the genocide itself again, the Tutsi were described as Hamites who had to be sent back to where they had come. Thus the ethnological errors of the nineteenth century recuperated an old Biblical myth that was, in turn, appropriated by the natives themselves on both sides of the ethnic divide.

It is worth noting that the Hutu in Burundi shared this same feeling during the massacres that followed the assassination of the first Hutu ever to rule Burundi (Melchior Ndadaye) in 1993. While it is easy to understand the frustration of the Hutu, it is less acceptable to accept the idea that was circulated along with other false myths that the Tutsi of Burundi should go back to their region of origin, which was said to be Egypt. These false myths help to explain some of the fallacies constantly recuperated by the outside world. *The New York Times* of Monday June 27, 1994, A-9, for example, reporting on the French intervention in Rwanda ("OpérationTurquoise"), talks of "a French-language flyer posted on the faded yellow wall of the immigration post at Cyangugu" (south-west of Rwanda) that reads: 'The Tutsi are out to exterminate us. We know you are a race of vipers, drinkers of Bantu blood.'" The unsaid in the flyer is that the Hutu are Bantu, thus natives, and their enemy is the Hamitic, Nilotic Tutsi.

The politics of conflict and warfare is always antagonizing, and in periods like the first half of the 1990s in Rwanda and Burundi, the young men and women of this generation were retaught the wrong dichotomies, the wrong myths, and the wrong theories. They were taught to fear and kill the ethnic other. It is indeed heartbreaking to watch thousands of people fleeing, and, among them, a young child, hardly five-years old, carrying a machete in his hands, the weapon that has killed thousands of people just as innocent as the child himself, or to hear a twelve year old boy on a TV special report boasting that he has butchered three persons, or even to read in a newspaper article how a Hutu man killed his nephews and nieces simply because their father was Tutsi.

Chapter Three proposes a close reading of the "Bahutu Manifesto" and an analysis of the 1959 Hutu revolution. Published two years before the revolution, the text of the manifesto reflects the appropriation of the Hamitic Hypothesis used to repudiate more the Tutsi (who had no doubt benefited from it) than its European authors, who had used it to exclude the Hutu from participation in the administration of the Kingdom. This document founded the Hutu ideology: Hutu solidarity (to òverthrow the Tutsi monarchy) and the depiction of the Tutsi as invaders and foreigners, whose place was outside Rwanda. Language plays a major role in a revolution and in the pre-genocide phase in the case of the Rwandan genocide, as it was for the Shoah. It helps to construct a discourse the aim of which Aimé Césaire has called, talking about colonialism, "chosification" (thingification).[7] It is a linguistic process through which the future victim is described as less than human, a foreigner, an animal (particularly a snake), or a monster to be eliminated before it eliminates the killers, thus convincing the latter that it is in their vital interest to get rid of the victim already rendered worthless through language. Language thus becomes the primary locus of extermination because it aims to inoculate the would-be killers against any sense of guilt, responsibility, and humanity. For example, in Louis Malle's movie *Au revoir les enfants*, the Gestapo officer says that Jean Bonnet (Kippelstein) is not French, "He is a Jew," he says.[8] Naming someone a Jew is condemning him or her. Previous to this discourse, of course, the genocide ideologues have done their extensive propaganda, and no more needs to be said when Jewish qualification in the case of the Shoah or Tutsi identity in the case of Rwanda is invoked. The 1959 Hutu revolution that ushered into a Republic constructed the Tutsi as a colonizing race and never sought to rectify this historical fallacy but instead made it its ideological foundation.

Chapter Three also explores the manner in which the leaders of independent Rwanda politically exploited the ethnic configuration codified by the colonial administration. I argue that in their official recognition of ethnicity, post-colonial regimes in Africa in general and in Rwanda in particular fostered economic and political competition along ethnic lines. Political practices like the so called "balanced distribution" of resources and places in high schools, in the institutions of higher education, and in the central administration and the military; the absence of democratic procedures of power sharing and transfer; the sorry mockery of the law and of the principles of justice which created a group of people who considered themselves above the law; a pathetic manipulation of the vulnerable parts of the population (the unemployed youth, the poor, and the illiterate population at large); and a decreasing economic performance; all legitimized, institutionalized, and secularized historical ethnic awareness, created new ethnic groups, subgroups, and conditions that rendered possible the kind of horror that shocked the world in April-July 1994.

Chapter Four tackles the issue of human rights in Rwanda from October 1990 to April 1994 to show how State-sponsored violence and terror created a culture of impunity for those aligned with the government. The many human rights violations since the outbreak of civil war in October 1990, decried by local and international organizations of human rights, piled up day after day, and the regime in place just ignored the different calls to restraint, as it was preparing the butchery of 1994. This chapter shows that human rights violations were indeed part of a plan to condition ordinary Rwandans to kill. The chapter ultimately suggests that it would make more sense for the international community to interfere forcefully in burgeoning ethnic or nationalist conflicts. The principle of noninterference in the domestic affairs of a nation should not apply when there is a real possibility that conflicts can build to proportions we observed with the Rwandan refugee crisis in July 1994. Within two weeks of the crisis, the international community authorized an intervention package that cost millions of dollars. This huge amount would not have been used if the four-year old conflict had been contained. The kind of zeal that the international community showed in helping the refugees, many of whom perpetrators of genocide and other crimes against humanity, would have been unnecessary if world governments had heeded the numerous calls and recommendations made by the different organizations of human rights that investigated human rights violations in Rwanda since October 1990. If we in the contemporary world believe in globalization, we need to draw practical consequences from the many conflicts going on in the world today. Letting conflicts build to climactic moments of horror will not protect us. The tremendous technological developments in the media have made it possible to live in what a critic has called "the historicity of the present,"[9] so that we will not escape the horror on our television sets or in the newspapers. We may even be asked to contribute money to alleviate the suffering of the people affected by the conflict. Many instruments of international law were crafted when most nations of the world were still trying to define themselves as nation-states. That time has passed when we had to worry about thwarting national sentiments; perhaps we need to redefine our views about interference in the national affairs of an independent nation. This is certainly a drastic proposition, but when a nation butchers its own people, what right does the world have not to intervene?

Chapter Five confronts the participation of ordinary Hutu in the killing of their Tutsi countrymen. I invoke the work of Daniel J. Goldhagen, Primo Levi, Hannah Arendt, and Tzvetan Torodov to construct a critical framework that I use to discuss the Rwandan case. I reject perspectives about the Rwandan genocide that build their argument around lines similar to the monocausal argument advanced by Goldhagen in his seminal if controversial book.[10] I use Primo Levi's concept of the "gray zone" to diffuse any sense that there was only one single motivation. I suggest that there was a maze of interests and motivations behind the participation of so many ordinary people in the genocidal frenzy. I use Todorov's theoretical construct to talk about the totalitarian regime and the construction of the "enemy" to be destroyed. Talking about the involvement of ordinary Hutu in the Rwandan genocide is in a way recognizing Primo Levi's and Hannah Arendt's suggestion that ordinary men are more dangerous than the few sadistic killers. Arendt's "banality of evil" is a painful human observation: no special attributes are required for a normal person to become a killer, and those who have organized mass murder in the history of humanity realized this reality before Arendt suggested a name for it. After this theoretical inquiry, I survey the multiple motivations that led thousands of ordinary Hutu to participate actively, zealously, and sadistically in the killing of their Tutsi countrymen.

The conclusion traces a framework of memory for the victims of the 1994 Rwandan genocide by invoking ways in which the memory of World War II and the Holocaust were lived in Europe after 1945.

Chapter One

Framing Rwanda:
Ethnic and Nationalist Conflicts in
the Post-Cold War Era

> In this new world, local politics is the politics of ethnicity;
> global politics is the politics of civilizations.
> --Samuel P. Huntington, *The Clash of Civilizations and the
> Remaking of World Order*

     The collapse of the Soviet Union and the subsequent dismantling of the communist regimes at the end of the 1980s and the early 1990s were hailed with enthusiasm all over the world. Politicians and social scientists contemplated a new world order and a more secure earth. Yet, in the same period, the Bosnian conflict in former Yugoslavia in 1992-1994, the resurgence of fighting in some republics of the former Soviet Union, in Afghanistan, in Angola and the numerous conflicts in Africa and all over the world irrefutably undermined this optimism. As James Woolsey, the first CIA director in the post-Soviet era, declared in January 1993 during his Senate confirmation hearing (and many leaders echoed his thought), the monsters may have died, but there are still venomous snakes out there already biting or lurking to bite. Less than ten years after the somehow prophetic assessment of the post-Cold War world came the September 11, 2001 terrorist attacks on the United States. Commercial jetliners were turned into flying bombs and hit the Twin Towers of the World Trade Center in New York City as well as the Pentagon, and a third attack tragically ended in Pennsylvania. Combined the three attacks killed several thousands of innocent civilians. In addition to the extreme evil of these mass murders, the frustration and humiliation of these attacks was derived from the fact that the United States and its western allies had successfully contained the mighty Soviet Union and the Eastern block during the Cold War but were not prepared for this kind of conflict, planned in the caves of Afghanistan by the Islamic fundamentalist Osama Bin Laden and his Al Qaeda network and involving people operating from cells around the world, including the United States. In a sense, traditional conflicts and warfare involving well-defined territories were somehow much easier to fight, but the redefinition of the ideas of nation and border in the global community now means that efforts have to be dispersed towards the myriad imagined communities that cut across nations. For example, the 9/11 terrorists and their networks imagined themselves through Islamic fundamentalism and a shared ideology of hatred of western values. This type of terror is without borders and as such is difficult to understand and contain.

The first Post-Cold War CIA director also discussed the "ethnic cleansing" carried out by the Serbs in Bosnia-Hercegovina as well as all the possible ethnic and nationalist troubles that now make up most of the international conflicts. Almost a decade later, the world watches the Israeli-Palestinian conflict escalating, the Northern Ireland conflict not completely resolved despite the Good Friday Agreement, the Republic of Macedonia dealing with a committed rebellion of Albanian nationalists, and a war involving at least seven nations in the heart of Africa (the Democratic Republic of the Congo, Angola, Namibia, Zimbabwe, Rwanda, Uganda, Burundi, and three rebels movements). Even though peace agreements have been reached in some of these cases, their implementation faces major obstacles that reflect the complexity of modern conflict and the paradox of the globalization movement. As there are few international conflicts, in fact as nations come together to form economic and political unions, intranational conflicts multiply. Even the war that has been dubbed the "first African world war" (the war in the Congo) had its origin in national ethnic strife. It was first launched by an ethnic group called the Banyamulenge in eastern Zaire whose Zairian citizenship was denied by the regime of Mobutu Sese Seko. As it will be seen later on, this ethnic question eventually had tremendous national, regional, and international implications. It is a telling reality of the New World order that the countries involved in the conflict are all members of regional organizations and also of the African Union that was officially launched by the Organization of African Unity in Lusaka, Zambia, in 2001. While this state of affairs certainly undermines the supranational organizations, it most importantly underscores the centrality of intranational conflicts in the contemporary world. Interestingly enough, the notion of "nationhood" is not the only stabilizing force in today's world. Thanks to the global economy and its main agents, multinational corporations, political entities do not necessarily correspond to geographical and economic entities. One possible consequence is that "disintegration of countries may not matter much to companies as long as they can continue to do business."[1] In fact, nations and groups in conflict may well be profitable to the corporations. The trade of diamonds and other rich materials did not stop in Sierra Leone and the Democratic Republic of the Congo despite the raging civil wars going on in those two countries for the last few years.

Who could have imagined that in 1994 a country as small as the tiny Republic of Rwanda in Central Africa could be the setting of a savage massacre of more than eight hundred thousand innocent people in just a few weeks? Who could have imagined that in the last years of the twentieth century, this same tiny nation would produce possibly the most challenging refugee crisis in modern history, when more than two million persons crossed the border to neighboring Zaire and Tanzania in June and July 1994? Who could indeed have imagined that as World War II Allies were pompously celebrating the Normandy invasion that eventually made possible the defeat of Nazi Germany, superlative barbarity was going on in Rwanda as the world was just watching the triumph of freedom over Nazism? Who could have imagined that almost fifty years after "Never Again," it was happening again and the powerful nations of this world reneged on their moral responsibility to stop the most dreadful genocide after the Shoah?

The ethnic and nationalist configuration of today's world conflicts constitutes a frustrating situation for world leaders as well as a cause for concern and material for intellectual pondering and research. A central phenomenon in contemporary politics, ethnicity is likely to remain a critical issue in the future because of its intricate nature. The result of a maze of historical, political, cultural, and economic elements, it keeps on metamorphosing, as it were, into new forms conditioned by struggles for power and economic interests. Along with nationalist passions, ethnicity has triggered many conflicts since the end of the Second World War.

The social scientist H. R. Isaacs reports that in 1975 ethnic violence alone had claimed more than ten million lives since 1945, a number that has increased at least by at least four million more since his book was published.[2] Much of this violence has followed the ethnic and nationalist upheavals at the end of the 1980s with the collapse of the Berlin Wall, the fall of the Soviet Union and of the communist regimes in Eastern Europe and efforts to establish democracy in Third World countries, particularly in Africa. Ethnic, nationalist, and religious wars seem to be such a common lot on the African continent that the Western media have become weary of them and report only and for some days on those conflicts that suddenly erupt in massive massacres. Rwanda and Burundi are certainly the most conspicuous examples of ethnic tensions on the continent, as their very recent history has shown.

Examples of nationalist conflicts are found in the cases of Sudan, Senegal (Casamance), Saharan Arab Democratic Republic (SADR), and the Touaregs of Mali and Niger. The birth of the Republic of Erythrea in 1992 was the clear consequence of nationalism. Of course, one must mention the 1967-1970 Biafra secession war that cost the lives of two and half million Nigerians.

Religious conflicts in Islamic Africa, most particularly in Algeria, Egypt, and Sudan, are the result of Islamic fundamentalism, which aims at toppling the non-Muslim governments to replace them by Islamic governments. In the 1990s in Algeria, the conflict between the fundamentalist FIS (le Front Islamique du Salut) and the military government plunged the country in turmoil and produced a situation of perpetual fear, especially in the intellectual milieus. In Egypt, the fear of fundamentalist attacks shrank the tourist industry of the country in the same period. In Sudan, the Muslim government (ruling according to the Sharia) has been engaged in warfare against the animistic and Christian south in the last two decades. Misery in southern Sudan is unspeakable. After twenty years of conflict, more than one million persons have been killed, three million are displaced inside the country, and one million have fled the country.

In general, since the 1990s there have been numerous conflicts on the African continent. Countries which experienced strife include Zaire (the Democratic Republic of the Congo since 1997), Liberia, Somalia, Sierra Leone, Eritrea, Ethiopia, Zimbabwe, Uganda, Angola, Congo (Brazzaville), Djibouti, Kenya, Mauritania, Mozambique, Nigeria, Cameroon (the antagonism with Nigeria over the Bakassi region), and more. It looks as if the continent is perpetually taken into a whirlwind. Meanwhile, older nationalist ideologies have not died in Northern Ireland (the conflict has claimed more than 3,100 lives in 30 years) and in Canada (the nationalist, secessionist movement in the province of Québec). In all corners of the world, ethnic and nationalist tensions are legion. Areas of conflict in the former Soviet Union following its disintegration include Chechnya, the Republics of Georgia, Armenia, and Azerbaijan. In Europe, the very conspicuous war in the former Yugoslavia often veils other militant nationalist claims, notably in Northern Ireland and Spain (The Basques). The frequent Irish Republic Army (IRA) bombs in Northern Ireland and in London before the Good Friday Agreement and the continuing Catholic versus Protestant antagonism constitute continuing evidence of a problem that has trailed for a long time.

In North America, the Indians' continuous claims in Canada and the United States, the Los Angeles riots in April 1992, the failed referendum in January 1993 in Canada to give Québec a semi-autonomy and continuous efforts by the Parti Québecois to achieve full autonomy are also examples of racial/nationalist discord.

A thorough census of all ethnic and nationalist troubles shows without equivocation a chaotic entanglement of conflict patterns and calculated political and economic interests in the local (national), regional, and international play of ethnicity and nationalism. Again, recent happenings in international politics are very eloquent.

After the invasion of Kuwait by Saddam Hussein in August 1990, the United States of America shepherded with an amazing rapidity and efficacy its Western allies as well as much of the international community and ousted without difficulty the Iraqi army. Of course, leaving Iraq to occupy Kuwait would have been a blessing of expansionist minds and a questioning of frontiers decided by colonial powers, and thus would be a dramatic precedent for the international community, which would certainly have to deal with more such claims not only from formerly colonized continents (Africa, Asia, and Latin America) but also from other countries with expansionist agendas. Had it not been for the amount of oil at stake in Kuwait, however, and the tremendous power it would give to a tyrant like Saddam Hussein, I do not believe the West would have shown the same remarkable zeal. Whenever and wherever the political and economic interests of the United States and the West in general are endangered, they use their military might to defend them.

The fuzzy concept of a New World Order much chanted after the fall of the Berlin Wall and the collapse of the Soviet Union (and thus of communism) was not strong enough to justify the massive deployment of the American troops, especially because it was ill-defined (and in fact could hardly be well-defined due to the complexity of world affairs). Nor was it convincing to advance the concept of territorial integrity of a sovereign nation. Other countries in the contemporary era have been attacked and maimed of parts of their territories, but no coalition was formed to dislodge the invaders. Cyprus and the Democratic Republic of the Congo are two cases in point.

For more than two years, the world watched with indignation the tragic events in former Yugoslavia where Serbs, Croats, and Bosnians were engaged in dreadful warfare. The same West which showed determination with the Iraq's invasion of Kuwait simply recoiled in front of Serbian ethnic cleansing against the Croats and the Bosnian Muslims and the Serbs' refusal of several peace plans. Religious, political, and historical considerations constantly played against the definite settlement of the conflict--former Yugoslavia has three major religions: Catholicism, Orthodoxy, and Islam. In two years (1992-1994), the conflict took more than one hundred thousand lives, and signs of resolution were rather thin until the United States government took the leading role in peace negotiations that led to the Dayton Agreement.

The African continent is probably the continent that breaks the record of wars. Having lived in the West for some time now, I know that anything that does not receive media attention is probably not going to bother any politician's agenda. For different reasons, countries such as Rwanda, Burundi, Angola, Sudan, the Democratic Republic of Congo, Somalia, Algeria, and many African nations have known in the recent past gruesome moments of turmoil and are still turbulent in many respects.

The world still remembers the Somali tragedy that compelled US President George Bush to send in troops to facilitate humanitarian aid to a people victimized by its own warlords, fighting to gain control to the point of starving the people and preventing humanitarian aid to reach those in need. In a year and a half, insecurity produced a terrible famine. Between 200,000 and 250,000 are said to have died.

The images shown on CNN were quite revealing on the impact that civil wars, fostered by tribal squabbles for domination, could achieve: a total disrespect and denial of life. The pictures also showed how unwatched cruelty of warlords can be to the expense of a whole people. This was to the mind of the world the first time the U.S (followed by European nations and some Asian and African countries) sent troops for purely humanitarian purposes.

As images pushed the US to go in to "restore hope," it is also images that pushed the West to withdraw armies. The image of a US soldier's naked body savagely dragged in the streets of Mogadiscio and that of the much brutalized Michael Durant were immortalized by television and newspapers images and pushed the US to review its rules of intervention on foreign lands. The images of Haitians fleeing in thousands and drowning in hundreds on the Caribbean sea have caused initiative after initiative in the US policy towards Haiti. Whereas the West had grown used to the Bosnian war, the gruesome images of a bomb falling in an open market in the city of Sarajevo in March 1994 prompted the US and its NATO allies to threaten the Serbs with airstrikes to abandon the siege of the city. The resolve was most convincing in that context. Had the TV images not been shown, the pressure would not have been created.

TV images cannot focus on all hot spots on earth. Thus, while they help the extremely explosive situations, they have created a dangerous psychology on world leaders: the psychology of the TV images commonly referred to, at least in the past years, as the CNN effect. Absence of this effect has easily kept a mask over other equally disturbing problems. One such case is Southern Sudan, where people have been dying, victimized by the civil war that opposes the government's troops to the SPLA which has its hold on Southern Sudan, composed mainly of Christians and animists, who oppose the Islamic rule of the Sharia. Even now as I am writing this line, I am looking at a dreadful image in Time (December 27, 1993) spread on two pages, of a Southern Sudan man, or rather a skeleton of a man dying of dehydration, whose only living signs come from his protruding white teeth on a black dead background and eyes and the words of an elderly Sudanese woman that say, "Where we live, there is no food, no water, and all the cattle have died." Of course, this is only an understatement of the whole reality. Those words do not express fully the tragedy of Southern Sudan, where, like in Somalia, death is the normal sight.

At least we saw these images of Somalia and occasionally of Southern Sudan, but there are spots, perhaps more dreadful than Somalia and Bosnia Herzegovina, that do not get any attention at all. Angola is one such spot. The peace contemplated with the 1992 elections did not come at all. The UNITA of Jonas Savimbi refused the outcome of the ballot, accusing the MPLA of Dos Santos of massive fraud. The war became even more dreadful than before. The fragments we get from time to time on CNN World Report are just eloquent enough to suggest the kind of human depravity that war can bring about. At certain times, hundreds of people die everyday from war wounds, from lack of medical care, from starvation, and more. The result of nineteen years of warfare ridicules the bond of humanity: between 250,000 and 380,000 dead, more than three million refugees, and three other million subject to starvation.

In October 1993, a coup attempt in Burundi led to the assassination of the democratically elected president. Incidentally, he was the first Hutu to rule the country after centuries of the Tutsi minority domination. The death of the President and several of his ministers triggered a level of violence that resulted in the death thousands of people of both ethnic groups—at least 200,000 persons since 1993. Besides the unavoidable reason of ethnicity, the deep reason is political. The fact that the coup was prepared by the high ranking Tutsi officers does not by itself imply that all the Tutsi on the hills were involved in the preparation of the putsch. The top officials, highest-ranking military officers, and the powerful civilians in government, who know about the political and economic advantages of being in the position of power, are really the ones to blame. As usual, the most appalling part of the story is that it is not those individuals in power who die of the tragedies they thread but the poor people of the hills from both ethnic groups who are manipulated for the benefit of those who are supposed to work for their advancement and welfare. The farmers on the hills, irrespective of their ethnic affiliations, live the same type of difficult life, share the same language and the same culture. In other words, they are united by the bond of neighborhood and laborious life, but those who are supposed to enlighten them always make sure from time to time to forge differences and sow dissension for their own benefits

For this particular case of Burundi, the high-ranking Tutsi officers knew very well how dreadful the consequences would be to the Tutsi on the hills. They were condemning them to death in the hands of the angry Hutu, who in turn would face the reprisals of the Tutsi military, thus feeding the historical fear created by a history of massacres started in 1972 when as many as 150 thousand Hutu were massacred by the Tutsi government. In 1993, members of the Hutu elite who escaped the coup called for resistance and revenge. For anyone familiar with the language they used, since the coup was taking place in the capital city and not on the hills, it was an overt appeal to the Hutu constituency to attack the Tutsi in general. The cases of Burundi and Rwanda show political elites so appalling as to take the population as hostages. The monstrous manipulation of the population through heinous propaganda playing on past fears exacerbates the ethnic question in both countries.

These cases clearly show that ethnic and nationalist conflicts are and will continue to be leading forces in world affairs. Unfortunately, as it has been seen, only those conflicts that present extraordinary danger to the political and economic interests of the West are the ones that are likely to draw quick diplomatic and/or military interventions and solutions.

Defining Ethnicity

The political complexity of "ethnicity" is reflected notably in the multiple definitions proposed by politicians, sociologists, and other social scientists. The terms used in its definitions seem to vary not only across the domains of study in which it is used but also across the geographical contexts to which it is applied and even across the historical periods it applies to. The European definitions differ in some respects from the American and the African.

Etymologically, the adjective "ethnic" and its derivative "ethnicity" derive from the Greek word "ethnikos," meaning "heathen." The root form of this word is "ethnos" or "nation," a term that was used to refer to the "non-Israelitish nations of Gentiles." Brian Du Toit cites *The Shorter Oxford English Dictionary on Historical Principles* as listing two meanings under the entry "ethnic": "A. Pertaining to nations not Christian or Jewish; Gentile, heathen, pagan. B. A Gentile heathen, pagan." Thus "ethnical" (the adjective used before "ethnic" came to be the standard adjective) came to be synonymous with "heathenish or pagan" while "ethnicism" (used before "ethnicity") meant "heathenism or paganism."[3]

In Europe, the use of "ethnic" occasionally referred to race or phenotype, but it was generally used "to designate differences in religion, behavioral forms, and life-style,"[4] thus clearly establishing a contrast between one's own group and the others and pointing to other possible subgroupings. Put simply, the markers used in the definition were not exclusive. The European social scientists frequently referred to social groups and subgroups in Africa and the Americas with terms such as "tribe" and "race."

Julian Huxley and A. C. Haddon complain about the misleading use of terms like "race," "culture," and "nation" and suggest dropping the term "race" from the terminology of scientific inquiry and adopting instead "ethnic group or people" for all contexts.[5] They advocate the use of *phenotypal groups or subgroups* when obvious physical differences are observable. An example that readily comes to mind is the distinction between people with black hair and skin and a broad nose, and those with wavy and curly hair with white skin and a narrow nose. Du Toit pokes fun at the open system of this European definition by suggesting that we would have "round-headed and broad-faced peoples as representing ethnic groups."[6]

As a general remark about the European definitions of "ethnicity," we can say that they encompass a wide range of groups and subgroups, including religious groupings, occupational groupings and, mostly, groupings built on phenotypal differences. The defining markers of 'race' are not clearly delineated.

In the Americas, social scientists generally tended to use the word "ethnic" to refer more to sociocultural than to racial differentiations. In *An American Dilemma*, for example, Gunnar Myrdal upholds ethnic attach-

ment as a consequence of "convenience and mutual protection" as applied
to Blacks and different immigrant groups.[7] He suggests that ethnic background and affiliation lead to ethnic cohesion. In *The Social System of
American Ethnic Groups*, W. Lloyd Warner and Leo Srole use the term
"ethnic" to refer to "any individual who considers himself, or is considered
to be, a member of a group with a foreign culture and who participates in
the activities of the group. Ethnics may be either of foreign or of native
birth."[8] In this definition, again, ethnic groups are viewed as sociocultural
rather than racial entities, though in reality the two may coincide--the example of Blacks and Whites in the United States is a case in point.

In short, while the British (and the Europeans in general) used
"ethnic" to refer to race (and a wide range of subgroupings of different
types), the American social scientists used the word in its sociocultural
dimension.

Brian Du Toit notes that this difference is even reflected in the
dictionaries written on both sides of the Atlantic. *The Oxford English Dictionary* gives the secondary definition of "ethnic" as "Pertaining to race;
peculiar to a race or nation; ethnological" while the secondary definition
of "ethnic" in *Webster's New World Dictionary* is "Designating one of any
of the basic divisions or groups of mankind as distinguished by custom,
characteristics, language, etc.; ethnological."

In 1952, Paul Walter reaffirmed this American definition in *Race
and Culture Relations* when he wrote that an ethnic group may "refer to a
distinct racial grouping, to one whose distinction is not racial but cultural,
or it may apply where both racial and cultural differences coincide."[9] Social psychologists have used the term "ethnic" with reference to both racial
and sociocultural differences. The idea of sociocultural differences, however, continued to be reaffirmed. In 1976, Frederick C. Gamst and Edward Norbeck edited a book entitled *Ideas of Culture, Sources and Uses*,
in which they argued that "an ethnic group is a recognizable sociocultural
unit based upon some form of national or tribal distinction, which lives
among other people rather than in its own country."[10]

Several defining characteristics of the concept of "ethnicity" ap-
pear in the previous overview. They are: specific major races, sociocultural groups, subgroups living among others in a foreign country, and cul-
turally-based groups whose criteria of definition include common language, history, and beliefs.

The word "ethnicity" is a relatively recent coinage; it appeared in
dictionaries in the 1960s. "Ethnocentrism" was used before that period.
Brian Du Toit writes, "it appears for the first time in 1961 in *Webster's
Third New International*, in 1972 in the *Supplement to the Oxford English*

Dictionary, and in 1973 in the *American Heritage Dictionary of the English Language.*"[11] But the new denomination did not change the basic meaning; instead, the term "ethnicity" came to be accepted as "a neutral, unemotional referent to those characteristics and qualities that mark an ethnic group, irrespective of whether the group is defined basically on sociocultural or basically on phenotypic grounds."[12]

It can be said from this overview that there are various ways of defining ethnicity, and no one definition applies to all situations. It is the context that defines ethnicity, and in a sense, ethnic identity is created by specific circumstances including linguistic, cultural, and religious communities as well as competition for national resources. The Bosnian problem is contextually different from the Angolan, from the Rwandan, from the Burundian, from the Irish. Subgroups within an ethnic group may fight against each other. An ethnic group may seek coalition with another group to topple an otherwise more important group. In other words, associations and dissociations may just respond to the political need of the moment. Does this mean then that there are no ethnic groups in cases with overt political and economic struggle? Does this mean that there cannot be any harmonious relationships between ethnic groups? Later in this chapter, I will argue that, in fact, conflict/war situations offer the best defining characteristics of ethnicity.

How was the term "ethnicity" used in the African context? To say that Africa is a mosaic of languages, religions, histories, and cultures is probably not enough to underscore the diversity that makes up its cultural complexity. A country like the Democratic Republic of Congo (former Zaire) counts more than 250 tribes, each with its own geographical area, language, gods, beliefs, and values; Nigeria more than 300; Benin more than 70. At the other extreme, countries like Rwanda and Burundi have three groups that speak the same language (respectively Kinyarwanda and Kirundi) and share the same religious beliefs and values. Is it right to call the Hutu, Tutsi, and Twa ethnic groups then? According to a now questionable and widely rejected historiography, around the third century, a large group of people called "Bantu" descended from the Lake Chad region and emigrated to different parts of Africa south of the Sahara in search of lands to cultivate. With the flow of time, they came to form different tribes scattered all around Africa south of the Sahara, each with its own culture and its own social, economic, and political organization. Except for some historically well-known empires like the Mossi Empire and the Empire of Mali, those different tribal organizations remained relatively independent until the advent of colonization. The 1884/85 Berlin Conference divided the African continent into different countries with new boundaries responding only to the arbitrary criteria set by the new European masters. Most African countries as we know them today are thus a creation of colonization, which put together people of different beliefs, languages, and cultures, and most of the time dividing communities which had lived together for long periods of time. This would have tremendous consequences as the colonial order sought to establish unifying elements like language and new organizational, economic, and political patterns.

After this brief background, let us see how the term "ethnic" was used with regard to the African situation. Here some conflicts of terminology around "ethnicity," "race," and "tribe" emerge from studies on the African organizational reality. Some social scientists, like the British, used the terms "ethnic reality" and "ethnic groups" without accommodating them to the local realities of Africa and without attempting any definitions other than the ones applied to European circumstances. For example, in a 1936 study, Seligman speaks of "racial groups," "language groups," and "tribes" without making any distinction and, in fact, using one for the other.[13] On the other hand, in 1947, S. F. Nadel published *The Nuba*, a study of the Korofan region of the Sudan, in which he explains that the concept of tribe "hinges on a theory of cultural identity, which ignores or dismisses as immaterial existing variations, and ignores or disregards uniformities beyond its self-chosen boundaries. The tribe exists, not in virtue of any objective unity or likeness, but in virtue of an ideological unity, and a likeness accepted as a dogma."[14] It appears from this passage that Nadel defines "tribe" as a subjective reality decided upon by members of a community who put boundaries where they want them to be along lines of the same language, culture, and social descent. In this line of thinking, a tribal grouping is mainly an ideological construct. The lack of an objective criterion points also to the lack of a centralized political authority grouping different tribal organizations and thus to the proliferation of small independent entities that can be called "tribes." Thus the concept of "tribe" is a socio-geographical reality, as people of the same tribe traditionally would cluster in the same geographical area as a closed group with the same language, a common ancestry, and a homogeneous culture.

While many African communities were organized along these tribal lines, there were here and there amalgamated societies created by the incorporation of other groups. The result is that the tribal reality disappeared without effacing ethnic awareness. A case in point is that of Rwanda and Burundi. This situation is at the basis of a terminological confusion present in the western media, in which one can read expressions like "tribal fighting in Rwanda," an expression that lost its sense certainly with the sixteenth century with the incorporation of all the components of the society, as it will be seen later. It is absolutely wrong to refer to any conflict in Rwanda or Burundi as "tribal" for the simple reason that there are no tribes in the two countries.

Many social scientists have stressed the fluid and flexible dimension of ethnicity. While local peoples used the social, biological, and political organizations of their own communities to identify or contrast themselves with other communities, the colonialist certainly saw in this subjectively drawn reality room for manipulation, for even traditionally tribal groups were social constructs always involving the categorization of "us" versus "them" in the competition for whatever political and economic interests were at stake. Ethnicity would thus be a set of characteristics and attitudes adopted by a given group at a given period of time and recognized as such by other groups and could comprise socio-behavioral, phenotypic, temporal, and spatial criteria adapted to competitive models in or outside the society.

With the advent of colonialism in Africa, different people with different cultures and languages and truly living as separate groups, were occasionally waging wars against each other to expand territory or to settle disputes of different types, but without the real existence of the idea of nation (except in some rare cases such as Rwanda, Burundi, and Ethiopia). Colonizers invented boundaries and nations for the sake of organizing their acquired territories and avoiding clashes with other European powers. The result of this arbitrary division was that a tribal group thus divided could go to, say, two different countries. In periods of ethnic warfare, these groups can constitute a complication of the problem. In the 1990s, for example, the question of identity and citizenship for the Banyamulenge, Tutsi of Rwandan origin who live in the provinces of South Kivu and North Kivu, was one of the major origins of war in the Democratic Republic of Congo.

In other words, ethnicity is so complex and involves so many parameters that it is difficult to capture and define it in any definite sense. Thanks to this complexity, economic and political competitions will easily manipulate it by emphasizing the aspects that better fit the situation. In times of tension, organized groups will activate those dimensions that favor their case.

Ethnicity and Open Conflict

We may perhaps resolve the confusion that surrounds any attempt to define ethnicity by looking at social practices and/or moments of open conflict and how they impact ordinary men. Situations of war are more

likely (rather than periods of peace and stability) to produce a clearly defined sense of ethnicity. In fact, it is in such a time that governments may .
not hesitate to adopt policies that encourage atrocities towards the undesired group and are likely to encounter little resistance in doing so. The
context of war helps to objectify the enemy, the future victim by defining
him, giving him physical and moral characteristics. In Rwanda, Burundi,
and the Democratic Republic of Congo in the 1990s, for example, ethnic
conflicts have convincingly shown that, in trying to achieve certain political goals, governments and their satellite parties and groups invoked ethnic myths and stereotypes to sharpen internal political mobilization. They
dug hard in the past and the present to explain both the success and failure
of their governments to contain what was perceived as threats from their
respective enemies. In Burundi, in 1993, the first Hutu president was assassinated by the Tutsi military less than four months after he took office,
and the consequence was a bloody pogrom in which Tutsi killed the Hutu
and vice versa. In 1999, the government of Laurent Kabila of the Democratic Republic of Congo, facing an armed rebellion backed by Rwanda and
Uganda, targeted an ethnic group called B*anyamulenge*. Close to the
Tutsi, this group dominated the leadership of the rebellion. The Banyamulenge who were caught in the government-controlled cities and regions
were atrociously murdered and others imprisoned and tortured. The Kabila
government easily succeeded in enlisting the population to kill the well-
defined enemy. Strangely enough, it is the Banyamulenge's rebellion
against the Kinshasa government of Marechal Mobutu that brought
Laurent Kabila to power.

   It is quite revealing then that war situations favor Manichean
processes, and governments can easily set up mechanisms to enforce and
intensify divisions. In the case of Rwanda, when the Rwandan Patriotic
Front (RPF) attacked from Uganda on October 1, 1990, the invaders were
immediately officially defined as Tutsi, and the Tutsi inside Rwanda, who
were not part of the rebellion, were associated with them through the invocation of old myths and stereotypes that I discuss in Chapter Two. The political discourse appealed to significant historical periods such as the Hutu
revolution (Chapter Three) as a way of mobilizing the Hutu, in a Manichean fashion: the Hutu against the historical enemy—the Tutsi. Policies
were initiated to restrict Tutsi movement and humiliate them through "lais-
ser passer" (a travel document that gave the bearer the permission to travel
inside the country) and other government documents required in times of
war, even in areas not directly affected by the conflict. Even though these
documents were required of everybody (Hutu, Tutsi, and Twa), Tutsi and
Hutu members of the political opposition experienced hard times in secur-

ing them, if at all. Since the objective of these documents was clear—to restrict the movement of those who were undesirable—a number of people simply did not bother to apply for them.

War situations help to define ethnicity by highlighting the physical, moral, economic, and cultural features of each group. For example, in 1990-1994 in Rwanda, the Tutsi were physically defined as tall, with aquiline nose and light complexion. Morally, they were defined in public and official discourse as people who could not be trusted because they are "liars," "snakes," "untrustworthy"; economically, they were said to dominate businesses in cities as well as the Roman Catholic clergy. Culturally, it was said, for example, that they were more likely to do the "ugushayaya" dance (an elegant, soft dance) as opposed to the "kinimba" dance of the northerners and northwesterners who liked to define themselves as "unsullied Hutu." The historical and ideological origin of these definitions will be discussed in Chapter Two.

My claim to use the war situation as a time to define ethnicity is further justified by the fact that in times of peace and relative stability, governments tend to make it anathema to use the categories of Hutu and Tutsi in an oppositional context. Official public definitions are inclusive; they talk of unity and development. Again, the examples of Rwanda and Burundi stand out. The Hutu government of Habyarimana in Rwanda since 1973 until 1990 officially promoted unity among the three ethnic groups (Hutu, Tutsi, and Twa), but it is the same government that implemented policies based on ethnic quotas and required all official documents including identity cards and school and job application forms to specify the ethnic affiliation of each individual. The same government prepared and carried out the 1994 genocide of the Tutsi. In Burundi, the Bagaza regime (1976-1987) prohibited the use of the two terms "Hutu" and "Tutsi." This "official" policy, however, did not prevent the same government from pursuing policies that favored the Tutsi. The same situation prevailed under the leadership of Pierre Buyoya, who toppled Bagaza 1987. Thus in times of relative peace and stability, ethnic demarcation is done through subtle, less violent policies. Methodologically, it becomes easier to define ethnicity in times of open conflict since social, political and economic practices follow a clearly defined ethnic logic, and thus the social scientist can work on verifiable practices. As I argue later on, the war situation offers unambiguous solutions to mixed ethnicity situations (which are the result of intermarriage between the Hutu and the Tutsi). The overwhelmingly Manichean politics and practices in times of ethnic strife offer the surest   elements to theorize about ethnic mobilization and identity, specifically on how people behave during turbulent periods as opposed to how they behave in times of peace.

The Competition Model: Olzak and Nagel

Another way of defining "ethnicity" is by looking at what moti-
vates ethnic mobilization in periods of (relative) stability. Olzak and Nagel
view ethnic relations as competitive. Their competition model looks at
ethnicity in terms of "functionalist and Marxist models of social change."[15]
In discussing the competitive nature of ethnic relations, they posit four
main, somehow contradictory hypotheses: First, modernization or "the industrialization, urbanization, and bureaucratization of market and political
organization will decrease ethnic heterogeneity, that is, it produces new
loyalties based on class, not ethnicity."[16] In other words, modernization
undermines ethnic awareness and identity. Second, paradoxically, "modernization and development spark ethnic movements"[17] as different groups
align themselves or mobilize for economic competition. Third, "modernization and development trigger ethnic movements" and "when resources
become initially available to an ethnic periphery, these regions are likely
to mobilize against a state center."[18] Fourth, ethnicity leads to a "focus on
the relationship between assimilation and mobilization of ethnic groups."
[19] Olzak and Nagel argue that "modernization increases levels of competition for jobs, housing, and other valued resources among ethnic groups.
This perspective holds that ethnic conflict and social movements based on
ethnic (rather than some other) boundaries occur when ethnic competition
increases."[20]

According to the competition model, groups mobilize along ethnic lines in the domains of labor, housing, marriage, education, the military, and other types of market competitions. How then does ethnic identity "supersede other potential loyalties and political cleavages" (Olzak
and Nagel 3)? In periods of peace, loyalties easily form across ethnic and
regional lines, whereas in times of unrest, the Manichean logic triumphs.
While competition theories are right when they assert that "modernization
affects ethnic movements by stimulating ethnic competition within increasingly homogeneous markets, which simultaneously breaks down small-
scale boundaries and increases the potential for mobilization on a large
scale"(Olzak and Nagel 3), the war/conflict situation breaks this down
with its binary oppositions. The O.J. Simpson trial in the United States in
1995 verifies this competition model. For the duration of the trial, negative
and positive attitudes towards Simpson came predominantly from Whites
and Blacks respectively. When the jury returned a "not guilty" verdict,
there was generalized jubilation on the African-American side and dismay

on the White side.

Outside the violent situation of war, a government associated with one ethnic or racial group may implement policies that favor that particular group. This was certainly the case during the 1973-1994 Habyarimana regime in Rwanda, which implemented policies of quotas based on ethnic and regional representation, but in reality the official policy was only a façade to exclude the Tutsi and the Hutu of the south, as we shall see later in the book.

The quota system drew a legal framework that recognized ethnic or racial identity as a basis for access to services. But what was really troubling about the quota system in Rwanda was that it was manipulated by those in power, in reality to exclude the undesired and give more access to resources and services to the dominant group, that is, people from Gisenyi and Ruhengeri, who controlled the central administration and the army. This is particularly devastating in developing countries (such as most African countries) where the private sector is underdeveloped and the public sector, controlled by the government, is almost the exclusive way to social mobility.[21]

Intrusive labor laws and ethnic or racial stereotypes can also invade the underdeveloped private sector and perpetuate segregation in labor markets. In the case of Rwanda, during the Habyarimana regime (1973-1994), it was required of employers of the private sector to report on the ethnic quotas of their employees. It was not difficult to see that these intrusive laws aimed at barring the Tutsi access to jobs. Interestingly enough, there was probably a high percentage of Tutsi in the non-governmental organizations and in such places as embassies where the national labor laws were not applicable.

In periods of peace, the distribution of the population into specific occupations is another indication of ethnic identity and awareness. In Rwanda, there were, since 1962 and probably before, ethnic enclaves that were likely to have more Hutu or more Tutsi. The national army, for example, was almost exclusively a Hutu affair (mainly the Hutu from Gisenyi and Ruhengeri prefectures). In 1973, there was only one Tutsi officer in the National Guard (which would later become the Rwandan army), and in 1990, there was only one Tutsi high officer in the Rwandan army. On the other hand, probably as a way of countering this segregation, groups suffering from discrimination will tend to join ethnic enclaves that can escape complete control of the government. According to Olzak, "an ethnic enclave is a structure in which members of an ethnic population exploit a common occupational niche, participate in common ethnic institutions and organizations, and form a dense interaction of network communication, information, socialization, and marital endogamy."[22] For example, in Rwanda, at least until 1994, there were a disproportionate number of Tutsi priests in the Catholic clergy and in businesses. In cases such as Rwanda, ethnic enclaves tend to produce ethnic awareness in domains that are perceived as not having tremendous political implications. These enclaves are likely to hold because they do not constitute a direct threat to the administration.

Unlike industrialized situations that produce new ethnicities based on the dynamics of production, today's ethnicity in Rwanda and Africa in general is deeply rooted in pre-colonial and/or colonial times. This situation satisfies one of the aspects of the primordial theory of ethnicity, the view that ethnic identification remains unchanged despite other social transformations, probably because industrial development is not significant enough to shake primordial inclinations. In Rwanda and elsewhere in Africa, ethnicity is manipulated and exacerbated for economic and political ends. Therefore, two clear conclusions can be reached. First, ethnic divisions were codified by the colonial power, and the independence and the promise of economic development did not dissolve them. Instead, they have intensified and strongly emerged in moments of crisis, for example during the apocalyptic killings of Tutsi and moderate Hutu in 1994.

Second, ethnic mobilization is still strongly based on archaic forms of social organization and identification, to the contrary of what Nagel writes about the production of ethnicity in industrialized nations: "The view of ethnic organization and identity as rooted in earlier epochs, reaching forward to shape the attitudes and behavior of current group members does not mesh well with a multitude of examples of the production of ethnicity"(31). What I want to suggest here is that even when a new group is created in a country like Rwanda, it stems from existing ethnic configurations, and in times of crisis original configurations prevail. But, as I said earlier, an important phenomenon took place in the southern part of the country, that is, ethnic intermarriage. The situation now is that many people have both Tutsi and Hutu blood, so that it is not clear what they are in terms of the traditional Hutu/Tutsi dichotomy. It would be interesting to conduct a systematic study of how mixed households behaved during the 1994 pogroms.

Ethnicity as a Political Construct

This angle of ethnicity is based on the belief that "ethnicity is largely an ascribed status that is situationally activated" and "ethnic boundaries are flexible, spatially and temporally fluid, and permeable—permitting the movement of personnel across them."[23] This was certainly the case in pre-colonial Rwanda where Tutsi, Hutu, and Twa were more social class markers than the codified ethnic labels that they have been constructed to be since the German and especially Belgian colonial administrations.[24] Policies based on ethnic and regional preferences in independent Rwanda created layers of Hutuness in addition to Tutsi ethnicity. During the First Republic (1962-1973), the President (Grégoire Kayibanda) was from Gitarama prefecture in central Rwanda. As a result, the Hutu of Gitarama had more power than the Hutu from other regions of the country. During the Second Republic (1973-1994) (under President Juvénal Habyarimana from Gisenyi), the Hutu of Gisenyi and Ruhengeri liked to qualify themselves as "purs et durs" (unsullied *and rough)*, obviously casting themselves as the real Hutu as opposed to the Hutu of other regions whose Hutuness may have been tinted by Hutu/Tutsi intermarriage. It is the "Hutu purs and durs" of the north who dominated the army, the single most important institution in the country, because it was the primary center of power. This way of defining Hutu ethnicity was a strategic calculation aimed at mobilizing the Hutu of Gisenyi and Ruhengeri to support the Habyarimana regime. The resulting ethnic taxonomy was as follows: (1) the Hutu of Gisenyi and Ruhengeri; (2) the Hutu of other regions; and (3) the Tutsi. There was a time, however, between 1973-1980, when it was alleged that the Tutsi of Gisenyi was better off than the Hutu of southern regions. After the Rwandan Patriotic Front invaded Rwanda in 1990, the Rwandan government launched a sustained campaign to promote, for political convenience, a Manichean taxonomy: Hutu versus Tutsi. Since the same government had distributed social, political, and economic favors to the Hutu of Gisenyi and Ruhengeri, this new taxonomy did not hold. Before the RPF invasion, there was more animosity between the Hutu of Gisenyi and Ruhengeri (and an adjacent part of Byumba) on the one hand and the Hutu of the rest of the country on the other hand. Regionalism was by far a more acute problem than ethnicity. The Tutsi had tacitly understood that as long as they did not try to agitate for political and military positions and stayed in safer enclaves (such as business and the Catholic clergy), they would have peace. In fact, between 1973 and 1990, there was no pogrom against the Tutsi in Rwanda. The Rwandan intelligence services, however, in the hands of "purs et durs" Hutu from the North close to Habyarimana, were obsessed with ascertaining the ethnic group of all civil servants. Since the Tutsi had understood their position, the intelligence services focused more on the Hutu of the South. In the 1980s, the *République des Nordistes* (Republic of Northerners, meaning Gisenyi and Ruhengeri), as it was commonly referred to in the South, was more concerned with regional confrontation than with the Tutsi problem. As we shall see in Chapter Five, the political parties that formed in 1991 reflected more regional concerns than ethnic antagonisms, even if ethnicity was part of the political discourse, especially on the side of parties allied with the government of Habyarimana.

Ethnicity as a political construct was unequivocally displayed in Burundi in 1993. In the presidential and legislative elections, the voting population of Burundi, without displaying it overtly in opinion polls taken before the election, voted along ethnic lines, and thus the Hutu popular majority voted one of its own into office. Ethnic mobilization in this case aimed at achieving political advantages with the attendant social and economic dividends that would follow with the control of government. The FRODEBU victory would certainly lead to labor redistribution and more opportunities for the Hutu of Burundi. This ethnic redrawing of the political landscape would certainly restructure the other sectors of national life. As I argued before, in such countries as Rwanda and Burundi, control of economic organization and processes is a direct consequence of the control of the political organization and processes. In developing countries this seems to be true by and large because competition is mainly located in the political arena, and control of political power also gives access to control of economic processes.[25] If it is obvious that ethnic affiliation will give access to the sharing of power, the process leads to a more overt case of politicization and legitimation of ethnicity. Consequently, "the role of ethnicity [is] both an antecedent as well as a consequence of particular political processes."[26] Ethnicity constructs political processes, enhances (sub)regional loyalties within a dominant group and, more importantly, reinforces existing ethnic groups—all these elements are constitutive components of the "structure of political access and content of political policies."[27]

Ethnicity, "Punishment," and Isolation

The establishment of Bantustans in Apartheid South Africa and the Indian reservations in the United States isolated specific racial groups in specific geographical areas with the goal of controlling them. This strategy punishes and controls the other and leads to a more acute ethnic awareness. During the 1959-1962 Hutu Revolution in Rwanda, the same strategy was used as a way of dealing with internal Tutsi refugees, who were denied the possibility of returning to their houses and instead were directed to "Tutsilands" such as Bugesera, a malaria-infested region. Willame writes that the resettlement of internal Tutsi refugees in the prefectures of Kibungo and Kigali was conceived and defended by the colonial administration and the Hutu revolutionaries (who would soon be the leaders of the young republic) as a way of pacifying the country.[28] Free of ethnic upheaval, Kigali and Kibungo offered relative security to the Tutsi. To encourage Tutsi resettlement in those two regions without legally forcing it, the colonial administration established refugee camps, aid, and distribution of land for farming and stockbreeding for those willing to stay.[29]

More recently in Burundi, as a way of stopping Hutu rebels from attacking the capital city of Bujumbura, the government of Major Pierre Buyoya decided to implement (between September 1999 and July 2000) a policy of "regroupement" in areas surrounding Bujumbura where different rebel movements operated.[30] The fact that the rebellion was Hutu and the regroupement affected almost exclusively the Hutu could not but lead to more ethnic awareness that the Tutsi were oppressing the Hutu through the "regroupement" policy[31] which forced people to leave their houses and live in squalid makeshift, inhuman, and altogether miserable conditions.

The situations presented in this section are more likely than not to mobilize ethnic or racial awareness and ethnically structure future political events such as elections, because they constitute a hardly veiled recognition of ethnicity as a defining element in political practices. Extreme if relatively peaceful consequences of this policy can be seen in Belgium where the Dutch-speaking Flemish and the French-speaking Wallons are geographically separate; in Fiji, where the Parliament has an equal number of Fijians and Indians in the House of Representatives (an attempted coup by the "Fijians" in 2000 was justified by its leaders as a reaction to the strong influence of the Indians); and in India, where untouchables were given a quota in Parliament and in the civil administration.[32] These situations legitimize, institutionalize, create, or solidify ethnic and regional awareness.

Ethnicity, Language, and Culture

Language and culture are other factors that may structure ethnic or racial awareness and mobilization in the competition model. This is, for example, the case in Belgium and Canada. In Belgium, the Flemish and the Wallons tend to be politically organized along linguistic lines. The Parti Québecois in Canada is a language/culture party whose base is in the French-speaking province of Québec, which has tried a few referendums to secede from Canada. In different countries of the world, groups that feel excluded or fear future political exclusion may organize along the language/culture line. Examples include the German speakers in Belgium and the Italian and Portuguese groups in Québec.[33]

Paradoxically enough, there has never been such a linguistic or cultural problem in Rwanda and Burundi. People in both countries speak the same language (Kinyarwanda and Kirundi respectively) and share the same cultural and religious constructs. As Nagel rightly puts it, however, "the speaking of a common language ... does not automatically produce ethnic unity, group identification, an organizational substructure, or a shared culture."[34]

Another question that we might want to look at briefly is the problem of linguistic policies and their impact on ethnic configurations. In Rwanda, everybody speaks and understands one language: Kinyarwanda. It is the language of daily interactions. In this respect, Rwanda (along with Burundi) enjoys a unique linguistic position in Africa, but colonization was carried out in French. French was the language of administration and school instruction. Since colonial times, French has been the language of instruction in primary school, high school, and university. Knowledge of French and English is a sine qua non of access to paid jobs and to powerful positions. Yet, only 2% of those who finished primary school could go to high school until the 1980s.

In recent years, the rate has increased to about 20%. Proficiency in the two languages is a social determinant, especially since fewer than 10% of Rwandans can use them. Does this mean that this elite minority has constituted a new ethnic group? The internal reactions to the conflict in Rwanda have shown that this linguistic determinant is not yet strong enough to weaken the traditional ethnic division of Hutu/Tutsi and the created regionalist awareness in periods of strife.

Ethnicity and Resource Redistribution

If access to resources is an important ingredient in the construction of ethnicity, it follows that policies which designate certain groups for remedial or special treatments such as affirmative action in the United States, the distribution of education scholarships and low-interest loans as well as land will lead to ethnic awareness or mobilization along these lines. However, these boundaries tend to run across ethnic groups. For example, affirmative action in the United States targets traditionally underrepresented groups such as women (of all races), Blacks, and Native Americans. Interestingly enough, there is a popular misconception that it is for Blacks only, even though white women seem to have benefited more from the policy. Moreover, redistribution may produce other undesirable effects such as what is termed reversed racism in the United States, where, for example, affirmative action has prompted the claim that white males are discriminated against if merit is not the only criterion used in the screening of job applications.

The Twa of Rwanda and Burundi have not taken advantage of affirmative action policies initiated to uplift them, probably because of a general lack of involvement in national affairs. On the other hand, the effort to correct past inequity through regional and ethnic balance in Rwanda from the 1960s to 1994 has led to claims of injustice and to ethnic and regional awareness. Thus while affirmation action practices may respond to the demand of social justice, they are more likely to create ethnic or regional tension when their implementation is perceived as responding to political convenience, as it was the case in Rwanda under the Second Republic (1973-1994). In the 1970s and 1980s, Colonel Aloys Nsekalije used his position as minister of national education to send disproportionate numbers of natives of Gisenyi and Ruhengeri to high schools. It was not unusual for the communes of Karago and Giciye, the heart of the "sacred region" of Bushiru, to have at least 150 pupils each sent to high schools while some communes in the "south" could get fewer than ten places. Nsekalije's argument was that the south had had more than its share under the First Republic, and regional redistribution was necessary to redress the injustice of the past.

Ethnicity as a Palimpsest

During the relatively peaceful years of 1973-1990 in Rwanda, the Hutu of the South, not the Tutsi, were perceived as the threat to the northern grip on power. As a result, discrimination in job placement, educational opportunities (especially placement in high schools, the national university, and study abroad scholarships), development projects, and the military was common practice. Since 1962, it is only at a time of conflict that the Hutu versus Tutsi dichotomy came to the front; otherwise, the regional antagonism, though not as deadly as the several ethnic instances of turmoil, has preoccupied the politicians at the helms. There is no denying that the political parties that surfaced in Rwanda in 1991 were mostly reactionary forces to the hegemony of the clique from Gisenyi, Ruhengeri, and to some extent part of Byumba adjacent to Ruhengeri. People from different social classes in this region somehow came to believe in the 1970s and 1980s that the country belonged to them, because they were the Hutu "purs and durs."

Depending on situations, multiple layers of ethnicity can rise and fall and mobilize for specific purposes. Within these layers there can also be other layers based, for example, on class. What is, for example, the relationship between educated and salaried workers and mostly illiterate farmers on the hills of Rwanda and Burundi? After all, no matter who is in power, both Hutu and Tutsi farmers, who make up more than ninety percent of the whole population, live in the same economic conditions. The competition takes place in cities, where the educated elites live a western style of life. In countries where representative democracy is nonexistent, the competition for power mostly takes place away from the majority of the population. Does this social, cultural, and economic context permit us to associate the Hutu and the Tutsi of the countryside to the salaried Hutu and Tutsi who, by comparison, have a very comfortable life? Or do these farmers simply become ethnic pawns whenever the administration needs to play the ethnic card? If indeed we accept the proposition that ethnicity is a political construct, then it follows that what we call ethnic strife is primarily grounded in politics. It is not far-fetched to argue that in the absence of a democratic culture that allows for a peaceful transfer of power following democratic elections, those in power and/or those who seek power will use violence to attain it, and will use ethnicity because it is engrained in the collective consciousness of the people after a whole century of deadly experimentation that started with the German and Belgian administrations.

The situation is not very different in Burundi. In 1966, Michel Micombero staged a military coup, and since then Burundi has been mostly ruled by presidents from the southern region known as Bururi. Ethnic violence, especially since 1993, has blurred the overwhelming hegemony of the Bururi region over both the Tutsi and Hutu of other regions. In 1972, the Micombero government committed a genocide against the Hutu elite—at least 150 thousand Hutu were killed, and thousands went into exile in the neighboring countries of Rwanda, Tanzania, and Zaire. A handful of others fled to Belgium and other western nations. The following year, Micombero conceived a school reform program (actually implemented under the Bagaza government, 1976-1987) that transformed most high schools in the countryside into teacher training schools, but the Bururi lycées were not affected.

Unlike the training schools that formed elementary school teachers and did not offer the possibility of admission to higher education, lycées offered a general education that led to higher institutions such as the military academy, the national university, and other institutions of higher education. Furthermore, the school reform program established that each child would go to a high school of his or her region. With only a few exceptions, the Bururi region was left with the surest passage to the high administration cadre of the Republic of Burundi or to the possibility of becoming a commissioned officer in the Burundian army, the real power broker in the country since 1966. The reform also meant that the Hutu of Bururi more than the Tutsi of other regions had more chances to go to institutions of higher education and to the military academy. What's more, the school of non-commissioned officers (Ecole des Sous-Officiers) was also in Bururi. It comes as no surprise that among the Hutu in the Burundi army since the mid-1960s disproportionate numbers are from the Bururi region. Most of the leaders of the Hutu rebel movements that have destabilized Burundi since 1993 are from Bururi. Many Burundian exiles I have spoken to agree that the regional question (they refer to it as the "Bururi question") is central to the Burundi problem.

Despite this regional mapping of power, how do we explain that in times of strife, Hutu and Tutsi of all regions are easily set against each other for the ultimate benefit of the elite? Does it tell us that ethnicity is such a powerful tool that it easily brings people together in such a blind manner? The 1972 mayhem against the Hutu and other pogroms have installed the psychology of fear, the fear of being exterminated by the other objectified in the ethnic other.[35] In over a century, the elite has developed different strategies to manipulate this ethnic fear.

Another important aspect of ethnicity that cannot be overlooked is that of the ethnicization of the military, a development that reinforces the political (and economic) construction of ethnicity. After the excitement of independence in the early 1960s in Africa and the disillusionment that followed, came a time known as the period of "military coups." The military rulers, whose practices were heavily influenced by the totalitarian regimes of the Communist block, relied substantially on the military (to whom they gave many privileges) to stay in power. They gave the soldiers preferential wages and controlled the distribution of important positions in the central administration. In Rwanda, the Tutsi were systematically refused access to the military because they could collaborate with their "brothers"(refugees in neighboring countries) to reconquer power. Also, the President had to have men of confidence to deter any attempt of the southerners to regain power. As a result, an overwhelming number of military recruits were Hutu from Gisenyi and Ruhengeri. This added to the awareness on the part of the Tutsi and Hutu of the south that the political rhetoric was void of meaning.

Ethnicity, Nationalism, and Global Economy

The world's political economy is nowadays defined by the new concept of "global economy." This concept is founded on the premise that people can exchange goods, services, and money all over the world (free trade), that money can be traded and moved all over the world (free movement of the capital), that things can be made anywhere in the world (free movement of production), and that one can buy anything from anywhere in the world (open consumer markets). These attributes affect different nations in different ways. The fundamental assumption is that global economy encourages national industries to produce for export rather than for local demand. It favors corporations in the sense that it encourages wealth accumulation rather than local needs, these being best served through increased national wealth. The forces of global economy (rather than national policies) decide much of the orientation of the economy (the law of the capital). Needs of national economies are served by world markets, which puts pressure on governments to join the global economy. This philosophy was enacted at least three times in the course of 1993. In North America, clearance was given to the North American Free Trade Agreement (NAFTA), an agreement that has created the world's largest free trade zone with at least 376 million consumers (the U.S, Canada, and Mexico). The European Community has now adopted a new currency, the Euro. The General Agreement on Tariffs and Trade (GATT), also known as the Uruguay Round, was finalized as planned and will dramatically diminish tariffs on goods throughout the world, with the beneficial consequence of creating new jobs. The meeting of East-Asian and Pacific Heads of States (the US, Canada, Japan, Taiwan, China, Singapore, Malaysia, Indonesia, Thailand) in Seattle, Washington, in November 1993 (and annually thereafter) marked the beginning a future economic organization.

Obviously, then, the world's best economies are playing a new game: opening to the world. But others, especially African economies, seem to be sleeping on their unsuccessful dealings at home. The annual meeting of the Organization of African Unity officially launched the African Union in Lusaka, Zambia in 2001, but it will not work as long as dozens of conflicts are still raging on the continent and there are so many dictators still at the helms. So what becomes of them in this "globalizing" world when, because of perpetual warfare, they cannot even feed their people? Is there any hope that one day they will enter global politics and global economy? Even the regional economic organizations have rarely worked satisfactorily. The Organization of African Unity (OAU), which was created in 1963, has little to credit itself for, except the independence of African nations. Any sense of independence and unity, however, is constantly undermined by continuing dependence on the financial help of the former European masters and by chronic conflicts on the continent.

The major problem of this organization is the lack of mutual consideration and confidence in each other. As a result, the many conflicts that have erupted since independence days have instead been solved with the help and pressure of West European and North Americans nations. Until recently, most negotiations concerning African conflicts have taken place in European capitals with European and American facilitators, not on African soils and with African facilitators. This lack of mutual respect is coupled with the lack of financial and logistic means to implement policies. The recent case of Rwanda has shown little enthusiasm on the part of African leaders, unable to transcend the personal animosities. Of course, the lack of logistic and financial means was cited as an explanation of the inaction, but the political will itself was dramatically lacking. The same reasons explain, to some extent, the negligible presence of Africa in the dynamics of global economy.

Democracy, the sine qua non of true development, was often despised by the leaders of independent Africa. To my mind, the biggest mistake made by the first leaders of independent Africa was to dismantle the political oppositions that had existed in the fight for independence and in the early years of the respective Republics. To achieve ethnic harmony was the excuse they used to topple democratic institutions.

African independence was also achieved in the heat of the Cold War, another element that did not help the advent of a democratic culture. Siding with the West or with the communist block was cause enough for a President to be defended by the one or deposed by the other. Africa thus became the ideological battleground with Presidents leaning on the side that offered the best protection. The Cold War consequently produced dictators in Africa who managed to rule for decades at the expense of true democracy and to the misery of their people. Those who were not abandoned by their protectors continued to rule: Houphouet Boigny of Ivory Coast, a protégé of France, died at the age of 88, still President. Mobutu Sese Seko of Zaire, one of the most terrible dictators of independent Africa, was a long-time ally of the United States of America. He was toppled by a rebellion in 1997 after 32 years of rule. Since the Cold War was over, the Americans no longer needed him to counter the communist threat previously posed by the Marxist regime in Angola. From the 1960s to the 1990s other regimes came and went with the wish of foreign powers. When military coups and death became the only ways of relinquishing power, it goes without saying that the transfer of power would not be smooth. This three-decade practice created a political tradition that encouraged violence and war as expedient ways of conquering power. Bad habits die hard, and it will take time and strong commitment to reverse this mentality. If we agree that democracy is a process (not a state), one cannot expect many African nations to become democracies overnight. The passage from dictatorship to democracy will be a long and sometimes violent road, as it will be hampered by poverty, illiteracy, the scourge of HIV/AIDS that decimates millions of Africans every year, and myriads of other problems that the Western democracies have put behind them a long time ago. Decades of dictatorial military regimes have left Africa an almost pathetic case of underdevelopment. Some European Africanists have even suggested that Africa has refused to develop. Today, while everybody else is busy threading economic ties, African nations are still fighting their tribal and/or ethnic wars, using large chunks of their budgets to purchase weapons, and dealing with embarrassing leaders. The regional organizations do not resist the national/regional conflicts.

In 1978, Rwanda, Burundi, and Zaire launched a regional organization called "La Communauté Economique des Pays des Grands Lacs" (The Economic Community of Countries of the Great Lakes) (CEPGL), but this organization was often vulnerable to political dissensions due mainly to the politics of ethnicity in Rwanda and Burundi. In both countries, there are three ethnic groups: the Hutu, the Tutsi, and the Twa. Rwanda was under the Tutsi rule for four centuries until 1959 when a revolution deposed the Tutsi monarchy and proclaimed a Republic ruled by the Hutu. No such thing happened in Burundi, which continued to be governed by the Tutsi minority even after the recovery of independence until June 1993 when a Hutu president was elected (and killed only four months later). The ethnic tensions in both countries with different groups being in power meant that the free movement of people and goods was not possible.

Since independence, the two countries have been confronted with ethnic conflicts. The 1959 social revolution in Rwanda led several hundreds of thousands of Tutsi out of the country to neighboring Uganda, Burundi, Zaire, and Tanzania. Several ethnic upheavals forced Burundian Hutu to flee to Rwanda, Zaire, and Tanzania. With this situation of "refugee exchange" between Rwanda and Burundi, Burundi receiving Tutsi refugees from Rwanda, and Rwanda receiving Hutu refugees from Burundi, the regular attacks launched by those refugees to return to their homelands always created a tense situation in the region from the 1960s to the 1990s. I remember the heated broadcast exchanges in 1972 between the Rwandan president (Grégoire Kayibanda) and the Burundian president (Michel Micombero) when ethnic tensions in Burundi caused an estimated 150 thousand deaths among the Hutu ethnic group (mostly the elite) massacred by the Tutsi-dominated army. In the 1960s, the Rwandan refugees, especially those living in Uganda and Burundi launched at least six attacks, but these were driven back by the government army. What is interesting and can shed some light on the horrendous carnage that took place in Rwanda in 1994 is that each time the refugees attacked, there were massive government-organized reprisals against the Tutsi of the interior. For example, it is estimated that in 1963 more that ten thousand Tutsi were massacred in Rwanda following an attack of the refugees. This reaction does not mean that the massacred people were in any way associated with the attack except for their belonging to the same ethnic group as the assailants. As it will be discussed later on, this became a common practice on the part of the Rwandan government that each time something dramatic was happening or was about to happen, they tended to use the Tutsi as scapegoats. An example of that took place in 1973 when the minister of defense, Major General Juvénal Habyarimana and a group of officers (mostly from Gisenyi and Ruhengeri), wanted to seize power. They instigated a general unrest in the country, leading to the killing of the Tutsi for no particular reason--this time there was no refugee attack. The unrest offered him a pretext to take power by a military coup with the promise to restore peace in the country. No sooner had he taken power than peace was established, as if by enchantment.

This politics of ethnicity is not of the nature to foster good relations between Rwanda and Burundi. Therefore, it should not be surprising that organizations such as the CEPGL (Rwanda, Burundi and Zaire) or the Organization of the Kagera Bassin (Burundi, Rwanda, Uganda, Tanzania) are very sensitive to ethnic tensions. With the ethnic conflict in Rwanda since October 1990 and in Burundi in October 1993, it is almost normal that the two organizations have ceased to exist in practice, though in principle they are still in place. Between October 1990 and April 1994, Rwanda and Burundi accused each other of helping the rebels attacking the two countries. Though the invaders came from Uganda to attack Rwanda, the Rwandan government accused Burundi of being an immediate transit for recruits joining the Rwandan Patriotic Front. In the same manner, the Burundian government was accusing Rwanda of hosting and training an underground political organization called PALIPEHUTU or The Hutu People Liberation Party to topple the Tutsi government in Burundi. These mutual accusations were not necessarily unfounded.

Refugee attacks against Burundi mostly came from Tanzania. They were also followed by organized massacres of Hutu inside Burundi. Numbers in 1972, 1988, 1991, and 1993 reached dramatic levels. In 1988, I had the misfortune of watching corpses of Burundians floating on the Akanyaru River, which flows near my native hill. The corpses came

from the carnage of Ntega and Marangara where the Tutsi army had mercilessly massacred the Hutu and thrown their bodies in the Akanyaru River
(between Rwanda and Burundi)--a method that probably inspired the Hutu
militia of Rwanda in April, May, and June 1994.

The result of this ethnic play is that the regional organizations
could hardly survive the tensions between the two governments, one led by
an ethnic majority (Hutu of Rwanda) visibly oppressing the minority, the
other led by an ethnic minority (Tutsi of Burundi) visibly oppressing the
majority. Thus, any lasting solution to ethnic violence in Rwanda and Burundi will necessarily come from an inclusive consideration of the problems of the two countries (and of the whole region of Central Africa, for
that matter).

Other regional economic organizations such as the Preferential
Trade Area (PTA), which includes countries in eastern and southern Africa, are undermined by the same political situation of distrust fueled by
ethnic politics. This kind of environment hinders the free movement of
persons, goods, and money, sine qua non of a free trade area. Concerning
the free circulation of persons, countries fear that, due to continuous political tensions and warfare in the region, unwanted elements can easily enter their territories. As for the circulation of money and goods, the ever
urgent need of strong international currencies (especially the American
dollar and generally currencies from the developed world) in the majority
of the countries makes the regional currencies unwelcome.

While the rest of the world was busy making economic associations with immediate neighbors, the African nations were projecting a
fully integrated African economic community sometime after 2025, according to the OAU meeting in Abuja, Nigeria in 1991. It may well be the
case that this community does not see its birth, or if it ever does see one, it
may be determined by the forces already in place, giving it a direction that
will favor the already existing markets of North America, Europe, and
South-East Asia. Or like its political counterpart, the African Union, it
may lack solid democratic foundations and the means and ways of implementing any economic policies. For any economic and political union to
emerge, a number of conditions need to be fulfilled.

If African nations do not learn to solve their ethnic, regional, and
religious problems, there will always be conflicts. A democratic culture
empowered by solid and nonpartisan national institutions appears to me to
be the only way of achieving peace, without which development is absolutely impossible. The judicial system of each nation must be refined to
serve true democracy, not individual dictators and their cronies. Most of
all, the political elite must show restraint and stop using the easily manipu-

lated population for selfish political and economic advantages. The respect for national laws and human rights must be defended by justice; if not, there is no possibility of democracy.

We all know that men, being what they are, need constraining principles that limit their hegemonic impulses that make them want to dominate and grab everything. The raison d'être of any government is to ensure equal opportunity for all. Stories from all over Africa show that authorities tend to place themselves above the laws of their nations, and little by little take their families and friends in the same place, as they move to manage the country as their own property. As I will suggest later on, the horrendous carnage that cost the lives of hundreds of thousands of Rwandans in 1994 was the result of a group of people, a minority from one region of the country, who were exempted from the law of the land and eventually convinced themselves that they could do anything without being bothered. In a rehearsal mode, they selectively killed on small scales for three years since 1990 and then in April 1994 unleashed a well planned killing machine that they had carefully engineered through propaganda and a culture of impunity. They wanted to exterminate a whole ethnic group and a whole political opposition so as to maintain themselves in power.

Most African countries depend to a great extent on international donors, who help to balance budgets, build roads, hospitals, and other infrastructures. It makes no sense for international assistance to continue putting money in development projects if these are later destroyed by internal upheavals. In addition to aid, it makes more sense to focus on bringing about a democratic culture, within which at least the basic human rights are respected and the values of life and liberty honored.

Chapter Two

The Hamitic Hypothesis and Rwandan Historiography

The Bahutu display very typical Bantu features.
--Ministère des Colonies (Belgian Ministry of Colonies), *Rapport sur l'administration belge au Ruanda-Urundi (1925)*

The Mututsi of good race has nothing of the negro, apart from his color.
-- Ministère des Colonies, *Rapport sur l'administration belge au Ruanda-Urundi (1925)*.

Two theoretical approaches have been broadly applied to Rwandan ethnic studies: essentialism and functionalism, both of which, unfortunately, atomize the fluid reality of ethnicity. Essentialism posits primordial ethnic processes. Even though this approach can certainly explain the processes involved in ethnic mobilization, it can also be dangerous in that it can lead to the assumption of cognitive predispositions and to the stereotypical labeling of groups of people or collective labeling, including the denial of humanity to the negatively labeled group. This approach, for example, explains Goldhagen's theory underlying his controversial book *Hitler's Willing Executioners: Ordinary Germans and the Final Solution* (discussed in Chapter Five) in which he maintains that cognitive anti-Semitism ran deep into the collective German (and European, for that matter) cultural mindset. Of course, Hitler and his cronies had used essentialism in defining the Jews as inferior beings, as less than human, as a gangrene that needed to be taken out of the German social body. Horowitz calls 'essentialism' the mistake of "'pseudospeciation', the treatment of members of other groups as if they were members of different species, which manifestly they are not. Denial of common humanity has produced unspeakable brutality against members of other ethnic groups"(75). Thus the most dangerous aspect of essentialism is that its casts the other, dominated group as "other," bad, evil, and as such it must be eliminated or continually victimized.

Functionalism views society as a functional, static, and conflict-free entity as if clear-cut and firm boundaries separated the different social components. As Horowitz cautions, however, "even as conceptual convenience often demands a static idiom, it needs to be remembered that the phenomena are reciprocal rather than unidirectional."[1] Furthermore, social and ethnic groups are in constant interaction in both peaceful and violent periods. As the previous chapters have shown, there are layers of factors in this interaction. Elements of ethnic conflict are not necessarily prior to it, for "they take place partly in anticipation of conflict."[2] They can be simultaneous to it, and acute ethnic awareness is certainly posterior to ethnic violence. In the cases of Rwanda and Burundi, ethnic strife tends to obliterate cross-ethnic boundaries based on ethnic factors in the process of creating Manichean patterns of social behavior. This is certainly the case in post-genocide Rwanda, where people have been easily categorized as Hutu (collectively guilty of genocide) and Tutsi (victims of Hutu mass killings). Despite this teleological import of functionalism that makes ethnic groups discreet and fixed agents of history and social structure, there is room to claim that it offers a theoretical framework within which to understand the leading ideology of ethnicity in pre-colonial, colonial, and postcolonial Rwanda.

Broadly speaking, functionalism views society as organized along the functional needs of the various institutions, the cultural patterns, and the personality traits of individuals. Rules and role assignment, selection, socialization, and consensus are given central, fundamental prominence. Within this framework, small social organizations are integrated in the superordinate value system of the society. The system itself is structured as goal or structure-oriented. Specific roles are assigned to individuals and groups of individuals. Organizations such as schools and the army are relevant, efficient, and stable in as much as they adapt to and advance the determined goals of the system. Conflict is dysfunctional and threatening because it undermines the efficient production of desirable social relations and values.

Applied to the situation of Rwanda, functionalism would mean that the categories of Hutu, Tutsi, and Twa are always discreet and are assigned, as in the colonial and postcolonial historiographies, the respective roles of farmers, livestock breeders, and hunters, a taxonomy that is far from representing the labor picture in Rwanda. Moreover, it can lead to what a Rwandan historian has condemned as "the absurdity of some debates on the part of the so-called intellectuals who aim at the exclusive appropriation of anterior heritage, such as cattle, metal and so on."[3] The functionalist approach carries the danger of systematically classifying the Hutu, the Tutsi, and the Twa in the three categories of farmers, livestock breeders and hunters, thus denying the essence itself of Rwandan nationhood since the sixteenth century. Pushed a little bit further, it would easily simplify the complex issue of ethnic relations in Rwanda (and in the Great Lakes region in general) and consecrate a fallacious ideology of origins that has produced the historiography that led to the independence of Rwanda and the constitution of its social, economic, and political institutions.

Proponents of both functionalism and essentialism have failed to note that these two approaches are not mutually exclusive in the case of Rwanda. The functionalism of colonial historiography will later become, and coexist with, the essentialism of leaders of independent Rwanda. Essentialism marked the ethnic ideology and policies of the Hutu-dominated governments from the 1960s to 1994 in casting the Hutu as the victim and the Tutsi as the invader of Hutu land and the oppressor, thus making him the scapegoat of the two Hutu governments' failures.[4] This essentialist logic is certainly part of the logic of the 1994 Rwandan genocide, as it was part of the Shoah. The killing machine of 1994 used the ethnic functions prescribed by the colonial agenda and turned them into ethnic bias and stereotypes to oppress and annihilate the other—the other being the Tutsi and their moderate Hutu sympathizers. Thus it is not surprising that "the son of the farmer" (mwene sebahinzi) was a favorite expression used by the infamous extreme RTLM to refer to the Hutu, calling upon them to compete in eliminating the Tutsi. In the period between the 1950s and 1994, essentialism and functionalism were used in selective political instances to promote the Hutu ideology. Functionalism allowed ethnicity to be constructed in cultural narratives whereas essentialism produced ethnic features and attributes as innately determined. At the time of mass killings, the former fed on the latter.

The functionalist approach works particularly well with myths and mythologies that legitimize the cultural, political, and even economic values and beliefs of the foundations of a given society. The goal of such myths is "to strengthen tradition and endow it with greater value and prestige, by tracing it back to a higher, better, more supernatural reality of initial events."[5] The socio-political system of pre-colonial Rwanda was very much organized along these mythical configurations, according to the historiography that guided Rwanda since the 1950s. The tradition that these mythologies produced operated a remarkable shaping of the Rwandan society, assigning to its components roles that looked like divine decrees, and the resultant social organization somehow "a divinely ordained social structure in which each individual was assigned a specific caste, and each caste a specific rank."[6] Let us look at several myths and the ways they assigned roles to the groups in the society.

The first, found in a dynastic poem entitled "The Story of the Origins," has it that at the origin of history of Rwanda there was Kigwa, who fell from heaven and had three sons: Gatwa, Gahutu, and Gatutsi.[7] When he decided to choose his successor, he entrusted each of the three sons with a pot of milk to watch over during the night. At daybreak, Gatwa had drunk the milk; Gahutu had fallen asleep and in the carelessness of the sleep, had spilt the milk; and only Gatutsi had kept watch throughout the night, and only his milk pot was safe. So it was clear to Kigwa that Gatutsi should be his successor and by that fact should be exempt of any menial tasks. Gahutu was to be his servant. The utter unreliability of Gatwa was to make him only a clown in society. As a result, Gatutsi received cattle and command whereas Gahutu would acquire cattle only through sweat and services to Gatutsi, and Gatwa was condemned to hunger and gluttony and would not acquire cattle.

Like all myths in all communities, this one was not a piece of mere fiction, but an attempt to imagine a reality enacted in the unwritten law of the Rwandan society. It became a moral justification of the perpetuation of a minority rule, dictated, as the myth wants it, by a divine order. Pierre Smith notes that different versions of the same myth construct the same functional vision of the Rwandan society. One such version says that the three sons of Gihanga were challenged to build a house on a rock. Only Gahutu succeeded in bringing the necessary material and completing the task, thus demonstrating his technical know-how and his taste for manual work.[8] In yet another version, Gatutsi keeps his pot of milk safely and receives cattle as a result. Gahutu drops some milk on his hands, and this constitutes his predisposition for work. The woman drops some milk on her bosom, and this is a sign of motherhood. As for Gatwa, he drinks all the milk, and thus nothing except gluttony will be his mark. Another version, notes Smith, has it that Gihanga pronounces the judgment that Gatutsi will milk the cows, Gahutu till the fields, and Gatwa hunt.

Another version that clearly reflects the functionalist view of society has God telling the Tutsi that they are the only interesting group and giving them weapons to get rid of the other two, but the Tutsi thought about the role of the other two and refused. God said the same to the Hutu, but they thought about the protection and justice they received from the Tutsi and they also thought about the Twa who made the pots and amused them; they also refused. When the Twa's turn came, they immediately charged forward without any consideration, but God stopped them in good time and cursed them. As a result, they would not bear arms except at the service of the Tutsi.[9]

The second myth is found in the Banyiginya dynasty. Its phrasing is after a text published in the late 1950s when the minority was fighting the mobilization and attack of the Hutu majority. According to this myth, the ancestor of the Banyiginya is Kigwa, who arrived on a hill (locality) called "Rwanda rwa Gasabo" with his brother Mututsi and their sister Nyampundu. They arrived with cattle, goats, and fowl in selected pairs of male and female. They had a Mutwa with them called Mihwabiro, who closely followed them. They carried bows as weapons. They practiced hunting and forgery (blacksmiths). The land they joined was inhabited by the Bazigaba, whose king was Kabeja. In small groups then in larger ones, Kabeja's subjects talked to the newcomers. They received, first free of charge, afterwards in exchange of services, big game meat. Kabeja's men did not know the blacksmith craft, so they would give their services to receive hillhooks and hoes from the family of Kigwa. The ties between the servants of Kabeja and the family of Kigwa eventually became so close that the former left their first master and made themselves servants of Kigwa.

What this myth does repeatedly is to assign different roles, again establishing the Tutsi as shrewd in the successful attempt to enslave the Hutu. According to this myth, the Mutwa is already enslaved. The Hutu offered themselves into servitude on their own, without being forced to do so. Like the first, this myth establishes the traditional Rwandan society as a functional one, one in which roles and social categories are clearly defined, without any ambiguity. These stories are posterior to the realities they describe and interpret. They emphasize the intelligence, shrewdness, and agility of Gatutsi. As for Gahutu, he is good as a service provider. As for Gatwa, he is irredeemably a glutton, a clown, and a pariah.

One narrative explains how different groups received different levels of intelligence. The inclusion of the King (Umwami) and women here clearly shows that these stories were imagined in an attempt to explain and confirm social stereotypes:

> God invited everybody to get the intelligence contained in a pitcher of beer. The King arrived first, took the straw and drank to his thirst, leaving only a small quantity in the pitcher. Gatutsi then came and drank comfortably a sufficient quantity. When Gahutu's turn came, there was only a small quantity of liquid left, and he stood up, saying, "I didn't have enough to quench my thirst!" As for Gatwa, he ate the lees. As women did not have anything at all, it was decreed that they would use their husbands' intelligence.[10]

Another myth, which prevailed until the end of the monarchy at the end of the 1950s, concerns the divine omnipotence of the King. The popular tradition wants the King to be the incarnation of the deity *Imana* (God). He was viewed as the embodiment of the virtues of the system; he was the source of prosperity. Thus was he given divine attributes. The very moment a Tutsi prince became *Umwami*, he ceased to be a Tutsi. He embodied the three components of the Kingdom—Tutsi, Hutu, and Twa. He became God. He was addressed as "Nyagasani" (Lord). He was all beautiful--even when physical traits pertained to the contrary. His generosity did not know any limits. He could provide power and wealth and could withdraw them, as he pleased. He rendered justice, and all things and beings were, as by divine decree, his. For example, there was a saying that all cows and women of the kingdom of Rwanda belonged to the King. In a word, the king was "a faultless work of art, chiselled by chosen tools.... The nobility issued of the sacred groves of Rwaniko.... The hero of manifold beauty whose decision cannot be swayed, and whose memory will live for ever in Rwanda."[11] Popularly perceived as divine, the Mwami's power was sacred. He was guided by advice of repositories of esoteric codes and rituals embodied in the Abiru (a college of esoteric advisors).

In accordance with the societal functional organization and despite the claim that he transcended all ethnic groups, the King was a Tutsi, a role assigned through the other myths and consolidated in the last one. That is to say, the Tutsi supremacy was ultimately sealed in the assumed divine endowment of the King. It was a sacrilege to rebel against either the social role assignment or the King: "The King and the Tutsi [were] the heart of the country. Should the Hutu chase them away, they would lose all they have and Imana would punish them."[12] Due to the perpetuation of this legend, the Hutu were believed to be fearful. Consequently, through carefully marshaled myths, the Tutsi managed to affirm themselves as a master race, Imana's elect as it were, superior in military craft, showing courage and intelligence, and certainly because of all these qualities, called to be wealthy.

These myths made their way through the cultural life of Rwandans, who came to accept them. This acceptance was sealed in popular sayings, proverbs, and folktales. For examples, all folktales began as follows: "Let me tell you a story and stretch it so that even the traveler from afar will find it tied to the pillar of the house. Dead are the dogs and rats, giving way to the cows and the drum. Once upon a time, there was...." The cows and the drum are symbols associated with the King. Popular sayings such as "I'm not a Muhutu of your father" (Si ndi umuhutu wa so) assign the role of servant to the Bahutu. This particular saying thus simply means: "I'm not your father's servant." The noun "umuhutu" (singular)-abahutu (plural) was used as a synonym of servant-servants. Other sayings such as "Nta nyiturano y'umuhutu" (You cannot expect gratefulness from a Muhutu) put the Bahutu in an unworthy, shameful position only concordant with their social role of servants.

Other vehicles of minor literature such as proverbs carried the same ideological theme in both Rwanda and Burundi. In both Rwanda and Burundi, there are several ethnic proverbs that say it all. One says, "If you teach a Hutu to shoot a bow, he'll shoot an arrow into your stomach" (said by the Tutsi), and the other side has it that "If you polish the teeth of a Tutsi, tomorrow he'll bite you" (said by the Hutu). Other proverbs include "utuma abahutu abagira benshi" ("one who sends Hutu as messengers sends many," that is, "If one chooses Hutu as messengers, one better send many" implying that Hutu cannot be trusted as messengers); "Umuhutu ntashimwa kabiri" ("A Hutu is not thanked twice" implying that "A Hutu can do well once, but not twice"); "Umuhutu yabonye urupfu ruhita ati garuka undarire" (Literally, "A Hutu, upon seeing Death pass by, said "come back and have me for dinner" meaning that the Hutu are careless); "Inkunguzi y'umuhutu yivuga mu batutsi" (meaning "A Hutu brings bad fate to himself by singing his own praise among the Tutsi"); "Umututsi umuvura amaso akayagukanurira" (Literally, "you heal a Tutsi's eyes and he uses them to stare at you"); "umututsi umusemberera mu kirambi akagutera ku buriri" ("you let a Tutsi sleep in your living room and during the night he invades your bed [for your wife]," referring to the stereotypical unruly sexuality of the Tutsi); "umututsi umuvura amenyo akayaguhekenyera" ("you heal a Tutsi's teeth, and he grinds them against each other to show his hatred for you"); "umutwa ararengwa agatwika ikigega" ("when a Twa satisfies his hunger, he burns the barn" meaning that the Twa are incapable of looking beyond the present); and "inzira ngufi yamaze abana b'abatwa" (literally, "the shortcut has decimated the children of Twa" (meaning that the Twa can be easily deceived; they are gullible).

Like many others in Rwanda and Burundi, these sayings and proverbs are expansions of the other myths we have looked at. In the construction of a fixed ethnicity, people imagined their ethnic belonging and moral characteristics through this type of discourse, among other narrative forms.

It is obvious that myths had a tremendous physical and psychological impact on the three ethnic groups. The cultural, social, and political force of the myths was such that the Hutu were powerless, exploited, oppressed, and terrorized.[13] More than this, the set of myths discussed above reflect a code of values that organized ethnic relations in Rwanda, relations of inclusiveness and exclusiveness, solidarity and inequality. This binary system is obviously skewed toward exclusiveness and inequality. In other words, what the myths achieved was to establish what Maquet has called the "premise of inequality,"[14] a careful premise of a functional hierarchy that distributes roles not just to ethnic groups but also to other categories, such as gender.[15]

It will be seen later on how these different myths were politically exploited by both the Hutu and the Tutsi at the eve of the 1959 Hutu Revolution, and even more in the post-independence era. Though fictitious in nature, the different myths are cultural realities shaping social relations and regulating daily interactions. Just as the Christians believe in the Bible and the Muslims in the Koran, these myths were part of the daily fabric of Rwandan life. They were functional constructs, but political manipulation since the 1950s turned them into essentialist, inescapable realities that dictated national policy. They constitute, since the turbulence of the social revolution of 1959, what Malinowski would characterize as "a living reality, believed to have once happened in primeval times, and continuing ever since to influence the world and human destinies."[16]

Colonization and Ethnic Stereotypes and Theories

The European explorers who wrote about the Rwandan society loaded their writings with stereotypes and produced theories that were inadequate. It is remarkable, however, that there is consensus in their description of the behavior of the Hutu and Tutsi. This consensus, I believe, is more due to European aristocratic bias and the grand metanarratives of the Enlightenment. The end of the nineteenth century in Europe was characterized, among other things, by dualistic systems that analyzed other systems in binary oppositions, in terms of inclusiveness and exclusiveness, solidarity and inequality. This period was the pinnacle of expansionist thinking in Europe, which pushed it to explorations and colonization in the first place, for economic and cultural hegemony.

To appreciate fully how the Europeans shaped Africa (and the rest of the world, for that matter), we need to understand how they annihilated, misrepresented, and devalued Africa to recreate it in their own image in the name of what Rudyard Kipling dubbed "the white man's burden" in a poem of the same title in 1899. In the last four centuries, Europeans devalued Africa through at least three projects that they undertook together, with the backing of a battery of philosophical and literary texts. Those campaigns include the Atlantic slave trade, colonization, and the Cold War. The Big Chain of Being, the Enlightenment philosophies of the seventeenth and eighteenth centuries, and various narratives in the same period promoted discourses that reduced the status of Blacks to a subhuman species in order to justify European cultural, economic and political aggression. The likes of Sir Francis Bacon, Peter Heylyn, William Bosman, David Hume, and Immanuel Kant cast Africans as failing the Enlightenment test of humanity. The tenet of this philosophy was Reason, supposed to reflect in arts and sciences. Any people who did not display these characteristics in the European manner were deemed inferior to Europeans. Numerous writings reflect the presence of arts and sciences as the litmus test that Europeans, projecting their own ideals on the people they subjugated, applied to their colonies around the world. A few examples should suffice to show the inexplicable violence with which the Europeans treated the colonized world.

Colonization followed the same process of undermining the values of the colonized. By definition, colonization is negation of the other. The pretext of "civilization" as an excuse is hardly a veiled way of casting the colonized as the center and the colonized as the margin. The margin's attributes in the colonizer's mind are savagery, violence, chaos, cannibalism, disease, ignorance, and total damnation; whereas the center is the locus of civilization, order, control, reality, and authenticity. Abrogating this racist dichotomy, Aimé Césaire proposed revising the colonizer's equation "colonization=civilization" with the colonized's own equation "colonization=thingification."[17] Colonization works in several stages: negation of the colonized's values, naming the colonized, replacing the colonized's values with the colonizer's system. Césaire characterizes the result of this process as follows: "I am talking about societies drained of their essence, cultures trampled underfoot, institutions undermined, lands confiscated, religions smashed, magnificent artistic creations destroyed, extraordinary possibilities wiped out."[18]

Morgan Goodwyn, who opposed the racist ideas of his contemporaries, summarized well the general account of Africans and non-Whites outside Europe in these terms:

> [a] disingenuous and unmanly Position has been formed; and privately (as it were in the dark) handed to and again, which is this, That the Negro's though in their Figure they carry some resemblances of manhood, yet are indeed no men...the consideration of the shape and figure of our Negro's Bodies, their Limbs and members; their Voice and Countenance, in all things according with other mens [sic]; together with their Risibility and Discourse (man's peculiar Faculties) should be sufficient conviction. How should they otherwise be capable of Trades, and other no less manly imployments [sic]; as also of Reading and Writing, show so much Discretion in management of Business; ...but wherein (we know) that many of our People are deficient, were they not truly Men?[19]

In "Of National Characters," the Scottish philosopher David Hume represents one of the most racist ideas that Goodwyn was trying to counter. Hume wrote:

> I am apt to suspect the Negroes, and in general all the other species of men (for there are four or five different kinds) to be naturally inferior to the whites. There never was a civilized nation of any other complexion than white, nor even any individual eminent either in action or speculation. No ingenious manufacturers amongst them, no arts, no sciences. On the other hand, the most rude and barbarous of the whites, such as the ancient Germans, the present Tartars, have still something eminent about them, in their valour, form of government, or some other particular. Such a uniform and constant difference could not happen, in so many countries and ages, if nature had not made an original distinction betwixt these breeds of men. Not to mention our colonies, there are Negro slaves dispersed all over Europe, of which none ever discovered any symptoms of ingenuity; tho' low people, without education, will start up amongst us, and distinguish themselves in every profession. In Jamaica indeed they talk of one Negro as a man of parts and learning [Francis Williams]; but 'tis likely he is admired for every slender accomplishment, like a parrot, who speaks a few words plainly.[20]

Immanuel Kant agreed with David Hume in these terms:

The Negroes of Africa have by nature no feeling that rises above the trifling. Mr. Hume challenges anyone to cite a single example in which a Negro has shown talents, and asserts that among the hundreds of thousands of blacks who are transported elsewhere from the countries, although many of them have been set free, still not a single one was ever found who presented anything great in art or science or any other praise-worthy quality, even though among the whites some continually rise aloft from the lowest rabble, and through superior gifts earn respect in the world. So fundamental is the difference between these two races of man, and it appears to be as great in regard to mental capacities as in color. The religion of fetishes so wide-spread among them is perhaps a sort of idolatry that sinks as deeply into the trifling as appears to be possible to human nature. A bird feather, a cow horn, a conch shell, or any other common object, as soon as it becomes consecrated by a few words, is an object of veneration and of invocation in swearing oaths. The blacks are very vain but in the Negro's way, and so talkative that they must be driven apart from each other with thrashings.[21]

The same Kant claimed correlation between the color of the skin and the level of intelligence. He wrote, "This fellow was quite black... a clear proof that what he said was stupid."[22]

There are many other examples that could be cited, but these should be sufficient to render the intellectual emptiness and violence that Europeans imposed on the continent of Africa (and on the colonized lands in general) since the Enlightenment up to (at least) the end of the colonial period. This imagined intellectual, cultural, and religious emptiness was then to be filled by European values.

This racist taxonomy shaped by the Europeans' philosophical, cultural, and anthropological bias led to multiple fantastic narratives about the groups they found in Rwanda. Contrary to their expectations, they found a centralized, well-organized nation that contradicted their view of Africa as a space of cultural and political emptiness, of savagery and chaos that cried for European Enlightenment. They had to find an explanation in their Eurocentric cultural sphere. They imagined the Tutsi rulers as some 'mutants' of Europeans who had conquered the Hutu and the Twa because of their superior intelligence and, of course, their relatedness to Europeans. It was, they surmised, these Hamites, these 'European cousins' who were responsible for the sophisticated civilization in the central region of Africa. The physical descriptions of the Tutsi, Hutu, and Twa as well as their psychological attributes, using measures so far unknown to Rwandan culture (height, nose shape, skin color and physical movement and posturing) started the steadfast codification of an otherwise fluid system.

A quick perusal through exploration literature presents the Tutsi as extremely reserved. Mecklenburg wrote of them, "one received the impression of being in the presence of an entire different class of men, who had nothing further in common with the "niggers" than their dark complexion."[23] Of the Tutsi of Burundi, Meyer wrote, "the longer one has traveled in negro countries, and the better one has got acquainted with the negro characters, the more one is impressed with the proud reservedness of the Tutsi. There is no restless curiosity, no noisy, partly fearful, partly good-hearted welcome, as with most other negroes. The tall fellows stand still and relaxed, leaning over their spears while watching the Europeans pass or approach, as if this unusual sight did not impress them in the least."[24] Along with this somehow positive picture, Meyer says of the Batutsi of Burundi that they are lazy and opportunist, that they rarely speak their mind and often lie especially to strangers so that their interlocutors have always to guess or take what they hear with a grain of salt. The whole picture of the Batutsi of Rwanda and Burundi, as it transpires from the literature, is that they are rich, powerful, lazy, shrewd, unscrupulous, arrogant, and merry life-loving.[25] A report from the Belgian Department of colonies ten years after Meyer's observation would push the description further:

> The Mututsi of good race has nothing of the negro, apart from his colour. He is very tall, 1.80 m. at least, often 1.90 m. or more. He is very thin, a characteristic which tends to be even more noticeable as he gets older. His features are very fine: a high brow, thin nose and fine lips framing beautiful shining teeth. Batutsi women are usually lighter-skinned than their husbands, very slender and pretty in their youth, although they tend to thicken with age....Gifted with a vivacious intelligence, the Tutsi displays a refinement of feelings which is rare among primitive people. He is a natural-born leader, capable of extreme self-control and of calculated goodwill.[26]

In the literature and consistent with the binary and largely essentialist approach of the moment, the Hutu were depicted as inexplicably servile, boisterous, cowardly, without dignity, and tied to the stream of bondage to which they had been subjected. Meyer writes of them, "due to four centuries of terroristic rule, they have become slaves in thinking and acting, though not so slave-like in character as the Banyarwanda under their Hamitic despots."[27] A 1925 colonial report describes them as displaying

> very typical Bantu features.... They are generally short and thick-

set with a big head, a jovial expression, a wide nose and enormous lips. They are extroverts who like to laugh and lead a simple life.[28]

As for the Twa, a colonial document describes the group as totally marginal:

> Member of a worn out and quickly disappearing race...the Mutwa presents a number of well-defined somatic characteristics: he is small, chunky, muscular, and very hairy; particularly on the chest. With a monkey-like flat face and a huge nose, he is quite similar to the apes whom he chases in the forest.[29]

Nevertheless, it is erroneous to liken totally the situation of ethnic relations in Rwanda and Burundi, for in the latter, the Ganwa princely ruling dynasty, a special subgroup within the Tutsi ethnic group, complicated demarcation across ethnic boundaries. The Ganwa were superior to the other Tutsi. Even in Rwanda, a strictly delimiting approach is definitely dangerous, due to the fluid nature of ethnic affiliation.

This brief discussion of stereotypes, which certainly existed before the arrival of the European explorers, but which were systematized as social and political institutions, suggests that ethnic differentiation goes hand in hand with the mythological and cultural stereotyping in any given society. The result of stereotypes is polarization of social groups for easy control, and in the case of colonial Rwanda, for the Tutsi to stay in power. We will see later that even after the Tutsi monarchy, this politics of polarization will continue to be exploited by the Hutu majority for the same reason. One thing I often heard in Rwanda was that the Tutsi were arrogant and cruel (said by the Hutu) and that the Hutu lacked tact and were gluttonous (said by the Tutsi).

Social mythologies are not reflections or representations of some metaphysical reality, nor just a statement of a desired social order, but actually the creation, interpretation, and perpetuation of that reality. At the end of the day, myths are so imbued in the collective mind that they become the force through which people imagine themselves as members of their society. They become the conscience through which people view themselves (or at least that is the ultimate goal of those who promote the ideologies circulated by the myths). For example, in the northwestern part of Rwanda (Ruhengeri and Gisenyi) where I worked for six years, I heard of schoolteachers who taught their pupils that the Tutsi are very cruel people, even though many of those poor pupils did not even know what a Tutsi or a Hutu was. A Tutsi family I knew very well told me one evening that their daughter came home from school inquiring about that terrible, cruel creature called Tutsi that her teacher had talked about. Shortly after the outbreak of war in October 1990, two children of a high-ranking Hutu officer in the Rwandan army surprised their parents and their guests, who were talking in the living room. To the embarrassment of the officer, one child declared that he was a Hutu and the other that she was a Tutsi. Obviously, they had learned this vocabulary from school. Once ethnic identities (or any identities for that matter), as flawed as they might be, become part of public institutions (such as schools, political practices, and everyday discourse), they inscribe themselves in the collective consciousness. Education to correct the distorted history of a nation and uproot ethnic bias does little to change the situation and, in fact, may be in the eyes of some as a validation of old stereotypes. For example, after the Tutsi genocide in 1994, the decision of the new government, dominated by the Rwandan Patriotic Front, to issue new identity cards that do not mention the bearer's ethnic affiliation and to embark on a program of national reconciliation has been viewed by a number of Hutu, especially in the exile communities around the world as ways of establishing and maintaining Tutsi dominance over the Hutu. There are, as I write, Hutu who still believe that the Tutsi are an alien race and Rwanda should be a Hutu country, as there are a number of diehard Tutsi who are convinced of Tutsi superiority. This posture of polarization that is used continually throughout the history of humanity and certainly in particular force today is essentially moral and normative, for despite new philosophical trends and aesthetics (for example the postmodern aesthetics) that suggest otherwise, there is always something functional, binary, and prescriptive in our societies, even in the most liberal societies, especially in times of conflict. So the so-called "premise of inequality" in Rwanda produced the kind of psychological inhibitions desired by the myths and wrought other psychological anxieties and fears that have crept into post-colonial Rwanda and Burundi. It will be used to justify other practices similar to those of the *ancien régime* even when carried out in different times and by different ethnic groups.

    The colonial rule itself did not help to correct the wrong stereotypes; in fact, it froze and codified them and established them as social and political institutions. It will even encourage the status quo confirming the Tutsi as "intelligent, refined, and courageous" and thus born to rule over the "cowardly un-witted" Hutu. The reversal of this polarized situation resulted in a terrible bloodshed because it was not simply a political reversal but a psychological reversal as well, which may explain the animosity of the Hutu extremists against the Tutsi in Rwanda and the resistance of the Tutsi military in Burundi to a democratic rule in 1993. At the same time, it suggests that fear and suspicion of the ethnic other will be there for another time to come, for no one can heal psychological traumas in one generation.

As the German and later the Belgian colonialists used their racial and class biases in dealing with Rwanda (and Burundi), they identified with the Tutsi, who were tall and appeared to be refined and intelligent. They considered the Tutsi as a group distinct from the Hutu and the Twa and created the theory according to which the Hutu came from the Chad region and the Tutsi from Ethiopia. They had it that the Tutsi descended from the Biblical figure of Ham. Using John Speke's racist theory of origins, the Germans and the Belgians associated the Tutsi to the Hamites. Thus was the Hamitic Hypothesis introduced and became the most devastating myth in Rwandan historiography.

The Hamitic Hypothesis

Much has been written about the Hamitic Hypothesis, but it is necessary to recall it here for the central role it played in the creation of ethnic categories in Rwanda since the colonial period. In its dealings with Africa, Europe has always displayed its superiority complex and, of course, did not hesitate to look for justification of the inferiority of Africans, even in the Christian epic, the Bible. The story of Noah and his son Ham was the chosen text to carry the European projection of African inferiority. In Genesis (the book of Judeo-Christian origins) IX, we read that "when Noah awoke from his drunkenness, he learned what his youngest son Ham had done to him. And he said: cursed be Canaan, the last born of Ham." In Judaic historiography since the sixth century A.D., the Babylonian Talmud has it that the African carried the curse of their ancestor Ham and that they are black, degenerate, and condemned to slavery.[1] In the nineteenth century, egyptology dramatically revised the Hamitic myth to make Hamites indigenous to northeast Africa with their proper civilization. It is this civilization that European explorers in the second half of the nineteenth century are going to exploit to construct their myths of African origins and characteristics.

In explaining the 'superiority' of the Tutsi, the Europeans imagined the Hamitic myth that placed the origin of the Tutsi outside of Africa, a myth in line with the historical, cultural, and intellectual emptiness they had imposed on the "dark continent." Their logic was that no group this good could come from this continent.

The Nile explorer John Hanning Speke, in his *Journal of the Discovery of the Source of the Nile*,[30] claimed that the establishment of interlacustrine kingdoms was the result of the conquest by a superior race with a superior civilization whose origin he placed in Ethiopia. When he discovered the kingdom of Buganda in 1857-59, he linked its civilization to a Hamitic race, the Bahima, also called Galla or Abyssinians. He maintained that the Galla of Southern Ethiopia were the ancestors of the Tutsi/Bahima of the Great Lakes. This hypothesis was uncritically accepted and diffused by other nineteenth century explorers and by early twentieth-century missionaries and colonialists (who worked hand in hand for the colonial undertaking). Father Pagès argued that the Tutsi originated from ancient Egypt.[31] De Lacger posited that they had come from either Melanesia or Asia Minor.[32] Father van den Burgt profiled the Tutsi as European ideations of beauty, thus capturing the canon of beauty using European standards: "We can see Caucasian skulls and beautiful Greek profiles side by side with Semitic and even Jewish features, elegant golden-red beauties in the heart of Ruanda and Urundi."[33] As for Mgr Le Roy, "The Bahima differ absolutely by the beauty of their features and the light colour from the Bantu agriculturalists of an inferior type. Tall and well-proportioned, they have long thin noses, a wide brow and fine lips. They say they came from the North. Their intelligent and delicate appearance, their love of money, their capacity to adapt to any situation seem to indicate a Semitic origin."[34] The European fantasies about Tutsi origin sometimes bordered the ridiculous. Prunier mentions such different origins as "a primordial red race," "India," "the Garden of Eden," and "the Continent of Atlantis."[35]

All in all, narratives of Tutsi superiority placed their origin from without Africa, closer to the Europeans' own origins. For more than sixty years, these narratives informed the European dealings with the Rwandan society. The Germans and then the Belgians used the system of indirect rule based on an extreme mapping of their own hypotheses about race relations in Rwanda, with the dire consequence of developing a huge superiority complex among the Tutsi elite and an inferiority complex among the Hutu. The two egos, one bloated, the other flattened, are going to collide in a lethal rage since the 1950s and ultimately culminate in the 1994 genocide. Franche comments that explorers and missionaries

> Had read Aristotle, Ptolémée, John Speke whom they quote. The great Aristotle had written that the pygmies lived in the "Mountains of the Moon." It was thus true. Speke offered a theory making of Tutsi descendants of Semitic Hamites. Because he based his theory

on the Bible, it could be only true. Since then, explorers' and missionaries' narratives spoke of the Twa as "Pygmies," "Myrmidons," "dwarves" whereas the Tutsi were described as absolute rulers of a fabulous kingdom, men who were delightfully described as "biblical figures" and giant size, "Caucasoids," our cousins somehow, who reigned over the Hutu, "poor Negroes" of Bantu race. The [explorers and missionaries] found in Rwanda what they wanted to find there, what had been said about it before they went there. [36]

Consequences of the Hamitic Hypothesis

The Speke theory had tremendous consequences in various domains such as linguistics, anthropology, and politics. Sir Johnston, the first British colonial commissioner in the Uganda Protectorate was the first to link the Hamitic myth and the different late nineteenth-century narratives, as he linked the Tutsi/Bahima to pastoral invaders called Bacwezi from Ethiopia.[37] It is these invaders of a superior race, the theory goes, that conquered the inferior race, the Hutu agriculturalists. The Belgian colonial administration and the Catholic Church based their political choices on this pseudo-scientific theory and established a system of indirect rule centered around the Tutsi. Pierre Ryckmans, a Belgian administrator of Rwanda in the 1920s, had this to say about the Tutsi:

> The Batutsi were meant to reign. Their fine presence is in itself enough to give them great prestige vis-à-vis the inferior races which surround them.... It is not surprising that those good Bahutu, less intelligent, more simple, more spontaneous, more trusting, have let themselves be enslaved without ever daring to revolt.[38]

This "meant to reign" political principle implied that the Hutu were systematically ignored for administrative positions. The Mortehan Law of 1926 not only abolished the three-fold functions of chefs (umunyabutaka 'land prefect', umunyamukenke 'grazing land prefect', and umunyangabo 'army/security' prefect), it also led to the Tutsization of the administration, as the Hutu *sous-chefs* were systematically replaced by Tutsi. Later on, when the Belgian colonial administration attempted to remedy the outrageous Tutsization of the country by replacing illiterate Tutsi chefs with educated Hutu, the Catholic Church strongly opposed the move, again using the "meant to reign" ideology. Louis de Lacger reacted in these terms:

> But experiments of government by the commoners did not generally

yield good results. The Bahutu promoted to "chefs" lacked prestige and authority. They looked inferior in the presence of the lords that they appeared to unseat.[39]

Another eminent member of the Catholic Church, Bishop Classe, also opposed Resident Mortehan's 1926 new law arguing that

> If we want to position ourselves from a realistic point of view and if we seek the interest of the nation, we have in the Tutsi youth an incomparable element of progress that everybody who knows Rwanda cannot underestimate. Thirsty for knowledge, desirous of knowing what comes from Europe as well as imitating the Europeans, entrepreneurial, sufficiently aware that ancestral customs have no justification, nevertheless keeping the political know-how of their forefathers and the intelligence of their race for the governing of men, these young men constitute strength for the good and the economic future of the country. Let anybody ask the Bahutu if they want to be governed by the commoners or by the nobles; the answer is clear; their preference goes to the Batutsi, and rightly so: born to reign, they have the flair for governing. That is the secret of their establishment in the country and their control of it.[40]

The same Bishop Classe forcefully buttresses his position for the Tutsization of the administration:

> The greatest mistake the government could make would be to put an end to the Mututsi caste. Such a revolution would lead the country directly to anarchy and to hateful anti-European communism. Far from promoting progress, it would undermine the government's action, by depriving it of auxiliaries capable of understanding and following it. That is the thinking and deep conviction of all the heads of mission in Rwanda, without any exception.... As a general rule, we will have no better, more intelligent, and more active chiefs more capable of understanding progress and even more accepted by the people than the Batutsi. It is mostly and foremost with them that the government will be able to develop Rwanda in all aspects.[41]

The Belgian colonial administration acted upon the recommendation of Bishop Classe. The Tutsi were favored for education and for administrative positions, at least until the death of Bishop Classe in 1945.

Many African anti-colonial writers have discussed the strong collaboration between colonization and Christianity. For example, the Kenyan Ngugi wa Thiong'o has dubbed it the Holy Trinity—the (colonizer's) gun and capital and the (missionary's) Bible. It is a truism that without the one, the other would probably not have worked as well as both did. It is from this perspective that we can understand why King Yuhi IV Musinga was deposed in 1931 by the colonial administration, forced into exile in Kamembe (southwest of the country), and replaced by his son, who took the throne name of Mutara III Rudahigwa. Yuhi IV Musinga and his sur-roundings had welcomed the Germans and the Belgians for political and economic convenience (for example, the Germans were instrumental in putting down insurgence in the North, especially the Ndungutse rebellion), but the Rwandan palace did not embrace Christianity. Rudahigwa's bap-tism in 1943 sealed the Christianization of Rwanda, following a well-known popular belief called "irivuzumwami" (the irrevocable word of the King, literally "what is said by the king"). Nobody would go against the king; in fact people would joyfully emulate his example. This was a great coup for the Catholic Church, but it also immensely benefited the colonial administration. Prunier notes that "the Belgians had never liked Musinga; he had fought alongside the Germans against them, he was haughty and unruly, his mother was a pest, he was openly adulterous, bisexual and in-cestuous, he never converted to Christianity and he obviously tried to hi-jack the white man's civilizing mission for his political benefit."[42] So the Catholic Church did not hide its great satisfaction with their own hijacking of the Kingdom in order to transform it into a model of Christianity and European civilization.

The Catholic Church was satisfied with the dramatic decrease of paganism, as pagan symbols disappeared from the royal court. The new king consecrated the kingdom of Rwanda to Christ the King three years af-ter his baptism. Since the German and particularly the Belgian colonial administrations, the Catholic Church has had a tremendous impact on Rwandan society. It led to changes in customs, values, and beliefs that prevailed in pre-colonial Rwandan society. It proclaimed traditional wor-ship (*kubandwa* and *guterekera*,[43] for example), polygamy, and adultery sinful and evil and encouraged obedience to authority (including its own), thrift, hard work, and Christian piety.

The Catholic Church used its overwhelming influence to rein-force its authority, notably through the naming process. It imposed the lin-guistic dichotomy of Christian (umukristu) versus non-Christian or pagan (umupagani). The Christian vocabulary should be shocking to the Rwan-dan cultural mind. The priest was referred to as "data" "mon père" (my fa-ther); God as "data wa twese" (father of us all), thus creating a new cul-tural and religious universe that blurred the traditional cultural and reli-gious cosmology, making the Rwandan Christians members of all these constituencies.[44]

The Hamitic Hypothesis and Rwandan Historiography

In ethnology, at the start of the twentieth century, Seligman affirmed that African civilizations were Hamitic, and African history had developed from the interactions between the Hamites, Negroes, and Bochimans (Bushmans). He claimed that the Hamites were pastoralist Europeans who arrived in waves with better weapons and more knowledge than the Negroes (who were farmers).[45] Eventually, ethnologists and linguists (such as Meinhof, who defended the Hamitic line in linguistics) included in the Hamitic race "the Berbers with blue eyes, the Toubous of Sahara, the Peuls, the Ganches of Canaries, but also, of course, ancient and contemporary Egyptians (excluding the Arabs), the Nubians, the Beja, the Abyssinians, the Galla (Oromo), the Danakel, the Somali, the Masai, the Hima, the Tutsi...."[46] An important aspect of the Hamitic hypothesis is that the Hamites are pastoralists as well as warriors and are superior to the farmers. European explanations of groups in the Great Lakes region of Africa considered the Tutsi, the Hima, and the Ganda as originating from the civilized Hamites. In ruling Rwanda, the Germans and later the Belgians founded their indirect rule on the superiority of Tutsi over Hutu and Twa and privileged them until the 1950s when they shifted their loyalty to the Hutu.

The historiography constructed by the colonial administration and its close ally (the Church) is the very one that has been transferred into history lessons and textbooks. Every young person who went through the Rwandan school system was fed with a history of Rwanda grounded in myths and hypotheses imagined by John Hanning Speke and the many explorers, colonialists, and missionaries who were influenced by him. The Europeans used the Hamitic myth in particular as a way of rationalizing a situation they did not understand and, in fact, creating one in their own image. Since then it has been a controlling cultural and political reality. First imagined as an analytical model, it was implemented as an administrative tool and used to decide who would govern, farm, go to school, and more. So Speke's fictional narrative was easily turned into practical meaning beyond the seed story of Ham and his sons. Interestingly enough, the European fantasies turned into physical features of the Hutu and the Tutsi bodies as well as in moral characters, intelligence, personal deportment (walking, speaking, eating, and more). Interestingly enough, the myth was appropriated by Hutu and Tutsi colonial and post-colonial leaders to shape their policies. The chronic fear that has been established in both camps continues to feed the dysfunctional relationships between the two groups as well as the discourse and international policy of the West. When there is an outbreak of violence in the region, reports abound with such bizarre expressions as "tribal violence," "Nilo-Hamitic" warfare, and so on and so forth.

The Rwandan historian, philosopher, and man of letters, Alexis Kagame, a Catholic priest, appropriated the official thesis of his Church epitomized by Louis de Lacger. Kagame brought together the European historiographical myths and the ideology of the Kingdom of Rwanda in a way that positioned him at the center of both. In *Inganji Kalinga (The Triumphant Kalinga)*, a reference to the royal drum named Kalinga, Kagame elaborated on the theory that the nyiginya dynasty, which ruled the Kingdom of Rwanda until September 1961, had unified the country by defeating and annexing smaller kingdoms. The narrative places the origin of the Tutsi in Ethiopia. Even though Alexis Kagame claims that the book will prove that the kingdom has its roots, a long history, and an ancestral culture, he embraces Louis de Lacger's hamitic "truths," with the originality of using them to promote a nationalist and Africanist ideology and redeem the history and culture of Africa and Rwanda lost to the same Hamitic hypothesis and other racist theories that claimed that Africa was without civilization, without history, and without any political structures. If any sense of organization existed, it was due to the invasion of 'European cousins', the Tutsi. In reality, Kagame's simple Africanist adaptation does not at all abrogate the Hamitic myth but, in fact, places Rwandan historiography within a European racist perspective. Also, Kagame's is a political historiography, apparently at the service of the Mwami's court, but it does, in fact, reinforce the European bias.

The history of Rwanda taught in schools from the colonial period to at least 1994 goes in the following historiographical line, heavily shaped by the Hamitic myth. Since roughly the tenth century, the three different ethnic groups (the Twa, the Hutu, and the Tutsi) have lived in what was known as Rwanda. The Twa, pygmoid people, arrived first and settled in Rwanda long before the other two groups, but they were few in number. They lived on hunting and picking wild fruit. The Hutu, belonging to the Bantu, arrived second. They were agricultural people, clearing forests to cultivate. Third and last to come were the Tutsi, pastoral and nomad people tending their cattle.

Compared to the other two ethnic groups, the Twa are of a low status in the society. Up to now, they do not seem to have made any real progress and continue to live on the margins of the society. The Tutsi are said to have come from Ethiopia. They came with their cattle and found the Twa and the Hutu already in place. Before any incorporation, the three ethnic groups had different societal and cultural life patterns.

The Ethiopid waves consisted of "small groups of warriors moving slowly with their cattle"--warriors because (perhaps among other things) "pastoral nomadic societies are usually warlike";[47] they had to face the danger of their herds being raided. They were usually small groups, due to the nature of nomadic life and cattle-feeding. As vegetation became scarce, they had to scatter the cattle, with the result of discouraging human concentration. Maquet maintains that "within the warrior band there was no political authority in the sense that there were no relations of physical coercion: among the warriors, one had certainly more authority than the others because of his ancestry, his ability, his intelligence, consequently, his opinions were usually followed."[48]

When they arrived, they found the Twa and the Hutu in place. The Hutu were living in small autonomous communities scattered in the region and shaped by patrilineal affiliation. Within one such community, "social order was maintained and conflicts were solved by kinship heads whose authority was based mainly on their position in the lineage: they were closer to the ancestors than the younger generations."[49]

While there was no institutionalized hierarchy or social stratification in the Tutsi pastoralist groups and in the agricultural communities, the new society became hierarchized. Though few in number, the Tutsi imposed themselves as the superior group, and the Hutu came to be considered an inferior stratum. The Tutsi used their control of cattle to obtain domination over the Hutu. According to this stratification, the Tutsi could require the Hutu to give services and goods. Only the Tutsi could be warriors (some historians, however, contend that many of the great 19th century army commanders [Abatware] were Hutu). Only the Tutsi could occupy administrative positions in the social structure. They constituted the Rwandan aristocracy with the numerous diffuse yet real privileges that an aristocracy is entitled to. Maquet writes, "they commanded an amount of social power much greater than the peasant [Hutu]; their opportunities to obtain what they wanted or to get things done were much better than those of the Hutu."[50] They institutionalized a feudal system called *ubuhake* (vassalage), "a relationship created when an individual with low social power (usually a Hutu) offered his services to and asked protection from a person with great social power (practically always a Tutsi)."[51] The two roles of *shebuja* (lord) and *garagu* (dependent) were social relationships of power, domination, and dependence.

The Tutsi structure of power gave both army and land to the Tutsi and very rarely to a small number of Hutu. The King was always Tutsi. He was a sacred King and his subjects mystically identified him with

Rwanda itself. He was the supreme ruler, but his power was shared by the Queen Mother. He was assisted by his court. All the services of the kingdom (the court, the armies, and the administration) were accountable to him.

Another characteristic of this social stratification was its fluid and flexible dimension. Because the Tutsi owned cows and land while the Hutu were economically dependent and their agriculture was for subsistence, it was generally assumed that the Tutsi was rich and the Hutu poor. A Tutsi who lost his wealth could lose his rank and become a Hutu, while a Hutu who managed to get land and cows and acquire the favor of the rulers could be raised a level to become a Tutsi. This was called "guhutura" (to shed off "hutuness"). This fluidity and flexibility thus transcended the physical differences of Hutu and Tutsi. The 1933-34 census carried out by the Belgian colonial administration did not take this into consideration. Instead the elements that were used to classify individuals included the ten-cow rule, oral information provided by the Church (which had them from neighbors), and physical measurements.[52] The ten-cow role is the most cited method the colonial rule used to assign ethnicity. It is said that a family with no or less than ten cows would automatically be a Hutu, whereas the owner of at least ten cows would be given the Tutsi stratum. Obviously, this was an arbitrary way of codifying and freezing the whole society; there were many *petits Tutsi* who did not own enough cows to qualify for their ethnicity, as there were a number of Hutu who owned enough cows to be classified as Tutsi. The social impact of this policy was never measured, but it probably meant a lot of ethnic changes. Today, the situation is even less clear due to a strong intermarriage in a great portion of the country. Today there are many people in Rwanda who cannot claim pure "hutuness" or pure "tutsiness."

This codification of ethnic groups constituted a clear institutionalization of ethnicity by the European master. The Belgian administration designed identity cards for every citizen of Rwanda. In addition to the usual information, the identity card bore the ethnic affiliation of each individual: Hutu, Tutsi, or Twa, and the patrilineage. This system destroyed the fluid and flexible dimension of ethnicity, since things being written, confined in writing, were hardly amenable to changes reflecting the economic position of the individual in the community. As it will be seen later on, this codification is going to be exploited by post-colonial leaders.

Towards the end of the nineteenth century, Rwanda was a Kingdom with all the attributes of a nation-state. The colonial power enlarged and made more rigid the differences between the Tutsi and the other groups. They guaranteed the Tutsi such advantages as school education and positions in the administration. The Germans and later the Belgians applied the policy of indirect rule. They used the existing political hierarchy, at the top of which was the King, to administer Rwanda, which was part of the territory known as Ruanda-Urundi.

The German colonial power brought its administrative perspective but based it on traditional chiefs. Though the power of the latter was dramatically diminished, the new administration kept the organizational patterns it found in place and in fact actually strengthened them in some aspects of domestic administration. It offered protection to the King and helped break the resistance in the northwest in exchange for allegiance to the European master. But the colonial power made sure to convert the rulers (chefs), whose legitimacy rested on traditional grounds, into officials appointed by the colonial authorities and accountable to them."[53] The Tutsi considerably increased their grip on the Hutu majority, as they continued to control the administration and use it for their own benefit. According to Maquet, out of 46 "chefs" in 1956, there was not a single Hutu among them, and out of 603 "sous-chefs" there was not a single Hutu,[54] guaranteeing that the colonial power maintained all the privileges of the Tutsi and their higher social power.

Despite their limited access to education during the colonial period, the Hutu elite quickly became aware of this situation of inequality. New ideas made them contemplate the possibility of a change. In the 1950s, the decade of independence movements on the African continent, the Hutu realized the power of their overwhelming number. They created a political party called PARMEHUTU to foster mobilization of the Hutu. In the same period, other political parties were created along ethnic lines. The parties that had no ethnic affiliations did not succeed in recruiting any significant number of members. In 1959, ethnic upheavals led to the Rwandan Revolution, which eventually deposed the monarchy and resulted in the proclamation of the Republic (1961), as well as the declaration of independence (1962).

Conclusion

The historiography imagined and imposed by Europeans and easily embraced by the Tutsi elite that benefited directly from it had by the late 1950s put in the public conscience that the Tutsi was a conqueror, a stranger from afar, and a colonizer like the Europeans. He had a different occupation, and he ruled over the Hutu and the Twa, supposedly erstwhile occupants of the land. As recently as 1978, Pierre del Perugia described theTutsi as a giant, mythological person who came from remote lands to impose his will and his civilization on the Hutu and the Twa. He claims that the pastoral Hamite reached the interlacustrine region at the end of the twelfth century. This pastoralist group brought cattle and a foreign tradition that organized the otherwise chaotic masses of the Bantu. Del Perugia also asserts that because of their physical size, the Hamites imposed themselves physically and morally on the Bantu. "The origin of their splendid race," Perugia writes, "remains always mysterious" and mythical.[55] They could be from as far as the high lands of Tibet.

Thus, from the first narratives by European explorers and missionaries to German and Belgian colonial administrators, to a few Rwandan historians (prominent among them Alexis Kagame) to history textbooks used in Rwandan schools since the advent of formal schooling (introduced by the colonial administration and the Church) to the present, the Tutsi were presented as foreigners and relatively recent immigrants who brought civilization before the Europeans themselves brought their own—in other words, they were distant cousins to the Europeans, and, more importantly, preferred allies in the "white man's burden."

Chapter Three

The Debris of Ham: From the 1959 Hutu Revolution to the Institutions of Ethnic and Regional Otherness

> For I am convinced that though they had no inkling of this, they took over from the old régime not only most of its customs, conventions, and modes of thought, but even those very ideas which prompted our revolutionaries to destroy it; that, in fact, though nothing was further from their intentions, they used the debris of the old order for building the new.
> --Alexis de Tocqueville, *The Old Regime and the French Revolution*.

In 1945, the death of Mgr Classe, a figure emblematic of the official Church and colonial thesis of Tutsi superiority over the other two groups, coincided with several factors that eventually led to the 1959 Hutu revolution. On the world arena, the end of World War II and the realization of the tremendous loss of human life (at least 61 million killed as a result of the war, six million of these being Jews killed just because they were Jews) and the overwhelming destruction of cities, infrastructure, and economies as well as the social misery that followed, resulted in an intellectual questioning of what the postmodern philosopher Jean-François Lyotard has termed "grand metanarratives" (*grands récits*) that had been used to justify the European civilizing (that is, colonizing) mission. When the Allies liberated the Nazi concentration camps, the world was shocked by the ultimate evil of genocide committed by Hitler's Germany against the Jews. There is no doubt that the subsequent questioning of European Enlightenment ideology following the atrocities of World War II created a liberating and open epistemology that rendered possible the steady voicing by the colonies of new and hitherto ignored ideas, including the demand for self-rule. The colonial powers would not give up their colonies without a fight. This point is often neglected in the discussion of the Rwandan revolution. As we shall see in this chapter, the Tutsi elite in power, using the language heard in the other colonies in the 1940s and 1950s, alienated the Belgian colonial administration by demanding immediate independence. In the logic of independence wars, this was like a declaration of war against those who had previously declared them "born to rule." Even though there was no conventional war between the Belgian colonial administration and the Tutsi rulers, the former could not just give independence to their former protégés without a fight.

On the Catholic Church's side, the period after 1945 saw the replacement of Walloon priests with Flemish priests from the working class and the lower middle class, who easily projected their plight of oppressed majority in Belgium to that of the Hutu in Rwanda. This change in the Rwandan Catholic Church was of paramount importance since the Hutu counter-elite was created in the Seminaries and in the precincts, and under the guidance, of the Catholic European clergy, chief among them Mgr Perraudin, whose bishopric nurtured and advised the Hutu movement founded by Grégoire Kayibanda, who would later become the first president of independent Rwanda. As the mix was changing in the European clergy, the number of their Rwandan counterparts had increased to equal that of Europeans. The Tutsi priests from dominant families and lineages, better educated than the few Hutu in the clergy, now understood that it was untenable to refute racial equality and also knew that self-rule was only a matter of years. If Belgium was to transfer power, then they needed to position themselves better than the less educated Hutu. The decree of July 14, 1952 allowed for the election of councils on different levels of government, but, as Maquet and d'Hertefelt note, "this was a process of diffusion of power but principally among the group which already possessed it, that is to say, the Tutsi caste."[1] Thus the empowerment of the indigenous Rwandan clergy challenged the new ideological line of the new generation of European priests. Moreover, this tension within the Catholic Church, along with the demand for self-government by the Tutsi elite, alienated the colonial and Church establishments. The European clergy countered this new challenge by the former protégés by offering sustained help to the Hutu on different fronts. First, they launched *Kinyamateka*, a periodical that was edited by one of the Hutu elite, Grégoire Kayibanda, a protégé of Mgr Perraudin. Kinyamateka quickly became the most circulated paper in the country. The circulation network of the paper consisted of the parishes all over the country. Second, the creation of cooperatives and associations gave economic opportunities and possibilities of exercising leadership to the rising Hutu counter-elite. As Prunier notes, "slowly, in various parts of the country, the Hutu, who now felt that they had support from one of the leading institutions of the white man's system, started to organize, creating mutual security societies, cultural associations and, in the north, clan organizations among some of the quasi-Bakiga clans which had submitted most recently to the colonial power."[2] By the end of the 1950s, these developments had created new centers of power that challenged the traditional economic and political structure.

On the social and political levels, as Catherine Newbury aptly shows, the changes in the social and administrative structure of certain Rwandan institutions such as ubuhake (vassalage) seriously undermined the traditional mediation of power relationships.[3]

Previously controlled by families and lineages, the *ubuhake* and other forms of dependence, exploitation, and oppression were replaced by mandatory labor for the local chiefs and for public works (demanded by the colonial administration and implemented by local chiefs) and by taxation, which also became an individual burden, not the burden of corporate families or lineages. This new arrangement little by little empowered the individual by "turning collective relations of social subordination into individual relations of economic exploitation."[4] On the judiciary level, the introduction of European forms of justice (courts) also weakened the authority of traditional chiefs as it reduced the necessity of seeking protection from the traditionalist form of clientship—as we have seen, previously, the *shebuja* was expected to protect his clients. On the economic side, the introduction of cash economy diminished the prestige of cattle economy and further undermined clientship, previously the sole manner of acquiring cattle (the primary measure of wealth in traditional Rwanda). Both the Hutu and the Tutsi participated in the new cash economy.

The Explosion of the Hutu-Tutsi Problem

The second half of the 1950s was marked by the public display of the rift between the colonial administration and its former protégés as well as the radicalization of social discourse among the major political players, resulting in a turbulent situation that eventually led to what is commonly referred to as the social revolution of 1959. This period is the degree zero of any attempt to understand the 1994 Rwandan genocide, as it produced what one scholar has referred to as the "founding narratives of the Rwandan tragedy." [5] The period not only reversed the political landscape but also created the ethnic and political discourse that served as the ideological basis of independent Rwanda. The shibboleth rhetoric of the moment created two ethnic poles that have since generated fear and suspicion and become part of the collective consciousness, especially at moments of strife.

The year 1957 was particularly significant. Christian teaching and formal schooling had produced in a part of the Rwandan elite, both Hutu and Tutsi, a desire for democracy, freedom, and progress. That trend radicalized month after month. Probably the most dramatic event of the year was the publication of "Le Manifeste des Bahutu" or the "Bahutu Manifesto" in March 1957. Heavily influenced by the Hamitic Hypothesis, the signatories of the manifesto, all of them of Hutu extraction, blatantly reacted in very strong terms against what they called the Tutsi colonization. They said that the fundamental problem was not that of Tutsi-Belgian (the question of immediate independence demanded by the monarchy), but that of the Hutu versus Tutsi, arguing that it was then unbearable to live under the unjustifiable domination of a group that made up only 14% of the population.

The manifesto argued against *ubuhake* (vassalage) and the indirect rule practiced by the Belgian administration, which was accused of not doing enough to put an end to the obstacles that barred the emancipation of the Hutu from the yoke of the Tutsi. The document defined the problem as follows:

> The problem is primarily a problem of political monopoly enjoyed by one race, the Mututsi; political monopoly which, given the present structures, becomes an economic and social control; political, economic and social monopoly which, in view of the de facto selections in formal schooling, eventually becomes a cultural monopoly, at the great expense of the Bahutu who are thus condemned to remain eternal menials, and worse, after an eventual independence

they would have helped to conquer without knowing what
they were doing.[6]

In the manifesto, the Hutu proposed immediate domestic solutions they believed could ease the tensions. Those included a dramatic
change of the mentality according to which the elite could come only
from the Tutsi, repeatedly referred to as the Hamitic race. On the economic level, they called for an immediate suppression of forced, free
labor imposed on the Hutu masses; the legal recognition of the right of
land possession by individuals; the creation of a fund of rural credit to
promote rural initiatives in agriculture and various crafts; an easy access to the fund by the common Hutu; an economic union between the
Belgian colonies and the metropolis; and the right of free speech.

On the political level, in order to prevent the victory of the
Hamitic domination over the Hutu and the Twa, the signatories asked
for laws and customs to be codified. In other words, they wanted to get
rid of the esoterism surrounding the law in the country and strongly opposed what was known as "the custom of the Nation," according to
which justice was rendered following non-written laws, which favored
absolutism and individual interpretations void of any social sense and
discouraged private initiative. The nine Hutu intellectuals also demanded that elections be held on regular intervals. This, they suggested, would give a better chance to the Hutu to get access to the administrative positions at all levels.

On the educational level, the nine called for a quick revision
of the manner in which admissions to high school and to university
were conducted. In this respect, they demanded that racial criteria be
considered in the process. What they saw as obvious ethnic segregation
was the foundation of certain stereotypes used against the Hutu, namely
that the Hutu were poor and intellectually incapable and had bad manners. "Intellectual inability remains to be proved," they argued, "and
poverty is part of the social system; concerning manners, indeed im-
provement is needed."[7]

All in all, the nine Bahutu intellectuals who signed the manifesto wanted the "integral and collective promotion of the Muhutu."[8]
They asked the Belgian colonial administration and the Tutsi administration to carry out a positive action for the political and economic
emancipation of the Hutu masses. They rejected the Mututsi as a role
model for the Muhutu and instead asked for the respect of racial differences within the Rwandan culture. To make sure that the indirect rule
of the Belgian administration benefited everybody, the signers demanded that the labels "muhutu," "mututsi," and "mutwa" be main-

tained in the identity cards for fear that favoritism would increase once disguised. Keeping ethnic labels would also ensure that statistics were available to verify the treatment of the different groups in high school and university admission as well as in public employment. This labeling became the foundation of the quota system in 1962-1994.

This manifesto appealed very straightforward and very strongly to an ethnic group--obviously the term "race" was used in accordance with the prevailing European conception defined in the first chapter of this book. My reading of the manifesto is that it was a list of grievances, the basis of a future political program. It listed all the things the government was doing improperly and asking it to change the ways and means. At this time, the document was dubbed as a list of observations about the state of Rwanda from the Hutu perspective. The King and his advisers, however, refuted the claims of the Hutu, arguing that there was no Hutu-Tutsi problem. Although seen as a reformist, King Mutara III Rudahigwa had to deal with hardliners in the Tutsi aristocracy who did not want to share power with the Hutu and preferred the status quo.

Despite its many merits demanding social justice, the manifesto presented an ambiguous attitude towards the colonial power. It is not easy to decipher a clear line indicating the way the Hutu wanted to deal with the colonial administration, though it is known that it was the period when the latter was shifting its favors from the Tutsi to the Hutu, and this shifting was going to play a key role in bringing down the monarchy, especially since 1959. Moreover, the manifesto did not acknowledge that both Hutu and Tutsi peasants (called petits Tutsi) lived in the same economic conditions. All were subjected to forced labor. One evidence of this was that persons from both groups were fleeing to neighboring countries (Uganda, Tanganyika and Congo) to get away from forced labor. One very negative result of the manifesto was its strong polarization of the ethnic groups, by calling the manifesto "the Bahutu Manifesto" and thus excluding the Tutsi peasants and setting a bad precedent for future ethnic relations. After independence, the new leaders vigorously promoted Hutu solidarity.

Reacting to the "Bahutu Manifesto," the Tutsi elite close to the Palace reacted with similar shibboleth rhetoric. Even though they did not issue a Tutsi manifesto, their writings appealed to their ethnic group in unambiguous terms. Probably the most important writings from the group came almost one year after the Bahutu Manifesto, in May 1958. It is known as the "Premier Ecrit de Nyanza" (The First Writing of Nyanza). Appealing to one of the myths referred to in Chapter One (that is, the story of the Kigwa family and the Kabeja servants), the writing stated the following:

The situation being as it is, one can ask how the Bahutu are now asking their rights to share the common patrimony. Those who should ask for the sharing of the common patrimony are those who have fraternal ties. But the relationship between us (Batutsi) and them (Bahutu) have always been based on servitude; there is thus between them and us no fraternal bond. In reality what relations do exist between Batutsi, Bahutu and Batwa? The Bahutu claim that the Batutsi, Bahutu and Batwa are the sons of KANYARWANDA, their common father. Can they say with whom Kanyarwanda had them, what is the name of their mother and what family she belongs to?

The Bahutu claim that Kanyarwanda is the father of the Batutsi, Bahutu and Batwa; but we know that Kigwa is by far anterior to Kanyarwanda and that consequently Kanyarwanda is by far posterior to the existence of the three races of Bahutu, Batutsi and Batwa, whom he found well established. How then can Kanyarwanda be the father of those he found already in existence? Is it possible to have children without existing first? The Bahutu have claimed that Kanyarwanda is our common father, the uniting element of all the Batutsi, Bahutu and Batwa families; but Kanyarwanda is the son of Gihanga, son of Kazi, son of Merano, son of Randa, son of Kobo, son of Gisa, son of Kijuru, son of Kimanuka, son of Kigwa. Kigwa found the Bahutu in Rwanda. Say then, please, how we, Batutsi, can be the brothers of the Bahutu through Kanyarwanda our grandfather.

History tells us that Ruganzu killed many "Bahinza" (Kings of small Hutu kingdoms). He and our other Kings killed the Bahinza and thus conquered the lands of the Bahutu of which those Bahinza were kings. The details of this are found in "Inganji Kalinga." Since then our Kings conquered the lands of the Bahutu by slaying their kings and have thus enslaved the Bahutu, how come now these can claim to be our brothers?

We, the faithful servants of the King.[9]

As it appears from the closing sentence, this document was signed by twelve dignitaries (chiefs) of the court. What the document does is use one particular myth that was strongly established by then to make their points. This idea supports the concept that myths are not just myths in the way we tend to think but sets of ideologies that come to be embraced as realities, even though they are originally imagined. So to use the mythological characters to claim difference and superiority was another way of solidifying the other myths about Tutsi superiority, including the Hamitic Hypthesis that called the Hamites the civilizing agents in central Africa. Myths have always shaped political ideologies and practices in all societies and continue to do so, even in this age we call postmodern.

With the two writings, the polarization was complete; positions of the two main contending forces were clearly defined. This polarization is one of the reasons that led to the disastrous events that took place in the year 1959 and marked the beginning of what was called the "Rwandan Revolution." Hostility was so open at the end of 1958 and no common ground of understanding was found until November 1959 when violence erupted, provoking the deaths of thousands of Tutsi and the flight of hundred of thousand of others to neighboring countries, especially Uganda and Burundi, between 1959 and 1962. It was definitely the result of an ethnic radicalization on both sides. The strength of the Bahutu was in their overwhelming number and in the support of the Belgian colonial administration, whereas the strength of the Batutsi was in their control of the political and social networks of national politics though seriously compromised by the Belgian leaning toward the cause of the Bahutu. The spark was started by rumors according to which a Hutu sub-chief, Dominique Mbonyumutwa, was attacked and killed by Tutsi youth on November 1, 1959 in the central region of Gitarama. Although Mbonyumutwa was attacked, he was not killed, but the anti-Tutsi violence started by the incident quickly spread to the rest of the country.

Death of King Mutara III Rudahigwa and the Formalization of Political Parties

The unexpected death of King Mutara III Rudahigwa worsened the relationship between the conservative Tutsi on the one hand and the Hutu and the Belgian colonial administration on the other. He died on July 25, 1959 in Usumbura (now Bujumbura), Burundi, where he was attending a meeting, several hours after seeing his Belgian doctor. Rumors circulated in the conservative milieus that he had been assassinated, poisoned by white men with the complicity of political parties opposed to the conservative UNAR. Having no children of his own, he did not leave any male heir to the throne, so his succession would be decided in the traditional manner by the Council of Abiru, the guardians of royal customs. The family of the deceased king had the most stake in the succession and it sought to impose its candidate, Jean-Baptiste Ndahindurwa, one of the brothers of the king.

The kingdom's supreme council, which comprised both Belgian and Rwandan members, had its own candidate whose name was not revealed. The Hutu elite that wanted a republic as well as the masses that wanted an end to mandatory work (demanded by local chiefs and by the colonial administration for public works) and to taxation also had a stake in this turn of events. The colonial administration itself, which professed to want a democratic regime without necessarily understanding its contours, had to be consulted, according to Article 15 of the July 14, 1952 decree. The royal court used the elements of "surprise," "fait accompli," "threat of violence" and "abusive appeal to customs"[10] and prevailed, thus publicly humiliating the governor and infuriating the other parties. As the speeches were translated to the governor, he vowed to reconcile good governance and the respect of customs. According to the July 14, 1952 decree, the counselor charged with announcing the new King had to inform the Belgian governor about the secret decision, and the latter would have to make a determination as to whether to accept him.

In this period of high and focused ethnic mobilization, it is the two parties with ethnic affiliation that were going to be the pivotal arenas of national politics. They continued to play a decisive role in the shaping of ethnic relations in the country. "L'Union Nationale Rwandaise" (UNAR) (The Rwandan National Union), created on September 13, 1959, was dominated by conservative Tutsi ideology, but it counted members from both ethnic groups. It received financial and diplomatic support from the communist bloc of the UN Trusteeship council, further deteriorating the difficult relation with the Belgian colonial administration. At this time, the conservative Tutsi were openly hostile to the Belgians and, on top of that, UNAR demanded immediate independence.

The other party was deliberately called "Mouvement Démocratique Républicain/Parti du Mouvement de l'Emancipation des Bahutu" (MDR-PARMEHUTU) (Republican Democratic Movement/Party of the Movement for the Bahutu Emancipation). It was created on October 18, 1959, but its leader, Grégoire Kayibanda, had started it in June 1957 as "Mouvement Social Muhutu" (MSM) (Muhutu Social Movement), but at the time it gained little appeal. It is important again to stress here the direct appeal to the Hutu masses. The MDR-PARMEHUTU leaders were certainly aware of the importance of this appeal given the overwhelming number of the Bahutu (approximately 85% of the population) and its direct opposition to the Tutsi organization. The manifesto of the party echoed and expanded the main themes of the "Bahutu Manifesto" of 1957 and its condemnation of the social injustice and domination of the Bahutu by the Tutsi backed by the colonial administration. MDR-PARMEHUTU accepted the idea of a constitutional monarchy, provided that the King should not be designated by the Biru, esoteric counselors of the Court. The Hutu leaders were not asking for immediate independence, probably to avoid antagonizing the colonial power, which was helping them.

The political discourse of the Parmehutu Party is replete with an ideology rendered through the lenses of the Hamitic myth: "Tutsi colonialists," "conquerors of the Hamitic race," "Ethiopoid race," "feudo-colonialist Tutsi," "the Hamite-Tutsi colonizer," "Tutsi caste," and "Tutsi colonialism" are examples that reflect the Hutu ideology since the late 1950s, especially in two documents: (1) Déclaration of Parmehutu (MDR)—Extraordinary Assembly of Ruhengeri, June 6, 1960; and (2) Call from Parmehutu (recently renamed Mouvement Démocratique Républicain) (Republican Democratic Movement) to all the anti-colonialists of the world[11]—two very ethnically provocative documents. The King is referred to as a "Tutsi sultan," a "colonial sultan," or a "feudo-colonial chief"[12] and the Tutsi are asked to "continue their way to reestablish themselves in their forefathers' land in Abyssinia, or make the resolution to accept democracy and, in that case, modestly come back to Rwanda."[13] This kind of discourse obviously led to official anti-Tutsi fundamentalism.

The solution advocated and implemented by the new leaders to curve what they called Tutsi domination in schools and in the administration was the system of ethnic quotas, called "équilibre ethnique" (ethnic redistribution) that gave 9% of placement in schools and public employment to Tutsi and 90% to the Hutu. These practices reinforced the already lethal binary cleavage between the Hutu and the Tutsi (that is, in the words of the Hutu leaders, the Bahutu-Bantu and the Batutsi-Hamites, aristocrats, colonizers, and imperialists.

The expression "rubanda nyamwinshi" (the great masses) used by post-colonial Hutu leaders under the two Republics was a clear reference to the Hutu; it became part of the political landscape since the 1960s. As Jean-Pierre Chrétien notes, "the situation has been regulated since the last thirty years on the use of double meaning: behind the apparently social and political terminology, the obsession remained ethnic. The reduction of the problem to a dichotomy shaped by mere arithmetics of number (concerning groups defined at birth and duly authenticated by registration on identity papers) allowed to cover discriminating practices, in a rhetoric that claimed to be democratic even under a dictatorship."[14] Chrétien also notes Christian references that blinded the Belgian and Swiss non-governmental organizations and gave the appearance of good faith to the Rwandan government's ethnic discourse and practices.

Two other parties also played a significant role in the shaping of the events. The first one is "L'Association pour la Promotion Sociale des Masses" (APROSOMA) (The Association for the Social Promotion of the Masses). This was an avant-garde movement that emerged before the other parties. As a political party, its original aim was the promotion of the masses, both Hutu and Tutsi, but its membership attracted only a marginal number of Tutsi. At least in its name, this party acknowledged the precarious plight of both Hutu and "petits Tutsi." Tutsi who did not belong to the high-ranking families and lineages shared the same living conditions on the hills as their Hutu neighbors. It is from this organization that a more radical PARMEHUTU emerged. Later on, APROSOMA radicalized its views and adopted very strong anti-Tutsi and anti-King sentiments to the point that the King felt that it was more dangerous than PARMEHUTU. The third party was "Le Rassemblement Démocratique Rwandais" (RADER) (The Rwandan Democratic Union). A liberal Tutsi party, it was created by Prosper Bwanakweri, Chief of the territory of Kibuye in the northwest. He had been sent there, far from the royal palace in Nyanza, for his liberal views that annoyed the King and the conservative Tutsi. With the creation of UNAR by the more conservative Tutsi and its link with the communist block of the UN Trusteeship Council and its demand of immediate independence, the Belgian colonial administration recuperated Chief Prosper Bwanakweri to counter the conservative Tutsi ideology.[15] The party welcomed members from both ethnic groups; as a result, conservative Tutsi and Hutu did not like it. Besides, it was regarded as the creation of the colonial authority. Like the APROSOMA and MRD-PARMEHUTU, it was conciliatory vis-à-vis the colonial power by praising the work of Belgium in Rwanda and refraining from pressing for immediate independence. It would also accept a constitutional monarchy. The fact that all these parties were not opposing a constitutional monarchy in principle was probably dictated by the fact that Belgium was a constitutional monarchy, and that openly opposing this system of government would probably not be well perceived by the colonial administration, the real powerbroker.

The radicalization of views in 1957-1959 put in place all the necessary ingredients of a revolution. First, the Belgian colonial administration was openly challenged by its former protégés and was looking, as we saw with the case of Chief Prosper Bwanakweri, to counter the positions and demands of UNAR. Second, the all-powerful church, though divided between the indigenous clergy and the

European clergy, had produced a Hutu counter-elite in its seminaries. Thus, the colonial and religious duo had shifted sides. Third, both the Hutu and Tutsi elites adopted uncompromising positions mostly based on their ethnicity: the Hutu party viewed the Tutsi as a race of foreigners and colonizers who had exploited them with the help of the colonial power whereas the conservative Tutsi adamantly denied the existence of a Hutu-Tutsi problem and thus would not confront the grievances of the Hutu. Moreover, a number of them were imbued with the superiority complex informed by the Hamitic Hypothesis. All that was needed was a spark to trigger political upheaval.

The November 1959 revolution was preceded by the turbulent events discussed in previous paragraphs. As the major parties in the conflict radicalized their views, the conservative Tutsi tried to intimidate the Hutu leaders, especially Joseph Gitera, the somehow demagogue and unstable leader of the APROSOMA, and Grégoire Kayibanda, the founder of PARMEHUTU. During their public political meetings in the months preceding the revolution, UNAR leaders virulently attacked the Belgian colonial administration and the Catholic Church for their alignment with the Hutu cause. At the end of October 1959, UNAR called the Hutu opposition and Mgr Perraudin, a native of Switzerland who played the advocate for the Hutu as Mgr Classe had played the apologist for the Tutsi until 1945, traitors of Rwanda. The Kabgayi Bishop and his colleague of the diocese of Nyundo in northwestern Rwanda (the native Mgr Bigirumwami) denounced what they viewed as the ultranationalism of UNAR. When the colonial administration transferred three conservative UNAR chiefs (Kayihura, Rwangombwa, and Mungarurire) who were close to the royal palace, the King personally protested. As a reaction to the transfer of the three men, UNAR organized demonstrations in Kigali, the colonial police intervened, and at the end of the day, one person was dead and three were injured.

In this very tense climate, on November 1, 1959, in the territory of Gitarama, young members of UNAR attacked and severely beat the Hutu sub-chief Dominique Mbonyumutwa, who had refused to sign the resignation letter of traditional leaders who were protesting the transfer of the three chiefs. On November 5, 1959, an APROSOMA leader was murdered by a hit squad allegedly working for the conservative Tutsi. Other assassinations took place in the following days. Looting by organized groups often went hand in hand with massacres of Tutsi. The colonial police did not intervene, which led the Mwami to accuse the Belgians of complicity with the Hutu mobs and to threaten the mobilization of the Tutsi. Despite the joint plea by the court and the colonial administration, now epitomized by colonel Logiest, who was sent to Rwanda from Stanleyville in the Congo (now the Democratic Republic of Congo) in the wake of the violence, destruction of Tutsi property (houses, cattle, coffee plantations, etc.) continued. After five days, violence had spread to the territories of Gitarama, Gisenyi, and Ruhengeri, where Tutsi chiefs were attacked, killed or chased away, and their property destroyed. After a few more days, confusion, violence, destruction, and looting had spread to most territories, with different outcomes from different regions, depending on their ethnic mix. For example, in the territories of Nyanza and Astrida (now Butare), the number of chiefs and sub-chiefs hounded was dramatically different from the number of those chased in Gitarama, Ruhengeri, and Gisenyi. In the first case, there were more Tutsi in the two territories and less antagonism to the King whereas in the second case the three territories were predominantly inhabited by the Hutu, and the chiefs and subchiefs were unpopular.

UNAR, now fighting alone against the Hutu masses backed by the Belgian colonial administration and the Catholic Church (its European component), accused the last two of complicity with the Hutu, especially because it believed that this was not a Hutu versus Tutsi problem, but a conflict between those who wanted immediate independence (UNAR) and those who opted for the continuation of Belgian colonization (the Hutu, the Belgians, and the Catholic Church). Almost thirty years after the events, Colonel Guy Logiest, who played a pivotal role in the successful Hutu revolution, acknowledged in his memoirs what should obviously filter from the previous paragraphs, that is, the fact that the partiality of the Belgian administration was probably the most important element of the Hutu revolution, a proposition that validates Gérard Prunier's qualification of the Hutu revolution as "an ethnic transfer of power."[16] Colonel Logiest himself wrote:

> Some among my assistants thought that I was wrong in being so partial against the Tutsi and that I was leading Rwanda on a road towards democratization whose end was distant and uncertain... No, the time was crucial for Rwanda. Its people needed support and protection. My role was essential and it was important that I could play it till the final verdict which would come from the communal elections. Today, twenty-five years later, I ask myself what was it that made me act with such resolution. It was without a doubt the will to give the people back their dignity. And it was probably just as much the desire to put down the

morgue and expose the duplicity of a basically oppressive
and unjust aristocracy.[17]

The Belgian volte-face replaced the "natus ad imperium"
principle that they had applied to the Tutsi for four decades with an
ethnic majority (not a democratic majority), never encouraging independence on a democratic basis. From this perspective, if the Belgians
had been impartial or if they had intervened to impose public order, the
revolution would not have succeeded.

In the elections that were organized under the auspices of the
United Nations in 1960 and 1961, ethnic mobilization was still very
strong and not surprisingly the PARMEHUTU won overwhelmingly
for several reasons. First, now the polling stations were controlled by
the Hutu elite and the Belgian colonial administration. Second, the majority of Rwandans were illiterate, so even if they went to the polls, the
Hutu elite did the voting for them. Third, the UNAR was in a position
of irreversible weakness—the King was out of the country and the
Tutsi were demoralized by mass murder, exile, or internal displace-
ment, and the loss of their property.

"Party and society act on each other," Donald L. Horowitz
argues, and "nowhere is the reciprocal relation between party and society more evident than in ethnic politics."[18] This assertion is particularly
true in periods of open conflict, violence, or war, as it was the case in
Rwanda in the late 1950s and early 1960s, when political discourses
and practices created, promoted, and exacerbated ethnic awareness and
mobilization. In this context, emphasis is put on the manipulation of
masses uneducated to the political process whose only reference becomes their imagined or imposed ethnic affiliation. A political party
based on ethnicity does not have to suggest its ethnic orientation in its
name nor in its program. Its leadership, its practices, and word of
mouth can easily create a party dominated by one group and determine
the geographical support and distribution.

Post-Colonial Leaders and the Politics of Ethnicity

In the 1960s, the refugees who had fled the 1959 violence
launched several attacks to come back to Rwanda. Their attacks were
followed by severe reprisals against the Tutsi living in Rwanda. The
new leaders adopted policies that did to the Tutsi what the Tutsi rule
had done to the Hutu (with the exception that up to the unrest of 1959,
the Tutsi minority rule was not known to have used any ethnic cleansing on the Hutu), so that we can say, like Alexis de Tocqueville, com-

paring the French Revolution and the *ancien régime* it had toppled, that "they used the debris of the old order for building up the new."[19]

The political history of Rwanda since the 1950s is a history of antagonistic radicalization between the elite of the two ethnic groups whose thinking was grounded in a fallacious and racist historiography. The Rwandan Revolution of 1959, which professed to put an end to what the Hutu elite called the feudal and colonial oppression of the Hamitic race (the Tutsi) and Belgian colonization instead sealed the lethal binary antagonism between the Hutu and the Tutsi. The revolution gave rise to a society not primarily based on an economic and political program of government but on historical reversal, whereby the Hutu would simply occupy the terrain left by the exiled monarch and the Tutsi. In this sense, the revolution was a deliberately missed opportunity for the colonial administration, for the all-powerful Catholic Church, and for the Hutu elite led by Grégoire Kayibanda. Instead of a revolution for a democratic society, it was a change of players. The rhythm and tune of the dance stayed the same or became worse as the killing of Tutsi in 1959-61, 1963, 1966-67, 1972-73, and 1990-94 and the 1994 genocide demonstrated. Behind the words lurked a very dangerous anti-Tutsi ideology in the name of "rubanda nyamwinshi" (the great masses, that is, the Hutu) during the presidency of Grégoire Kayibanda (1962-1973) and Juvénal Habyarimana (1973-1994). The first, imbued with the idea of "foreignness" pinned onto the Tutsi by the Hamitic Hypothesis, proclaimed that he wanted to restore the country to its rightful owners, the Bahutu,[20] as the Tutsi were considered foreigners, invaders, and colonizers.

In 1960, the national committee of Kayibanda's party, Le Parti du Mouvement de l'Emancipation des Bahutu (PARMEHUTU), stated that "Rwanda is the country of the Bahutu and all those, white or black, Tutsi, European or those from other origins, who will let go their feudal and imperialist goals."[21] Thus a racist ideology sealed the end of the Hutu revolution, and the years that followed it became the foundation of political policies, statements, and practices that set the country on the wrong course. Instead of uprooting the racist ideology grounded in the whimsical Hamitic Hypothesis that had served to keep the Hutu in a subaltern position, the new regime instead appropriated it and made it its ideological reference to deny the Tutsi their deserved place in Rwanda, thus failing to give the country solid social and political foundations. Out of political convenience or sheer hatred of the Tutsi among the new Hutu political elite or a very narrow view of the past and the future of the country, the two republics that professed to be anchored in the 1959 social revolution sought to reproduce the Hamitic

Hypothesis in the mind of every Rwandan (through schools, probably the best place for indoctrination) and in all the professional sectors.

The practices were all too obvious to anybody. On the national radio and in the popular culture, there were songs and speeches that exalted the prowess of the Hutu. As I was growing up in the 1960s and early 1970s, I often heard the following song on national radio, and I also heard it sung by people going home from bars in the evening, "Ba Parmehutu tubavuge ibigwi, mwabaye imena ...nta n'impamba mwari mufite ariko muharanira rubanda rugufi" (Members of Parmehutu, you deserve songs of praise. You showed courage...you did not even have provisions, but you fought for the masses"). The national anthem "Rwanda Rwacu" ("Our Rwanda" or "Rwanda Our Country") contained verses that praised the MDR-PARMEHUTU party such as "Ndashimira abarwanashyaka bazanye repuburika idahinyuka" (I am grateful to the militants who brought about a republic that is trustworthy). In itself, the expression "Rwanda rwacu" has nothing of ethnic partisanship, but in the context of the early 1960s with MDR-PARMEHUTU proclaiming that Rwanda was a Hutu nation, it is easy to see how the first phrase of the national anthem could be construed as equally divisive. The word "abarwanashyaka" referred to above was also closely associated with MDR-PARMEHUTU; it was commonly associated with the militants of that party. Moreover, the Tutsi were called the "eternal enemy" of the Hutu, cockroaches, who were ruminating their defeat in 1959-62 and lurking to reconquer power by force, helped by the Tutsi who had not taken the path to exile. This kind of discourse was particularly cherished, following the attacks of Tutsi guerrillas from neighboring countries until 1966, the last year in which such attacks occurred. It is difficult to see how, as enemies of the republic, the Tutsi would be incorporated in the anthem as a national institution. In all fairness, other verses of the anthem call for unity among the Hutu, Tutsi, and Twa, but the first stanza obviously thematized and perpetuated the idea of a Hutu republic.

In early 1963, that is, only several months after independence, the few Tutsi members of the cabinet were fired and, after a semblance of trial, were shot for complicity with the "inyenzi terrorists," an expression cherished by the Hutu ideologues not only to refer to the Tutsi refugees who periodically, between 1960 and 1966, launched unsuccessful attacks on Rwanda but also to mobilize the Hutu. In the early years of the Republic, as with the 1990-1994 massacres of Tutsi and Hutu members of the political opposition, rumors of plots to assassinate Hutu leaders were circulated, and the PARMEHUTU took advantage of the tension to arrest, torture, kill or jail the Tutsi, as the national radio encouraged the population to get rid of those "Tutsi terrorists." Such was the case in 1963 when a group of Tutsi rebels attacked the Bugesera region from Burundi, and because of poor planning and lack of adequate military equipment, were easily defeated, even though they had initially succeeded in coming within fifteen kilometers of the capital city (Kigali). There were severe reprisals against the Tutsi living inside Rwanda: 10,000 Tutsi were killed in the prefecture of Gikongoro in December 1963 and January 1964. The Kayibanda government took advantage of the situation to get rid of moderate Tutsi politicians who had not gone into exile in 1959-1960.[22] The official justification of these horrendous massacres was that the normally moderate, tolerant, wise, and ordinary Hutu, the liberated former slaves of the Tutsi, were provoked to right anger by the arrogance of the feudal elements attacking the country with the help of their accomplices within. In reality, these massacres were organized in Gikongoro by the préfet, Nkezumugaba. Nobody was brought to justice in this case or any other instances that occurred at the same period in other parts of the country (such as Cyangugu where a cabinet minister, Otto Ruzingizandekwe, organized the massacres of Tutsi). Bertrand Russell denounced the massacres as the "most horrible and systematic human massacre that we have witnessed since the extermination of the Jews by the Nazi."[23]

The new leaders took advantage of the systematic categorization of the population into the three ethnic groups. The goal the new leaders had assigned themselves was to build a nation in which the three ethnic groups would work together, but it was indeed a very difficult task for several reasons. First, the new leaders talked about creating national unity but in fact they continued to draw political advantages from exploiting differences between Hutu and Tutsi. The Hutu majority had not yet forgotten the yoke under which it had lived for centuries. Second, the Tutsi refugees continued to launch attacks to force their return to power, fomenting an already strong anti-Tutsi sentiment in the country. Third, the Twa were certainly not apt to participate in any new kind of dialogue. For one thing, they had no exposure to new ideas through education. Consequently, they continued to live on the margin of the society. Clearly, there was an insurmountable gap between their stratum and the relative comfort of the two other ethnic groups.

The ethnic majority now in power used the resources that come from controlling the administration for their benefit, no doubt because they feared that sharing might give the Tutsi a new opportunity to reestablish control. Even though the constitution of the newly independent Rwanda stipulated that everybody, regardless of ethnic group, had equal access to the resources of the country, equity remained only theoretical. In 1969, as the Kayibanda regime had spent three years without any Inyenzi attacks, it was prey to profound internal divisions especially between the Gitarama (the President's region) and Gisenyi/Ruhengeri group. For several years, there had been claims that the government had done little to help the Hutu in schools and in the job markets. In 1960, the tenth congress of MDR-PARMEHUTU voted a new law known as "équilibre ethnique" (ethnic redistribution). Its rationale was that there were too many Tutsi in high schools and in institutions of higher education (the national university and the teacher training school, both in Butare).

The application of the ethnic redistribution policy started with the 1972/73 school year, and no Tutsi were admitted to those schools. In fact, Hutu student vigilante committees under the secret guidance of the country's security and intelligence chief, Alexis Kanyarengwe, chased Tutsi students from public and private high schools and from the two institutions of higher education. As for Tutsi civil servants, lists were posted at workplaces, and they were simply asked to leave. Four elements of explanation can be given for the 1972/73 unrest. First, the killing of the Hutu educated (at least one hundred-fifty thousands) in early 1972 in neighboring Burundi under the supervision of the Micombero regime (following an unsuccessful Hutu rebel attack in the south of Burundi[24]). As a result of these massacres, the situation between Rwanda and Burundi became very tense. On April 20, 1972, during the 12:45 pm news on the Rwandan national radio, a statement from the Rwandan Presidency announced that the Tutsi of Burundi had killed the Hutu, aggravating ethnic tension in Rwanda. The second explanation is that, according to the official determination, ten years after the social revolution of the Hutu, the schools, administration, and the Catholic clergy were still dominated by the Tutsi. Consequently, after the upheaval of 1972/73 and the July 5, 1973 military coup led by Major General Juvénal Habyarimana, a rigid control of ethnic statistics in schools, public employment, and the army grounded in the passé Hamitic myth became the social, economic, and political practice. Only 9% of places would go to the Tutsi, except in the military, which became the exclusive domain of the Hutu—it is worth noting that under the Habyarimana regime, the Hutu of Gisenyi and Ruhengeri overwhelmingly dominated the army. Third, the ethnic card played at this particular juncture also aimed to hide the very serious regional rift between the Hutu of Gitarama and the Hutu of Gisenyi and Ruhengeri, so it became convenient to use the Tutsi as scapegoat and a means of mobilizing the Hutu around the idea of a threatened "hutuness." Fourth, it is commonly assumed that the unrest was fomented by army officers from Gisenyi and Ruhengeri to show that the Gitarama-dominated Kayibanda government was unable to rule the country. The northern officers used the prevailing chaos as an excuse to stage a military coup. Otherwise, how could one explain that immediately following the coup, peace was restored as if by enchantment?

The "équilibre ethnique" under Kayibanda and "équilibre ethnique et régionale" (ethnic and regional redistribution) under Habyarimana in the name of a certain idea of distributive justice discouraged competition, individual ambition, and entrepreneurial spirit, but it also became the primary foundation of social, economic, and political practices. This distributive policy also aimed at keeping the Tutsi in check, as if saying, "we know where you are; try anything, but avoid politics; we do not want your daughters to marry our Hutu soldiers," thereby treating them as strangers in their own country.

We may note here that in the pre-colonial and colonial Rwanda, there was economic and political competition within the Tutsi aristocracy that often involved alliances from outside the group. For example, the Tutsi needed Hutu clients to fight rivals or defeat neighbors' claims on their properties, and the Hutu needed Tutsi for protection. But there was little or no competition between the Hutu and the Tutsi because the system made it very difficult. What was different in independent Rwanda is that competition was not open and alliances harder to construct, especially because, since independence days, regular ethnic conflicts created a climate of animosity and revenge, which did not inspire any confidence. The competitive spirit was undermined by unequal chances because the economy and politics were controlled by the governing Hutu majority, especially from Gisenyi and Ruhengeri. Easy access to resources, goods, and services presupposed membership in the ruling majority. Coming from the same region as the President was of course by far the best shot, as Hutu from the south were also largely discriminated against.

To counter their exclusion, many Tutsi (especially in the south) attempted, some successfully, to change their ethnic identity and become Hutu, in accordance with the fluid and permeable forms of precolonial social strata. This conversion of many Tutsi to Hutu is a clear example of the situational character of ethnicity, which is determined by the economic and political advantages at stake. But this conversion did not reach a high level of success, as the new administration was vigilant in discouraging the process. I know a young man from my native commune Muyira (in the province of Butare) who managed to use this shift to get to high school and to the national university. After he received his bachelor's degree in English in 1987, it was discovered by the secret services that he was actually a Tutsi, not a Hutu as he was marking on his official documents (identity card and school documents). He was obliged to go back to his "tutsiness" and that was the end of his studies. Even though he was one of the best in his class, the discovery meant that he could not pursue his studies further. His name was Jean-Baptiste Mugemana; he was killed in Nyanza during the 1994 genocide.

The 1973 Coup and the Regional Factor

A political exploitation of the ethnic mapping was institutionalized after July 5, 1973 when a military coup--this was a fashionable way of conquering power in those years in Africa--brought a military man from the north to power. Several interesting phenomena could be noticed since then. First, the civilian president who was deposed and who originated from the central part of the country was accused of having favored his region of origin. But Juvénal Habyarimana institutionalized regionalization on a very large scale, creating two poles, the North (his region of origin, actually two districts of the ten that make up the country, Gisenyi, Ruhengeri, and a small part of Byumba adjacent to Ruhengeri) and the South (the rest of the country, the most reviled being the prefectures of Gitarama and Butare). He institutionalized the so-called balanced distribution of the limited places in high school, the national university, the military, and the administration along regionalist and ethnic lines ("équilibre ethnique et régional"), but it overwhelmingly favored the "région sacrée" at the expense of Tutsi and southern Hutu. This policy created great ethnic and regionalist awareness, especially in the 1980s, but regional animosity was by far a more acute political problem in that period, as Hutu politicians from the south were made the scapegoats of the economic difficulties that surfaced due to the sharp fall of prices of coffee and tea on the international markets. There was a very short period at the end of the 1970s when it was commonly said in the south that a Tutsi from Gisenyi and Ruhengeri was better treated than a Hutu from the South. This proposition does not necessarily mean that the few Tutsi living in those two prefectures were treated well; if anything, it reflects the deep bitterness created in the south by what was perceived as the hegemony of the north.

The policy of "balanced distribution" was a clear legitimization and institutionalization of ethnicity and regionalism at the expense of merit. The political rhetoric proclaimed that the policy aimed at fairness among the different components of the country and that it would foster understanding and unity, but the results were dramatically disappointing. Not only was the distribution unfair (not respecting the percentage of different ethnic groups and different regions), but it also made people think about their region and their ethnic group. Some years into the military regime, the myth of "Hutu purs et durs" surfaced. It referred to the unsullied and rough Hutu, meaning Hutu from the north. It was a discourse aimed at revisiting Kayibanda's proclamation of Hutu ownership of Rwanda. The Hutu of the south were sullied by intermarriage with the Tutsi, the thinking went, and a number of them were Tutsi passing as Hutu. The new myth translated into practices that made southern Hutu aware that they were discriminated against and marginalized.

Though it was never publicly admitted, there was an underground struggle for power between the Hutu of the north, who controlled the economic, military, and political machinery of the country, and the Tutsi and the Hutu of the south. The propaganda machinery of the totalitarian single party covered up the problem with slogans chanting unity and peace.

With the presence of the rubric "ethnic group" on identity cards and all official documents (job application forms, military entrance forms, and various administrative documents), it was quite easy to control access to national resources. Many competent persons were refused positions in the administration, or places in high school or at the national university simply because they were Tutsi or were from the south. An autocratic and totalitarian regime forced people to sing and write that everybody was fairly treated and that there was unity among the three components and other subgroups (north-south, for example). Every adult Rwandan, ipso facto a member of the single political party known as "Le Mouvement Révolutionnaire National pour le Développement" (National Revolutionary Movement for Development) founded in 1975,[25] was forced to spend at least one afternoon a week in a session called "animation," praising the President and the action of his government. This cult of personality glorified Habyarimana for having saved the country from destruction and all kinds of disaster and for having brought peace, unity, and development in Rwanda. Every year there were local, regional, and national competitions to determine the groups in public and private institutions that put up the best show. As a university lecturer in Rwanda from

1986 to 1992, I participated in these sessions every Wednesday afternoon (2-5 pm). One could be a lousy performer on the job, but if one showed strong commitment during these sessions, his or her job was secured, and many promotions were based on one's fanatical participation. During these sessions, low-level employees who were skilled at creating songs and dances for the president acquired a sense of power over their superiors, which in turn increased their commitment to the cult. The common themes of the sessions included necessarily the 1959 Hutu revolution and the entitlements it brought the Hutu; the 1973 moral revolution (to my knowledge, nobody ever explained the morality of that coup or any coup for that matter), reference to the military coup of July 5, 1973 that was supposed to safeguard the entitlements (the French expression "les acquis" was often used) of the 1959 revolution; Habyarimana as a savior of Rwanda; Habyarimana as the father of the nation (an expression used in many African countries to refer to their despots); the unity between the Hutu, the Tutsi, and the Twa; and development. The reality of ethnic and regional politics, however, was far different from the lyrics of "animation." While the Habyarimana regime gave a sense of security to the Tutsi, it continued to discriminate against them, excluding them from the military, rigidly controlling their admission into high schools and institutions of higher education, and carefully screening the ethnicity of employees.[26] Any commissioned officer in the Rwandan army who wanted to get married had to seek the approval of the military hierarchy, and this policy, in place since the Kayibanda years, aimed at preventing the officers from marrying Tutsi women.

When I finished my MA in English at the National University of Rwanda, before I was offered a job at the National University, security and intelligence agents from the secret service visited my commune several times, held meetings in the Burgmaster's office, checked my family file, and interviewed several elderly people in my sector to ascertain my father's ethnicity. This was indeed unusual for the entry-level position of lecturer at the National University. The next year (1987), the British Council offered me a scholarship to do postgraduate studies in England. When I applied for a passport, the immigration service, an office directly controlled by the Presidency, rejected my application. In fact, each time I went to the office to check the status of my application, the officers acted as if I had not applied at all. Soon, I gave up. This was the preferred way that the President's office used to stop "suspicious" people from leaving the country. These people included the Tutsi, people who were officially Hutu but, coming from the South, were suspected of having changed their ethnicity, and

Hutu who had fallen out of grace with the government because of their political ideas. An employee in the scholarship office in the ministry of higher education told me a few months later that the Presidency had denied me a passport because my ethnicity was dubious. As far as regional and ethnic politics in Rwanda was concerned, this was probably the end of my innocence. I have never felt that humiliated in my life, especially because the scholarship was based on merit and it covered all my expenses—neither the National University nor the Rwandan government were going to spend a single penny on me. Some people joked that my humiliation was not that harsh because there were cases when people were sometimes pulled out of planes on the airport tarmac (I knew a colleague and several other people who had been humiliated in this manner). The following year the British Council renewed the scholarship offer, and this time I got a passport, because of the insistence of the British Council representative in Rwanda and, most importantly, with the help of a very influential contact I had made during the year.

In the summer of 1989, the secret service conducted another visit to my commune and sector looking for the same information. The reason of this new search, as I later learned from a former student of mine who worked in the intelligence office, was that I was a candidate for sous-préfet (loosely the equivalent of a deputy-governor) in my native prefecture of Butare. In this totalitarian regime, people did not apply for political positions; they were chosen, and the processing of candidates took place, in most cases, unbeknownst to them. Since I was not chosen, I can only surmise that my ethnicity was still dubious. Another ethnic identity check came when someone wanted me to be on the development council of my commune a few months after the second check—this time the intelligence agents only interviewed the burgomaster and checked my family file. What these three examples clearly say is that the regime was obsessed with anybody occupying a political position (or getting anything for that matter) without the Presidency's secret service absolutely ascertaining the ethnicity and political perspective of the candidate. A friend of mine told me at that time, "if they do that to you because they are not sure about you, just imagine what they do to us."

This politics of exclusion translated into different reactions intended to compensate for the limited opportunities. High school and university education is a privilege in Rwanda (and indeed in most, if not all, African countries) and access to this education is highly competitive. Since the late 1960s, admission had often been decided along ethnic and regional lines, but this competition increased after July

5, 1973 when ethnicity and regionalism were institutionalized. When the Tutsi and the Hutu from the south realized their very limited access to education, they started building private schools. Thus it is not astonishing that the first private schools were built by parents in the south and were often identified as Tutsi schools. Though some schools had been issuing high school certificates since the late 1970s, it was only in the late 1980s that they gained government recognition. This was the case for two well-known and highly regarded schools, EFOTEC in Butare and APACOPE in Kigali. Many more private schools were built in the late 1980s (in almost all regions of the country and not necessarily along ethnic lines, but to compensate for the limited places in public schools). In other words, the emergence of private schools in Rwanda was a direct consequence of the official recognition of ethnicity and regionalism and their exploitation for economic and political competition. This politicization of ethnicity in the school system polarized in such a way that public high schools had a Hutu majority while private high schools had a population of Tutsi far bigger than their percentage of the whole population. We must note that the majority of Tutsi live in the South, according to the 1991 census.

Another way that Tutsi and Hutu of the south coped with the ethnicization and regionalization of resource distribution was to go to business. They prospered in commerce and helped their peers either to go to private schools or to do business themselves. In the late 1980s, diehard Hutu especially from the north began complaining that there were too many rich Tutsi businessmen, in the same manner they were complaining about the number of Tutsi in schools and in the administration in the second half of the 1960s.

In summary, the post-colonial policies, grounded in the exclusion discourse of the 1959 revolution that dubbed Rwanda as the country of the Hutu, amplified by regional politics during the two republics (Kayibanda 1962-1973 and Habyarimana 1973-1994), increased ethnic awareness and created a new ethnic subgroup, the Hutu of the south, who were marginalized just like the Tutsi under the 1973-94 Habyarimana regime. This, in part, explains the political dynamics when a multiparty system started in June 1991. As we are going to see in the next section, the ideologies of some of the new parties were curiously similar to those that preceded and accompanied the 1959 social revolution. Interestingly enough, the same pattern of bloodletting followed, with just some new players and mass murder of unprecedented proportions. Even though it was mostly the logic of the 1959 revolution that was invoked in the Hutu extremist propaganda, the real motivation came from the elite and military in the north who did not want the "entitlements" of July 5, 1973 to fade away after only about twenty years of their historic hegemony over the Tutsi and the south. Those twenty years had clearly shown that if Rwanda was a Hutu nation (begat by the 1959 Revolution), after July 1973, the Hutu of Gisenyi and Ruhengeri (north) were "more equal" than the Hutu of the south.

Ethnicity in the Wake of Democracy

The political rhetoric since the 1970s has been that of unity and fairness through balanced distribution of resources. That is what everybody, politician and common man alike, was supposed to chant aloud, at least one afternoon each and every week since 1975. That was the official ideology of the military regime. Needless to say, every effort of criticism, however well intentioned, was severely repressed. On October 1, 1990, thousands of refugees of the 1959 revolution and of the 1960s reprisals took arms and attacked to force their way back into the country. The majority of the rebels were Tutsi. This attack prompted the arrest of thousands of people suspected of collaborating with the invaders. Statistics compiled by Human Rights organizations after the massive arrests established that the prisoners were composed of a majority of Hutu from the south. It was later discovered that very few of those arrested had anything to do at all with the invaders.

In the subsequent democratic movement that was given a quick impetus by the civil war, political parties formed along ethnic and regional lines. The former single party remained strong only in the north (the region of the President). Of the three major opposition parties, one (PL) had a stronghold in the Tutsi population, another (MDR, the largest opposition party) recruited strongly from Gitarama and from among the Hutu throughout the country, and the third one (PSD) incorporated the two ethnic groups, and had its stronghold in the districts of Butare and Gikongoro, where the founders came from. All three opposition parties had their strongholds in the "south."

This ethnicization and polarization of politics had major consequences since June 1991. While the former single party once claimed everybody automatically as members (a party official once declared that even the fetus in a Rwandan mother was a member of the party), it had a hard time convincing those it had mistreated to support it. Losing this dictatorial ground meant fewer members in the party in July 1991. The party executive committee designed methods of intimidation to force people back, but many found in the opposition parties the voices they had been denied long since. The many grenade and bomb attacks launched by members of the former single party in 1991 and 1992 were thus meant to eliminate opposition leaders and frighten the population back into the party. The former single party and its satellites radicalized their ethnic stands more and more, possibly in the hope to form an ethnically based constituency. The foundation of the "Coalition pour la Défense de la République" (CDR) as an ultra-extremist party, ally to the MRND party, was meant to appeal to the Hutu constituency in the same way in which PARMEHUTU had appealed to it in 1959. But this policy again failed to attract the Hutu of the south.

This ultra-extremist movement was already in gestation in late 1990 when a journal called *Kangura* (whose editor was later one of the founders of the CDR) quickly became notorious for its heinous rhetoric against the Tutsi. The journal made the name of Tutsi sound like an insult--actually all the Hutu who opposed the Habyarimana regime were called "ibyitso" (accomplices of the Rwandese Patriotic Front which was synonymous with Tutsi since October 1990). In *Kangura* No. 6 of December 1990, the editor of the journal, Hassan Ngeze, issued what he called the "Ten Commandments of the Bahutu" (discussed in the next chapter). The ten commandments came out three months after the outbreak of the 1990 war. The excitement with which the edition was received was, to my mind, an omen of the evil intention behind not only the journal but also those in the high administration of the country who were supporting it in the background, providing it with sensitive information and encouraging it to speak against and condemn all the Tutsi and all those who opposed the Habyarimana regime. The government did not condemn the writing, but instead anybody who was pointed out by the journal as an accomplice of the RPF was in danger of losing his/her job or being killed in obscure circumstances. The targets were almost exclusively Tutsi and Hutu of the south.

Conclusion

This chapter sought to show that a sustained and prolonged propaganda grounded in the Hamitic Hypothesis and its appropriation by different historical forces in Rwandan history, including the German and Belgian colonial administrations, the Tutsi elite who benefited from it until the 1959 Hutu Revolution, and the Hutu leaders of

independent Rwanda and the different institutions (such as schools and
the military) that helped to make Hutu ideology a part of the Rwandan
collective consciousness, all veiled a more dreadful political and
historical dimension in recent Rwandan history: the July 5, 1973 coup
that put a region at the helms of the country. When the 1990 civil war
broke out in Rwanda, the leaders from Gisenyi and Ruhengeri started a
careful and coordinated campaign to appeal to Hutu solidarity to gain
back the Hutu of the political south. The desired ethnicization of the
conflict also aimed at obscuring the economic difficulties of the
moment. The problem of poverty and rare resources is a very serious
one. Ultimately, the northern military and intellectual elites were
struggling to keep control of the meager resources of the country. I
believe that the northerners were ready to use any strategy, including
killing people, to retain the direction of the administrative and
economic machinery instead of sharing equitably with the Hutu from
the South and the Tutsi.

Chapter Four

The Path to Genocide: Human Rights Violations as Genocide Rehearsals

> At that level, we move from trivialization to normalization. It's
> the transformation from 'trivial' to 'normal' and from normal
> to prescriptive.
> --André Sibomana, *Hope for Rwanda*

The Kayibanda and Habyarimana regimes deliberately opted
not to tackle the thorny issue of refugees, many still living in refugee
camps in very poor conditions in neighboring countries (Uganda,
Burundi, Tanzania, and Zaire). The answer to the refugees' request to
return home was that there was no land for them in Rwanda.[1] Prunier
aptly summarizes the reasons of the two successive Rwandan
governments' refusal to welcome the refugees back: the problem of
shortage of land was obvious because of "overpopulation, overgrazing
or soil erosion,"[2] but the real obstacle was ideological: "The realities of
the present Rwandese political life, the pervasiveness of the Hutu racial
ideology, the problem of the Tutsi image as reconstructed by that same
ideology—all these obstacles to their dream of an eventual return were

blithely ignored."[3] Particularly victimized by political problems in the host country were the Rwandan refugees under the repressive governments of Idi Amin and Milton Obote. As Prunier and Mamdani show, this political Ugandan factor played a crucial role in shaping the Rwandans' awareness of their "otherness" in Uganda and the eventual military solution to their predicament. Rwandan refugees formed associations to deal with recurring threats in the host country. Thus, they "created the Rwandese Refugee Welfare Foundation (RRWF) in June 1979 to help the victims of political repression after the fall of Idi Amin. In 1980 the RRWF changed its name to Rwandese Alliance for National Unity (RANU). RANU saw itself as more politically militant than the RRWF and openly discussed the question of an eventual return of the exiles to Rwanda."[4] When Yuweri Museveni, President of Uganda since 1986, started a rebel movement, the Popular Resistance Army, which became the National Resistance Army (NRA) in 1981 shortly after the controversial election of Milton Obote in December 1980, many young Rwandan refugees, reacting to the repression organized by the Obote regime, joined the NRA en masse in the 1980s.

Among the initial core group of the rebellion were two Rwandans, Fred Rwigema and Paul Kagame, who occupied high positions (army commander-in-chief and minister of defense, and chief of army intelligence respectively) in the Ugandan army after the victory of the NRA in 1986. After about three years, resentment against the Rwandan influence in the army and in business, failure to secure the massive naturalizations the Rwandan community had hoped for, the firing of Major-General Fred Rwigema from his influential position in November 1989, and other problems related to being foreigners, convinced the Rwandans in Uganda that they needed a more drastic move. It is in this context that RANU changed into the Rwandese Patriotic Front (RPF) in December 1987 at its seventh congress, where the determination to return home (through political pressure or military force if necessary) to Rwanda was affirmed.[5]

In the meantime, inside Rwanda, the Habyarimana regime was politically and economically collapsing. The first seven years of his reign were generally judged "good years" by many observers. In April 1980, the failed coup led by the intelligence director Théoneste Lizinde and the influential Interior Minister Alexis Kanyarengwe let the old ghosts loose. In the following years, the plight of the dignitaries of the first republic was revealed. Lizinde, it was clear, had played a major role, if not the major role, in the killing of the deposed President (Kayibanda) and his ministers along with other important persons (businessmen, lawyers, and civil servants), most for obvious political reasons and some for personal reasons.[6] Many of the dignitaries came from Gitarama, the center of power during the first republic, and part of the political "south" under the Habyarimana reign. Lizinde was first tried for his role in the failed coup, but when the death of the leaders of the first republic became a major embarrassment that could not be easily dismissed by the Habyarimana government, he was again tried in 1985. I was then a student at the National University of Rwanda, Ruhengeri Campus. Many students (including myself) skipped classes the first day of the trial. I remember that as Lizinde was entering the courtroom of the *Cour de Première Instance de Ruhengeri*, he stopped at the top of the steps, turned around, and looked at the préfet of Ruhengeri, Protais Zigiranyirazo (brother-in-law of Habyarimana), and squarely told him that Habyarimana and Serubuga (Army Chief of Staff, also from Gisenyi) should have come to the proceedings. Zigiranyirazo's presence at the trial exposed the magnitude of the event. Lizinde's own defiance spoke volumes as to who was responsible. Nobody would ever believe that the security chief had killed the more than fifty dignitaries without the knowledge of Habyarimana and his close collaborators from Gisenyi and Ruhengeri. In addition, the killing took place at a time when Habyarimana and Lizinde were very close friends. A former high school and college classmate who hailed from Rwerere commune in the Bugoyi region in Gisenyi once told me about a weekend gathering at Lizinde's house in the late 1970s. Present at the meeting were President Habyarimana, other dignitaries, and high school and university students from Gisenyi. Habyarimana and Lizinde spoke with each other as very close old friends.

The pounding of Lizinde in the official media in 1985 could not fool the public about the shared responsibility of the northwesterners in the death of the Gitarama dignitaries. The revelations about this case further poisoned the already sour antagonism between the north (Ruhengeri and Gisenyi) and the south (Gitarama and Butare in particular). In addition, it resulted in the complication of regional politics and created some subregional suspicion for a few years: Lizinde came from the Bugoyi region of Gisenyi whereas Habyarimana came from the more powerful region of Bushiru. Furthermore, the main conspirators came from the Bugoyi region and from Ruhengeri. Neither the failed coup, however, nor the publicized Lizinde trial with its sub-regional trappings, deflected attention from the main "north-south" plot.

In the same period, politicians from the south who dared to disagree or publicly criticize the regime were either jailed or killed in suspicious circumstances that were planned to make the murders look like accidents. For example, Felicula Nyiramutarambirwa, a member of Parliament from Gitarama, was run over by a truck after questioning the corrupt way in which road-construction contracts were assigned— the minister of public works in charge of the contracts was Joseph Nzirorera from Ruhengeri. Another road accident killed Father Silvio Sindambiwe for his candid writings about government corruption and abuses.[7] Months before his death he was submitted to the unspeakable ordeal of being hit with a pack of human feces in his face as a car passed by him on a street in Kigali. From 1980 to 1985, he was editor of the very respected *Kinyamateka, a* journal owned by the Catholic Church but was fired by the chair of the Episcopal conference, Archbishop Vincent Nsengiyumva, who gave into government pressure. The Archbishop, himself from the north, was a controversial figure. He was a member of the central committee of the single party (MRND) until shortly before the visit of Pope John Paul II to Rwanda in 1990. It was raucously rumored in Kigali that when the presidential couple quarreled, the president's wife would seek refugee at the Archbishop's residence. Ruhengeri and Gisenyi overwhelmingly dominated the army; they received the best investment opportunities, most scholarships (to Europe and North America), the best portfolios in the cabinet, and the directorships of the important public companies and projects. As Mamdani rightly puts it, "allocation of posts was to take place, first on a regional basis and then on an ethnic basis. In practice, then, 60 percent of posts would be allocated to northerners and 40 percent to southerners" (139). In their own words, "igihugu ni icacu" (the country belongs to us--literally "the country is ours"). One will notice the use of the northern dialect "icacu" that became currency among opportunists seeking favors from the powerful north—the standard form is "icyacu." This is no time for a discussion of the relationship between politics and language use, but suffice it to say that southerners, who used to make fun of the northern dialect, would do so at their own expense during the second republic. The Kinyarwanda spoken in the south was the standard and official dialect.

The economic crisis that hit the country in the 1980s exacerbated the other cleavages. In 1986, the prices of the major export item (coffee) collapsed on international markets, which meant that the producers (the farmers on the hills) received very low value for the tremendous effort involved in the production of coffee. At the end of the 1980s, people were complaining publicly on radio shows and actually bragging about destroying their coffee plants because they said these were not worth the effort any more. There was great anxiety in coffee producing regions such as Mayaga—my native commune of Muyira in Butare is part of this agricultural region. I personally knew dozens of individuals who left for Tanzania in that period looking for better economic opportunities. Tin, another source of foreign currency, also lost value on the world markets in 1984-86; as a result, Somirwa, the company that had the monopoly of tin mining, closed. In September 1990, the Rwandan government signed a structural adjustment agreement with the IMF and the World Bank, resulting in the devaluation of the Rwandan currency, price increase for basic commodities, and generalized financial malaise in the country.

The economic state of the nation in the second half of the 1980s increased internal struggle for control of the central administration, which could be used to embezzle part of the foreign aid. Competition became tight, even among the people from the northern provinces of Gisenyi and Ruhengeri. The phenomenon known as *Akazu* came out in the open. In Kinyarwanda, "akazu" means "little house." The expression was used to refer to a select group of influential persons from Gisenyi and Ruhengeri whose will controlled the working of the administration. The core of the Akazu was undoubtedly what was known as "le clan de Madame" (the clan of Madam), a reference to the wife of the President and members of her family and their close associates. Almost everybody who followed Rwandan politics knew their names: Protais Zigiranyirazo (préfet of Ruhengeri), Colonel Pierre-Célestin Rwagafirita, the rich businessman Séraphin Rwabukumba, Colonel Elie Sagatwa (secretary of the President), Noël Mbonabaryi, Colonel Laurent Serubuga, Colonel Théoneste Bagosora, and a number of other individuals who were ready to do the bidding for the core group. This group expanded after the RPF attack toward the end of 1990 to include Joseph Nzirorera, Captain Pascal Simbikangwa, Charles Nzabagerageza (who replaced Protais Zigiranyirazo as préfet of Ruhengeri in 1990), Casimir Bizimungu (cabinet minister)—all them from Gisenyi or Ruhengeri. Most of these individuals were notorious in their own ways—for example, it was common knowledge in Kigali that Joseph Nzirorera (from Ruhengeri), although of very modest origins (to say the least) and having earned a salary for only several years, had celebrated two billion Rwandan francs in his bank accounts. It was rumored that he was in competition with Aloys Nsekalije (from Gisenyi), one of the officers who staged the 1973 coup and a minister until the 1980s when he fell out of grace with Habyarimana. He, too, had celebrated his two billion in bank accounts. Unlike the politicians from the south, who were fired, quickly sentenced, and jailed for any small act of corruption, it was clear that northerners could embezzle millions of public funds or foreign aid without being bothered, since they were the ones calling the shots. As the Rwandans put it, "imbwa yiganye inka kunywa mu rugo irabizira" (literally, "a dog imitated the cow by defecating in the precincts and it was punished"). In Rwanda, cows spend the night in the family compound called *urugo*; they defecate there, and their dung is collected in the morning and put in a compost to be used as fertilizer in the future. The dog is supposed to go out of the compound and out of sight to defecate. The analogy in the proverb meant that officials from Gisenyi and Ruhengeri were free to embezzle the public funds with impunity, but if anybody from the south dared imitate them and stole even small amounts, the law came after him with vengeance.

The summer and early fall of 1990 augured some political changes. The French President François Mitterrand, a close ally of Habyarimana of Rwanda, declared at the annual Franco-African meeting in La Baule that future aid to African states would be tied to multiparty democracy. Shortly after leaving France, Habyarimana set up a national commission for political reform, a move interpreted in the intellectual milieus as a way of reluctantly accepting and preparing multiparty democracy—for one thing, his cronies in the single party MRND did not want this change, because it would break their monopoly on the affairs of the country. In the same period, a group of thirty-three intellectuals, most of whom were set to resurrect the defunct MDR-PARMEHUTU of the 1960s, signed a letter addressed to Habyarimana demanding multiparty democracy. Also, the same year, a new journal called *Kanguka* (*Wake Up!*) was launched. It was edited by a Hutu called Vincent Rwabukwisi and sponsored by the very wealthy businessman Valens Kajeguhakwa, a Tutsi and a former close business associate of some members of the Akazu but who was no longer on good terms with them. He actually used the columns of the journal to accuse the Habyarimana clique of having caused the failure of his business ventures. In the summer of 1990, he fled to Uganda, along with a close ally of his, a Hutu from Gisenyi (Pasteur Bizimungu) who was director of the state-owned Electrogaz, a water, electricity, and gas company. To the RPF leadership, the story of the imminent collapse of the Rwandan government was good news. Inside the country, as it became clear that multiparty politics would be soon allowed, opposition leaders were recruiting founding members and writing up their political platforms. In this period of transition and political commotion, before the national commission on political reform submitted its report to the president, the Rwandan Patriotic Front, dominated by Tutsi refugees in Uganda (children of the initial refugees who fled Rwanda in the wake of the Hutu Revolution of 1959) invaded Rwanda on October 1, 1990.

The reaction of the Rwandan government to the attack as well as the conduct of war from both sides led to severe human rights violations that fostered a culture of impunity that rendered, with several other factors, the genocide possible in 1994. The Habyarimana government and party exploited the founding Hutu ideology and other forces of totalitarianism to turn the ordinary Hutu citizens into executioners of their Tutsi neighbors. What this chapter demonstrates is that human rights abuses at a great scale from 1990 to 1994 eventually trivialized killing and evil to the point that they became normal in the eyes of the public. This trivialization of evil was helped by a sustained propaganda of heinous broadcast for four years, which planted fear and the instinct of self-defense in the face of the RPF advances, especially for those who were internally displaced. It also created a culture of impunity that the proponents of the final solution to what they called the Tutsi problem in Rwanda carefully exploited in April-July 1994.

Four days after the beginning of the war, during the night of October 4, 1990, there was intense gunfire for several hours in the capital city of Kigali. The following day, President Habyarimana announced that the fire had come from RPF elements that had infiltrated the city. This provided an excuse for the regime to arrest thousands of people in the capital city and in all parts of the country. Between eight and ten thousand were arrested and confined without charge, some for days or weeks and many others for months. Those arrested were suspected of being supporters or "accomplices" (ibyitso) of the Rwandese Patriotic Front. Statistics compiled by Human Rights organizations after the massive arrests established that the prisoners were composed of a majority of Hutu from the south (61%). [8] They were detained in very precarious and deplorable conditions, in addition to being severely beaten and/or tortured in the most inhumane ways. A number of them died in the prisons, and some were never accounted for. The situation changed a bit when the conditions of detention received the attention of internal organizations of Human Rights and the diplomats in Kigali. Their pressure led the government to release the detainees after about eight months.

In the early months of the conflict, several acts of massacres were committed in several parts of the country, notably in the Gisenyi and Ruhengeri districts. Different organizations of Human Rights wrote reports on some cases, but most small massacres were never investigated because of the difficult access to reporters and human rights

monitors. For example, civil servants and high school teachers from the
south working in parts of Gisenyi and Ruhengeri were summarily executed, harassed, or jailed, regardless of their ethnicity.

The arrests that followed the October 4-5, 1990 drill were the
most noticed because they happened in Kigali and other cities, but what
happened in remote parts of the countryside was quite gruesome. Most
of the massacres took place in the two districts of Gisenyi and Ruhengeri, closely associated with Habyarimana and in the northern dis-
trict of Byumba and part of Kibungo, where fighting was most severe.
Killings in Gisenyi and Ruhengeri targeted the Tutsi minority. The first
round took place in the commune of Kibilira (in Gisenyi), where there
was an important Tutsi population. The local, communal, and provin-
cial authorities were involved in the preparation, incitation, and organization of the population to carry out the massacres. For example, the
préfet and his assistant in the region (called *Sous-Préfet*) were present
at the meeting that ordered the local authorities to go and sensitize the
population, by spreading false rumors that such and such important officer from the region had been killed on the front.

The attacks were led by the local authorities called "respon-
sables de cellules, membres des comités de cellules"[9] and by civil servants (school teachers, communal police, and employees of technical
assistance projects). They attacked the Tutsi population and burnt their
houses. Some of the corpses were thrown in the Nyabarongo River.
Within forty-eight hours, 348 persons were massacred, several hundred
houses burnt, domestic animals slain (and eaten), and food provisions
and house equipment looted or destroyed. In the first round of killing,
the role of the authorities (the burgomaster and the sous-préfet[10]) were
so evident that they were fired and jailed, but they were liberated only
after some weeks without any formal charges being brought against
them. The burgomaster was given another job afterwards, and the *sous-
préfet* (who incidentally came from the south) died in obscure circumstances. The burgomaster, a native of that northern region, was hardly
bothered and remained vice-president of the MRND, the then single political party.

It is important to stress that all the persons arrested in connection with the massacres spent at most four weeks in prison and then
were relinquished without any charges or even any files at all. According to the *Rapport de la Commission Internationale*[11] (a major source
of information for this chapter), the authorities explained the massacres
in the same manner that the Kayibanda government had explained the
killing of ten thousand Tutsi in 1963, as we saw in the previous chapter. In the same logic, the Habyarimana government, ideologically

grounded, as it claimed, in the 1959 social revolution and the 1973 moral revolution, claimed that the RPF invasion, the incitation by a number of extremist Tutsi, and a wrong interpretation of received information about the complicity of the Tutsi in anterior attacks by the refugees called "Inyenzi" (cockroaches) in the 1960s had provoked the wrath of the local population. As in the 1960s, all the Tutsi inside Rwanda were considered "accomplices" of the RPF (an accusation also extended to the Hutu opposing the Habyarimana regime). This interpretation was spread and stretched at will by extremist Hutu inciting the Hutu population to kill the Tutsi. In subsequent attacks on Tutsi in the region, as the attacks spread to other parts of Gisenyi and Ruhengeri, the authorities repeated the same now formulaic justification: allegation of Tutsi provocation, spontaneous popular outrage, and Tutsi attacks on Hutu families. The subtext for international consumption was that the Hutu were acting in self-defense.

After the war broke out, the government immediately launched a propaganda campaign aimed at describing the conflict as a Hutu versus Tutsi one. The RPF was described in the official media and in official statements and speeches as a feudal and monarchist group seeking to restore Kigeli V Ndahindurwa, the Umwami (King) who was deposed by the 1959-1962 Hutu revolution (who was then living in Kenya and later migrated to the United States of America, where he still resides). The official discourse repeated over and over again was that the RPF would reinstate the very unpopular "ubuhake" (vassalage), uburetwa (forced work for chiefs), and akazi (mandatory public work), all of which were associated with Tutsi (and Belgian colonial) rule before 1959. By and large, this propaganda fell on easy ears in Gisenyi and Ruhengeri (already reputed for their historical hatred of the Tutsi and southerners) and among local, regional, and national officials (who, according to the logic of the single party system, were MRND representatives) and among extremist elements (mainly intellectuals) throughout the country, many of whom were actually natives of Gisenyi and Ruhengeri working in other regions. As it filters through the rest of this chapter, the 1959 Hutu revolution was the main source of ideological reference, and the preferred document was the 1957 "Bahutu Manifesto," a document whose content everybody who had been to high school was well familiar with. Thus was it forcefully put forward as an antidote to what was called in extremist circles the new Tutsi invasion. As *Kangura*, the preferred newspaper of Hutu extremism, put it three years after the outbreak of the war, the Tutsi who attacked Rwanda in the 1960s were basically the same as those who attacked in 1990:

> We began by saying that a cockroach cannot beget a
> butterfly. And that is true. A cockroach begets another
> cockroach. If anybody contests this, he is not with me. The
> history of Rwanda shows us clearly that the Tutsi have
> always been the same, that they have never changed. The
> malice and the evil are just as we knew them in the history of
> our country. ... Ever since the Tutsi were removed from
> power by the 1959 revolution, they have been on the watch-
> out. They have done everything to restore monarchy. ... We
> are not wrong in saying that a cockroach begets another
> cockroach. Who could tell the difference between the Inyenzi
> who attacked in October 1990 and those who attacked in the
> 1960s? ... Their cruelty is the same. The unspeakable crimes
> that the Inyenzi commit today against citizens recall those
> committed by their elders: killing, looting, raping girls and
> women, etc.[12]

In a way that evidently displays the 1959 Hutu social
revolution, the December 1993 special edition of *Kangura* had the
ironic title of "Batutsi, Bwoko bw'Imana" (Tutsi, Race of God) and a
picture of Grégoire Kayibanda, the father of the 1959 revolution, as
well as a machete on the left end of the cover. Between the machete
and the picture one can read these words: "NI IZIHE NTWARO
TUZAKORESHA KUGIRA NGO DUTSINDE INYENZI
BURUNDU?" (WHAT WEAPONS SHALL WE USE TO DEFEAT
THE INYENZI—COCKROACHES—ONCE AND FOR ALL?).
Kangura then recommends bringing back the Hutu revolution of 1959
to finish off the Tutsi cockroaches.[13]

The 1959 Hutu revolution is also advocated as an antidote to
Tutsi victory by another notorious propagandist/singer, Simon Bikindi
(now in the hands of the International Tribunal for Rwanda in Arusha,
Tanzania), whose lyrics exalting the Hutu and the 1959 revolution
regularly aired on national radio several years before the 1990 war. Not
surprisingly, his songs appealed to the Hutu masses and exploited the
Hamitic Hypothesis, the 1959 Hutu revolution, and the end of Tutsi
rule:

> Carrying chiefs, servitude, the whip, the lash, and forced
> work that exhausted the people, that has disappeared for ever.
> You, the great majority [rubanda nyamwinshi] pay attention
> and, descendants of Sebahinzi [sons of farmers], remember
> this evil that should be driven as far away as possible, so that
> it never returns to Rwanda. Tell the sons of Sebahinzi to
> come and take the antidote.[14]

This song, like much of the propaganda, reminded all the Hutu, metonymically referred to as "bene Sebahinzi" (a reference to the old functional division of ethnic groups, as described in Chapter Two) to be faithful to the 1959 revolution, maintain it, and carry it to future generations. Failure to do so would mean that the RPF Tutsi would win, scrap the "entitlements" the Hutu received from the revolution, restore monarchy and its old ways, and take Hutu land. One must remember the weight carried by the last element, as more than 90% of Rwandans—Hutu and Tutsi—live on subsistence economy, farming their small land. The singer obviously is playing on a very sensitive issue of subsistence and survival for the overwhelming number of cultivators.

The appeal to the 1959 revolution was also part of a sustained effort to regain the support of the southern Hutu, disenfranchised by Habyarimana and the northerners (from Gisenyi and Ruhengeri) since 1973. If the Hutu of the south did not get as much as those of the north, the propaganda went, it was because of Tutsi infiltration in the public administration (masquerading as Hutu) and their dominance of the private sector. According to the propaganda, the Tutsi had robbed the Hutu of the south of their rightful positions. This infiltration, it was repeatedly and forcefully argued, had led disproportionate numbers of Tutsi in high schools, institutions of higher education, and the Catholic clergy:

> The other calamity that *Kangura* is committed to publicize is the detestable habit that many Tutsi have adopted of changing their ethnic group..., which allows them to go unnoticed and to take the places normally reserved for Hutu in the administration and the schools. If this disease is not treated immediately, it will lead to the destruction of all the Hutu.... 85% of Tutsi have changed their ethnicity.[15]

The use of the same themes and strategies over and over before and during the 1994 genocide points to a concerted and sustained propaganda apparatus and a centralized coordination among the propagandists and the newspapers close to the regime. *Human Rights Watch* notes that its researchers found in Butare prefecture "a mimeographed document entitled 'Note Relative à la Propagande d'Expansion et de Recrutement' in which one propagandist tells others how to sway the public effectively."[16] The author of the note offers an analysis of lessons from Roger Mucchielli's *Psychologie de la publicité et de la propagande,*[17]informed by Lenin and Goebbels (minister of culture and propaganda of Hitler's Third Reich). According to *Human Rights Watch*, the author of the note

> advocates using lies, exaggeration, ridicule, and innuendo to attack the opponent, in both his public and his private life. He suggests that moral considerations are irrelevant, except when they happen to offer another weapon against the other side. He adds that it is important not to underestimate the strength of the adversary nor to overestimate the intelligence of the general public targeted by the campaign. Propagandists must aim both to win over the uncommitted and to cause divisions among supporters of the other point of view. They must persuade the public that the adversary stands for war, death, slavery, repression, injustice, and sadistic cruelty.[18]

To achieve these goals, the author of the notes recommends two strategies: (1) Stage events to validate the propaganda; (2) "Accusation in a mirror," a strategy that consists of accusing the enemy of evil acts that the ideologues and their supporters are committing and/or plan to carry out. Examples of the first strategy include the October 4-5, 1990 staged attack on Kigali discussed earlier in this chapter: it achieved the immediate goals of getting French, Belgian, and Zairian military interventions and offered the ideal security framework of arresting thousands of Tutsi and Hutu opposition members (largely southern Hutu). It would have been difficult for the regime to arrest thousands of people without any kind of justification, so the staged attack provided the desired drama. As the author of the note suggests, this tactic is not an honest one. The staged attack of October 4-5, 1990 achieved its goals, but after a few days it was becoming clear to the general public that it was deceitful.[19] The regime further justified the arrests of the "ibyitso" (accomplices of the RPF) by claiming that, in the words of one of its ideologues, Leon Mugesera, "they were found with stocks of weapons, supplies of ammunition, radios for communicating with the enemy, or compromising documents, such as descriptions of the authorities and plans to attack."[20]

As for the "accusation in a mirror," it works as follows: "the party which is using terror will accuse the enemy of using terror."[21] This strategy achieves at least two goals: (1) It convinces the honest, neutral, and opposing forces that they are in danger; (2) They are encouraged and indeed justified in adopting self-defense measures. As this chapter shows, these two techniques, especially the second one, were fully exploited before and during the genocide. In the months that followed the outbreak of the war, one newspaper, *Kangura*, and many propagandists distinguished themselves in the use of this technique (Leon Mugesera will be discussed as an example).

Launched in May 1990, *Kangura,* edited by the extremist Hassan Ngeze, quickly acquired notoriety for its virulent anti-Tutsi propaganda. The fact that the editor received government classified information from the President's office and from different ministries left nobody guessing about the support that he was receiving from the dignitaries of the Habyarimana regime. Largely ignored before the war, *Kangura* perversely achieved prominence with its No. 6 of December 1990 in which the editor Hassan Ngeze issued what he called the "Ten Commandments of the Bahutu":

1. All the Hutu must know that a Tutsi woman, wherever she is, is working for her Tutsi ethnic group. Consequently, is traitor any Hutu:
- who marries a Tutsi woman;
- who makes of a Tutsi woman his mistress;
- who makes of a Tutsi woman his secretary or who protects her.

2. All the Hutu must know that our Hutu girls are more dignified and more conscientious in their role of woman, wife and mother. Aren't they more beautiful, better secretaries and more honest?

3. Hutu women, be vigilant and bring your husbands and sons back to reason.

4. All the Hutu must know that all the Tutsi are incapable of honesty in business. They only work for the supremacy of their ethnic group.
Consequently, is traitor any Hutu who
- associates with the Tutsi in business;
- invests his money or State money in a Tutsi-owned enterprise;
- lends money to, or borrows it from, a Tutsi;
- gives the Tutsi favors (granting import licenses, bank loans, building lots, public contracts...).

5. The strategic positions, be they political, administrative, economic, military and pertaining to national security must be entrusted exclusively to the Hutu.

6. The education sector (schoolchildren, students, teachers) must be predominantly Hutu.

7. The Rwandan Armed Forces must be exclusively Hutu. The experience of the October 1990 proves that this demand is founded. No soldier or officer should marry a Tutsi woman.

8. The Bahutu must cease to have pity for the Batutsi.

9. - The Bahutu, wherever they are, must remain united, stick together and be preoccupied with the plight of their Hutu brothers.
- The Bahutu of the interior and of the exterior of Rwanda must continually seek friends and allies for the Hutu cause, beginning with their Bantu brothers.
- They must constantly counter the Tutsi propaganda.
- The Bahutu must be firm and vigilant against the Tutsi enemy.
10. The Social Revolution of 1959, the 1961 referendum, and the Hutu ideology, must be taught to all the Hutu and on levels. All the Bahutu have the obligation to publicize this ideology largely.
Is traitor any Muhutu who will persecute his Hutu brother for having read, publicized and taught this ideology. (My translation)

The excitement produced by this ideology of hate in extremist milieus (particularly in the prefectures of Gisenyi and Ruhengeri) was an omen of the evil intention behind not only the journal but also those in the high administration of the country who were supporting it, providing it with sensitive information and encouraging it to speak against and condemn all the Tutsi and all those who opposed the Habyarimana regime. The targets were almost exclusively Tutsi and Hutu of the south. The government did not condemn the writing, but instead, anybody who was pointed out by the journal as an accomplice of the RPF was in danger of losing his or her job and of being killed in obscure circumstances. As a matter of fact, many pages in the editions that came out after October 1990 focused on denouncing people *Kangura* called Tutsi masquerading as Hutu in public office. One must note that the author of the commandments brings in an international dimension, calling upon what he calls "Bantu brothers," or the Hutu of the central Africa to fight and defeat a vast Nilotic Tutsi-Hima conspiracy to enslave the Bantu. *Kangura Magazine*, created in early 1992 as an international edition of *Kangura*, specifically targeted the Burundi audience.[22] In *Kangura Magazine*, No. 5, January/February 1992, Bonaparte Ndekezi contributed a piece titled "Peuples bantous du monde entier unissez-vous" (Bantu people of the world, unite). He wrote:

There is indeed a diabolical plan prepared by the Tutsi and their related groups, targeting the systematic extermination of the Bantu population as well as the expansion of a Nilotic empire from Ethiopia in the northwest and from

Douala   to the sources of the Nile ...from Gabon to
Lesotho including the vast basins of the Kongo, the Rift
Valley of Tanzania...down to the Cape and the
Drankensberg Mountains. That crusade is already under
way in the Kivu province [of Zaire], in Uganda under the
Hima Museveni and mostly in Burundi.... What are the
Bantu peoples waiting for to protect themselves against the
genocide that has been so shrewdly and meticulously
orchestrated by the Hamites thirsty for blood and for
barbarian conquests and whose leaders dispute the gold
medal of cruelty with the Roman empire Nero.[23]

The MRND ideologue Léon Mugesera made the same claim that the
Tutsi aimed to establish in the Bantu region of the great lakes (Rwanda,
Burundi, Zaire, Tanzania, Uganda) a vast kingdom for the Hima-Tutsi,
an ethnic group that considered itself superior, on the model of the
Aryan race, and which used Hitler's Swastika as its emblem.[24]

Echoing Mugesera, *Kangura* and other extremist newspapers
kept coming back to this plan, referring to Tutsi as "Neo-Nazi," driven
by revenge for the 1959 revolution, expansionist, cannibals, who had
grown horns on their heads—an attempt to describe them as monsters. I
personally heard people in Ruhengeri who said that the Tutsi grew
horns on their heads. The "Nazi" qualification is a typical case of
"accusation in a mirror."   Habyarimana and his supporters were
inspired by Hitler, Goebbels, and the totalitarian regime, judging from
the wide use of violence as a political tool and, not the least, the fact
that copies of Hitler's *Mein Kampf* and films about National Socialism
were found in Habyarimana's Kanombe residence after his death and
after the evacuation of his family to France after April 6, 1994.

Reference was also made to a 1962 letter that resurfaced in the
wake of the Rwandan war. The letter spoke of a Tutsi plan to take over
central Africa, starting with the Kivu province in Zaire. More widely
discussed and still given credence among Burundian Hutu (particularly
those in exile) was a plan called "plan Simbananiye" after the extremist
Burundian Tutsi politician Arthémon Simbananiye who was minister of
foreign affairs during the 1972 massacre of Hutu in Burundi in the
government of Michel Micombero. At least one hundred-fifty thousand
Hutu (mostly educated) were massacred—this pogrom is sometimes
referred to as the intellectual genocide of the Hutu of Burundi. After the
assassination of Melchior Ndadaye, the first Hutu President of Burundi,
in October 1993 after only four months in office, the theory of a broad
Tutsi conspiracy became even more plausible for the Hutu of Rwanda
and Burundi, an event which dramatically helped the "Hutu Power"

movement in Rwanda. Speakers at rallies organized by Hutu Power parties and tendencies in the aftermath of Ndadaye's assassination demanded Rwanda's intervention to help the Hutu brothers in Burundi.

Human Rights and the Regional Factor in Political Parties

In the democratic movement that was given a quick impetus by the civil war,[25] political parties formed along ethnic and regional lines. MRND, the former single party, remained the strongest in the northern provinces of Gisenyi and Ruhengeri (the region of President Habyarimana), although it had members in all parts of the country.[26] In 1991, several political parties were founded. The most important were created in the summer of 1991. Le Mouvement Démocratique Républicain (MDR) (The Republican Democratic Party) aimed at recuperating the core ideology of the MDR-PARMEHUTU of the 1950s and 1960s. In launching it, its leaders strongly appealed to the 1959 Hutu revolution and promised to defend its "entitlements" (les acquis). As a witness of this particular juncture, I could see that the party aimed to appeal to the overwhelming Hutu population. Not surprisingly, they used the expression "rubanda nyamwinshi" (great masses, i.e. Hutu) in their original texts. They also exalted the work of Grégoire Kayibanda, the original founder of MDR-PARMEHUTU. That it was the largest opposition party leaves no doubt as to its Hutu ethnic base, the strongest of which was in the prefecture of Gitarama, the home region of Kayibanda. Particularly active in the party were families of the Gitarama dignitaries who were killed in the 1970s (by Habyarimana, Lizinde, and their northern collaborators). Interestingly, MDR was the only political party that presented any kind of challenge to the former single party MRND in the prefectures of Gisenyi and Ruhengeri for three main reasons. First, these two regions had been strongholds of MDR-PARMEHUTU in the 1950s and 1960s. Second, there were a number of families who had benefited from the party in the 1960s. To keep tabs on Gisenyi and Ruhengeri politicians and senior army officers, Kayibanda often created divisions among them. He would play Gisenyi against Ruhengeri, and within Gisenyi he would play on the Bushiru/Bugoyi regions. Those who had benefited from these divisions did not necessarily enjoy the same privileges under the Habyarimana regime. Third, not all Gisenyi and Ruhengeri intellectuals and officers embraced MRND politics of ethnic and regional division and the regime of terror that followed October 1990.

The other two important opposition parties created in the summer of 1991 were Le Parti Social Démocrate (PSD) (The Social Democratic Party), and Le Parti Libéral (PL) (The Liberal Party). The stronghold of PSD was in two prefectures, Butare and Gikongoro, but it also had significant following in the other prefectures of the south, from Kibungo in the east to Cyangugu in the southwest. Its members were recruited from both Hutu and Tutsi ethnic groups. It was dubbed "the party of intellectuals," who were probably suspicious of the populism of MDR and who were obviously disappointed by the totalitarianism of MRND.

PL recruited many of its members among the Tutsi businessmen and intellectuals, as well as Hutu (especially those of mixed ethnicity). Unlike the other three parties (MRND, MDR, and PSD), PL had no stronghold in any prefecture and rather it tended to depend on city recruitment (especially Kigali and Butare). As the Liberal Party was openly accused by MRND and CDR of being an antenna of the RPF inside the country, a number of its members were afraid of making their membership known, especially in Gisenyi and Ruhengeri, where they could be easily eliminated. Less significant, a fourth party called PDC (Parti Démocrate Chrétien) (Christian Democratic Party) was also launched in 1991. The fact that the Catholic Church in Rwanda had been very close to the Habyarimana regime and the Christian Democratic International had embraced the regime as one serving its ideology did not help the PDC. In the last quarter of 1991 and early 1992, a number of small and insignificant parties were created, most probably with the encouragement of President Habyarimana and his cronies who wanted to counter the now powerful partnership created by MDR, PSD, PL, and PDC.[27]

On the multiparty front, the most significant event of early 1992 was the creation of the Coalition pour la Défense de la République (CDR) (Coalition for the Defense of the Republic), a party composed of ultra-extremist Hutu predominantly from Gisenyi and Ruhengeri, who called the Hutu of the other parties traitors. This ultra-extremist movement was in gestation already in late 1990 when *Kangura* (whose editor was later one of the founders of the CDR) quickly became notorious for its heinous rhetoric against the Tutsi. Exclusively Hutu[28] and grounded in extreme ethnic and regional ideology, CDR accused MRND and MDR of failing to defend the 1959 Hutu revolution against the Tutsi threat, even though in many cases it functioned as the extreme, northern wing of MRND. Before the spread of Hutu Power, CDR carried the banner of Hutu extremism and did the dirty work that MRND could not afford to do in the open because of its claim to be a national party and the positioning for possible elections in the future. CDR's creation in 1992 is very significant: the Arusha peace negotiations were in high gear, and those who stood to lose much from power-sharing arrangements were looking for ways of derailing the talks. In contrast to the negotiation spirit, CDR called for the total defeat of the Rwandan Patriotic Front, the extermination of Tutsi and the Hutu who had embraced the political opposition to MRND, and the reinforcement of a Hutu State in Rwanda and in the Great Lakes region (particularly in Burundi). CDR militia "impuzamugambi" (those with the same goal) worked closely with the infamous MRND militia "interahamwe" (those who attack together) since 1992 and particularly during the April-July 1994 genocide. All in all, the launching of CDR in 1992 could be interpreted as another extreme strategy by the northerners to place the October 1990 war in the ethnic logic (Hutu versus Tutsi), the only logic that would undermine the determination of the political opposition to negotiate directly with the RPF.

By and large, through this overview of the political parties that were founded in 1991 and 1992, one can see that not much had changed ideologically since the 1960s, especially concerning the 1959 Hutu revolution. Three parties (MRND, MDR, and CDR) professed to defend the revolution and thus directly appealed to the Hutu. The Parti Social Démocrate (PSD), the Parti Libéral, and the Parti Démocrate Chrétien were the only significant parties not overtly based on ethnic ideology that attracted members from both Hutu and Tutsi. Perhaps one of the two changes is the regional factor in multiparty politics: Gisenyi and Ruhengeri and part of Byumba for MRND and CDR, Gitarama and generally the south for MDR, Butare and Gikongoro (and parts of Gitarama, Kigali, Kibungo, Kibuye, and Cyangugu) for PSD.

From the regional perspective, one new political region in the multiparty politics of 1990-94 was created: the north (western) region of Gisenyi and Ruhengeri with an extreme Hutu ideology ("Hutu purs et durs"). Having most benefited from the second republic, the military and intellectual elites from this region were not ready at all to share power neither with the southerners nor with the invading RPF, and from the very beginning of the conflict, the northerners vowed to defend the entitlements of the 1973 so called "moral" revolution that had put them in power. In other words, as they claimed to be defending the 1959 Hutu social revolution, they were in fact using it because of its national appeal to defend the 1973 "moral" revolution. Even though they appealed to Hutu solidarity (an idea from the 1960s) and focused on depicting the civil war as a Hutu versus Tutsi conflict, there is no doubt that if they had completely defeated the RPF, or if the 1994 genocide had completely succeeded and the genocidal regime had retained power, the northerners would have gone back to their regionalist segregation.

This ethnicization and regionalization of politics had major undesirable consequences since June 1991. While the former single party once claimed everybody automatically as members (a party official once declared that even the fetus in a Rwandan mother was a member of the party), it had a hard time convincing those it had mistreated to support it. Losing this dictatorial ground meant fewer members in the party in July 1991. The party executive committee designed methods of intimidation to force people back, but many Rwandans found in the opposition parties the voices they had been denied since the 1970s. The many grenade and bomb attacks launched by members of the former single party in 1991-93 were thus meant to eliminate opposition leaders and frighten the population back into their party. Habyarimana and his ideological allies radicalized their ethnic stands more and more, probably in hopes of forming an ethnically based constituency. The foundation of the "Coalition pour la Défense de la République" (CDR) as an ultra-extremist party, an ally of MRND, was meant to mobilize the Hutu constituency.

This treason was forcefully proclaimed in the obnoxious speech by Mugesera in a political meeting that was held in Kabaya, commune of Gaseke, prefecture of Gisenyi, on November 22, 1992. He called all the opposition parties accomplices of the RPF and added, "We can't have peace if we don't go to war." Revealing aspects of his speech are contained in the following excerpts (translated from Kinyarwanda):

> Thus, in a our prefecture of Gisenyi, this is, if not the fourth time, the fifth time I openly declare that it is they who started it; in the Gospels, it is said that if someone hits you on the cheek, you also present the other cheek. I tell you that that passage has acquired a new meaning in our party. If anyone hits you on the cheek, hit your enemy on both cheeks and so strongly that he will not get up again. To begin with, you will strictly prohibit in our prefecture any kind of flag, any hat,[29] and any access to a member of one of the said parties, especially if he tries to organize a meeting here. I mean the whole prefecture of Gisenyi without exception.
>
> [The MDR, PL and PSD parties] have plotted to let the prefec-

ture of Byumba fall in the hands of the enemy. (...) They have plotted to discourage our army. The punishment for irresponsible authorities that allow the enemy to do what he wants is known. The law is very clear on that point. "Will be condemned to capital punishment any person who is guilty of acts intended to sap the morale of the armed forces." Why is this law not enforced?

You know very well that there are accomplices (ibyitso) [of the RPF] in this country. They send their children to the RPF. These are facts that were reported to you and that you know very well.... Why don't we decimate those families and all the people who recruit for the RPF? (...) We have repeatedly asked for a census of those people and their listing so that they are brought to justice. And if this is not done, let us remember that saying, which is also written in our constitution: "Justice is rendered in the name of the people." And if justice cannot be rendered to the people, ... in that case, we, the people, betrayed by justice, will be obliged to assume our responsibility in order to get rid of those hoodlums! If you allow the serpent to bite without it being bothered, it will soon be your turn to be exterminated....

Brothers, militants of our Movement, the rhetoric I have just used is not to be taken softly. It is our duty, in the high spheres of the party, to make it clear to you so that when they begin shooting at you, you don't accuse us of not having warned you. At the same time, I would like to warn any person who has sent his child to the rebels. That person, his wife and all his family must join him before it is too late because the time has already passed when we should defend ourselves, since the law is no longer enforced.

The fatal error we made in 1959 was to let them [the Tutsi] leave the country. Their home is Ethiopia, and we are going to find them a shortcut, namely the Nyabarongo River. I must insist on this point. We must act forcefully! Get rid of them!

...Long live President Habyarimana!

Mugesera said that he was speaking for the President, who did not deny the fact. Nor did the President condemn the heinous speech. The same appeal was made at another place in the same prefecture of Gisenyi, the commune of Kibilira. The two speeches made echoes in the whole country, and the attackers cited the two speeches as reasons to burn houses and kill the Tutsi and other persons belonging to opposition parties. The Minister of Justice ordered the arrest of Mugesera, but the latter hid in a military camp.

A very significant development in the MRND was the creation in the second half of 1991 of a party militia, known as "Interahamwe" or "Those who attack together" or "Those who sing the same tune." Its ally, CDR, also created a militia called "Impuzamugambi" or "Those who have the same goal." These two militias committed the majority of killings that took place after their creation. Soldiers from the regular army and/or from the presidential guard unit trained the two militias in the methods of killing—different sources also affirm that the French soldiers were involved in the training of the militia. Actually, the two militias had a number of soldiers in their ranks. The militia worked closely with the local authorities in Gisenyi and Ruhengeri and also in other parts of the country, especially the capital city. The program announced by Mugesera was often cited by the local authorities to decimate the Tutsi and the Hutu members of the opposition parties.

The Bagogwe, a Tutsi group, was probably the most affected by the first wave of massacres. They lived near the natural forest of the high mountains and at the edge of Gishwati Forest, in the prefectures of Gisenyi and Ruhengeri. Their main activity always was, at least until the 1940s, cattle breeding, agriculture being only marginal. More recently, with pastures becoming scarce they adopted agriculture and sought paid jobs. They lived in several communes of Ruhengeri and Gisenyi. It was easy for the authorities to deny that the massacres had taken place, especially because they had taken the care to seal off the region by limiting movements between that region and the rest of the country. Prohibitions to travel even from one "secteur"[30] to another were implemented with the help of the myriad road and sometimes path barricades. This policy was designed to prevent targeted individuals from fleeing and human rights monitors and reporters from entering the region. The hassles involved in obtaining documents needed for travel from one region to another in the country were quite discouraging. With this kind of cover, many atrocities were committed and never reported. Afterwards, all the civil and military authorities adamantly denied the massacres ever having taken place.

In addition to the irrefutable evidence found by an international commission that investigated the killings in 1993, including common graves in the different places in the communes where the Bagogwe lived—one was even in the backyard of a burgomaster named Juvénal Kajelijeli--I saw with my own eyes, several dozens of widows and their children (all female) in the town of Ruhengeri, seeking access to the authorities to ask for help saying that their husbands and sons had been massacred. They were hurriedly loaded in trucks and returned to their places. They would not be given travel documents to leave the region. I knew of two particular young girls of approximately 15 years of age who tried to find household jobs in the city of Ruhengeri and could not because they were immediately identified and returned to their communes. The authorities feared that the girls could get in contact with human rights organizations or representatives of foreign diplomatic representations, which could further damage the image of the government.

Like the other Tutsi of the interior, the Bagogwe were called "Ibyitso" (accomplices) or "Inyangarwanda" (those who hate Rwanda). Many of them were also jailed for several months. Their cows were butchered and eaten and their belongings looted. The authorities used the "umuganda," a community work demanded of all adults on a weekly basis, and asked the population "to work," an expression that became synonymous with killing the Tutsi (and the members of the opposition parties). Even though that community work was in principle a good practice, it was so often abused by the authorities that after some years it began to be perceived by many as forced labor. Absence at "umuganda" was often regarded as more severe than absence at work. Many civil servants were fired because of bad attendance at umuganda, though performing well at their respective jobs. In the countryside, people were sometimes charged heavy fines for not attending. It is this same community work that was exploited by the authorities to incite the population to kill. They would call people for an emergency community service and then tell them "to work."

The massacres of the Bagogwe took place shortly after the RPF successfully captured the city of Ruhengeri on January 23, 1991. The success of the attack was quite an embarrassment for government. Scapegoats were needed. The Bagogwe, among others, were blamed for the success of the RPF. A large-scale campaign to massacre them was then mounted. Janvier Afrika, a former member of a select group called "escadron de la mort" (death squad), later disclosed that the meeting that prepared the massacres comprised the President of the Republic himself, his wife, two brothers of the President's wife (Elie Sagatwa and Protais Zigiranyirazo, the first being the particular secretary of the president and the second the former *préfet* of Ruhengeri), and other personalities close to the family of the President and that of his wife.[31]

The Bagogwe were taken in communal trucks and killed with stones, machetes, spears, clubs, and even guns, near communal offices. The local population meetings that were called on the hills by the local authorities excluded the Tutsi. Soldiers exhorted the population to kill with machetes, to cut the Tutsi into pieces. In the region of the President, in the communes of Gaseke and Giciye, prefecture of Gisenyi, the killings followed the pattern used in Ruhengeri. The two communes along with the commune Karago (commune of Habyarimana) form the region of Bushiru, where Habyarimana came from. According to the *Rapport de la Commission Internationale*, the order to kill came from the then Minister of Interior, the prefect of Ruhengeri, and the director of the prison of Ruhengeri: "Go and do a *special umuganda*. Destroy all the bushes and all the Inkotanyi who are hiding in there. And, more important, don't forget that one who cuts a bad herb must also destroy its roots."[32] It is important to stress the use of "umuganda" and "akazi" (work), which, in this context, meant to kill the Tutsi and their children. Many of the massacres were carried out in special "umuganda,' or even after ordinary ones. The persons arrested said they had carried out the massacres under the directive of the government. Those arrested affirmed they went with local authorities or were sent by them. They used spears, machetes, hoes, sharpened bamboos, and rocks, the same "weapons" used during the 1994 genocide.

The massacres committed in the commune of Habyarimana have remained unknown, though the Justice Ministry said in its 1992 report that 68 people had been killed there. The actual number is certainly by far higher. Those who carried out the massacres were not named. An acquaintance of mine, who was assistant prosecutor in the region (but a native of the prefecture of Kigali, considered as part of the political south), told me once that he and some of his colleagues knew massacres were taking place there, but they were prevented from investigating. Once, they tried to reach the area, but they were forced to retreat by a barrage of rocks from a mob obviously assembled by the local authorities.

Another method that was used in certain places, such as the commune of Mutura (also in Gisenyi), was to simulate attacks by the RPF in the region and afterwards proceed with massacres as a form of reprisal, following the well-known pattern of the 1960s. Both soldiers and civilians participated in the massacres.

The reaction of the authorities was generally favorable to the killings, and because of this, their responsibility was quite complicitous in that they prepared and/or encouraged the killings. The participation of the military force constituted further evidence of the direct implication of the authorities. After the creation of the MRND and CDR militia, certain massacres occurred after their meetings. Throughout the report of the international commission, it filters that there was collaboration among the communes, complicity of local authorities, collaboration between the civil and military authorities, fictitious presence of a suspicious person and an RPF recruiter, coincidence of attack dates, vocabulary used to name the operations (for example *umuganda* and clearing the bush), and generalized impunity—all these elements point to the existence of a high level coordination of operations.

The Bugesera massacres in March 1992 support the idea that attacks were patterned in the same way and thus were carefully prepared before hand by a high authority. The region of Bugesera is in the southern part of Rwanda. It comprises three communes in the *préfecture* of Kigali. It borders the Republic of Burundi. When the massacres of Tutsi took place there, it was very far from the war zone, but it has a military camp at Gako, the largest center of military training in Rwanda. At least four groups were involved: the military authority of the camp, the civil authorities (local and national), the militia of the MRND (Interahamwe), CDR (Impuzamugambi), and the national radio.

Before 1960, the region was almost empty. Large numbers of Tutsi moved there in the 1960s subsequent to reprisals that, as we saw in the previous chapter, followed the *Inyenzi* attacks in the 1960s. Later on, more Tutsi and also Hutu joined them, and among the Hutu there was an important group from the northwestern *préfectures* of Gisenyi and Ruhengeri, who migrated to Bugesera looking for land to farm. Since the outbreak of the 1990 war, the region, like most of the southern part, was accused by the government of sending young men to the RPF via Burundi. Many young men were arrested in 1991 and taken to the military camp of Gako, accused of preparing to join the RPF. Most would not be seen again.

On November 11, 1991, the burgomaster of Kanzenze, one of the communes that make up the region of Bugesera, held a meeting in which he said he was the burgomaster of the Hutu and pointed to an opposition leader on the communal level as the leader of the Tutsi and charged that he would see who was stronger. Weeks after that event, Ngeze Hassan, editor of the extremist journal *Kangura*, visited Bugesera on several occasions. During those weeks, mines exploded in the region causing the loss of some lives and the destruction of some vehicles. On the one hand, the authorities accused the Tutsi of complicity with the RPF; on the other hand, human rights organizations accused the authorities of encouraging tensions to prepare attacks against the Tutsi.

Mid-February 1992, five persons were arrested and detained in the military camp of Gako for a week and later transferred to a police brigade in Kigali, where they were beaten and tortured by the secret agents of the Service Central de Renseignement (Intelligence Bureau of the Presidency). They were liberated following the pressure of human rights associations.

On March 1, 1992, during a political meeting of the Liberal Party (one of the opposition parties), the local representative (a man called Gahima) enumerated the errors of the burgomaster (Rwambuka). Afterwards, an anonymous piece of writing accused Gahima of being a rebel, a murderer, and an execrable bandit.

On March 3, 1992, the national radio broadcast five times a special announcement presented as a warning from a group of human rights activists based in Nairobi, Kenya, according to which they had discovered a plot planned by Tutsi in Rwanda to assassinate prominent Hutu, especially leaders of the political parties. During the night of March 4, 1992, the opposite took place. The MRND Hutu attacked the Tutsi. They burned housed, looted goods, and ate cattle. The weapons used were: machetes, spears, clubs, and hatchets. The attacks and killings continued until March 9, 1992, despite the fact that there was a military camp and thus soldiers could have easily intervened to stop the carnage, and the region is only less than an hour from Kigali. The authorities in the capital city, in other words, were aware of what was going on. Third, the gendarmes who intervened later on just watched the attackers do the "work." An estimated 277 people died in the attacks. Fourth, an Italian volunteer, Ms. Antonia Locatelli, who used her telephone to tell correspondents in Europe what was happening, was shot by a gendarme. In fact, when human rights organizations and the diplomatic community began witnessing the scale of the pogrom, the authorities searched for ways of minimizing it, notably by pressing the refugees who had fled to parishes to go back home. The burgomaster had the water supply at the Nyamata parish cut. Ms. Antonia Locatelli told him that it was wrong and cruel to do that. That same night she was killed by two gunshots, a bullet in the mouth, another in the heart.

As in the other massacres, the authorities, including the members of the "cellule" (cell), the councilor, the burgomaster, and the director of the national radio (Ferdinand Nahimana), were all involved. The authorities on the lower levels even participated and directed the attacks. The burgomaster was also involved. He later tried to justify the massacres by suggesting that the Hutu had been provoked by the Tutsi, the same kind of explanation that had been offered to justify the massacres in the préfectures of Gisenyi and Ruhengeri. The burgomaster of Kanzenze was a member of the executive committee of MRND; thus he had a lot to say in the policies of the party.

The official justification was, as usual, alleged actions carried out by the Tutsi against the Hutu, such as anonymous tracts and false rumors warning that the Tutsi were about to kill the Hutu, but the official justification did not mention the tract calling the Hutu to kill Gahima and the Tutsi. Some people even went as far as suggesting that the Tutsi had burnt their houses to put the blame on the Hutu.

A witness (Janvier Afrika) who talked to the International Commission said that the Death Squad of MRND and CDR participated in the massacres. He himself had been part of the operation and desisted later on. He affirmed that the burgomaster arranged the purchase of supplies (machetes acquired at Rwandex Chillington in Kigali, gas for burning houses, and vehicles to transport the assailants) and organized the massacres. There were also "Interahamwe" who came from the capital city from the quarters of Remera, Cyahafi, and Biryogo, who were taken to Bugesera in two vans and one truck. Some soldiers from the presidential guard unit and from the camp of Kanombe participated in the attack. A soldier in the camp of Gako declared to the International Commission that the commander of the camp had provided approximately 150 soldiers to help in the operation. The soldiers disarmed the Tutsi telling them that there was no more danger, and then afterwards the killers came and did their work. Those who survived confirmed the participation of the military in the operation to the International Commission.

Following the Bugesera massacres, 466 persons were arrested, jailed for a short time, and most were sent home after some months following deliberate prosecution errors. There were no compensation for the victims. In the name of Hutu solidarity, CDR paid a lawyer to defend those arrested, but eventually all those arrested went home, some to harrass the survivors of the attacks. The gendarme who killed Ms. Antonia Locatelli was condemned to one year of imprisonment.

It is important to note the significance of the Bugesera massacres in the path to genocide. First, it was the first massacre to take place outside the Gisenyi/Ruhengeri axis. The organizers used the same strategies already tested in the Gisenyi and Ruhengeri massacres as well as the concepts contained in the note inspired by Roger Mucchielli's book, notably the use of lies and exaggerations, the staging of events to validate the propaganda, and especially the accusation in a mirror. As a witness of the events of 1990-July 1992, I contend that the rehearsal of a final solution to what was tacitly referred to as the Tutsi problem in circles close to the Gisenyi/Ruhengeri powerbrokers would not be complete without staging it in the south, and that is exactly what the Bugesera massacres permitted: to verify the feasibility of massacres in the political south.

After these massacres, the MRND and CDR militia committed other acts of terrorism, for example by planting small bombs in southern cities (Kigali, Ruhango, Nyanza, and Butare). It was clear that they targeted the region because it had rejected the two parties and had massively adhered to the opposition parties. Except for the case of Bugesera, the two parties had failed to arouse the population in the south to kill each other. Possible explanations of this failure are: (1) in general, the historical animosity against the Tutsi, observed even in the pre-War years in Gisenyi and Ruhengeri, did not exist in the south; (2) the southern opposition to MRND and CDR and their radical ethnic positions; (3) the high level of intermarriage between the Hutu and the Tutsi in the south, which led northern Hutu to accuse their southern counterparts of having sullied their Hutuness. The better integration between the Hutu and the Tutsi in the south meant that the Hutu in the south would be more difficult to manipulate into killing their Tutsi neighbors.

As a conclusion to this analysis of the pattern involved in different massacres since the outbreak of war in 1990, the majority of people killed were Tutsi but also a considerable number of Hutu from the south, who happened to belong to opposition parties. The authorities were in most cases characterized by slowness, weakness and indifference to intervene to stop the killings. In the beginning, it was the population that carried the attacks led by local authorities and government soldiers, but since the creation of the MRND and CDR militia, these played an important role in different operations of massacre and terror in collaboration with elements from the Presidential Guard and the national army.

Subsequent operations of massacres occurred in January 1993 carried out by the militia in the north under the supervision of local and central government authorities. The same pattern of preparation was used. As an example, "Africa Watch" (volume 5, No.7) reports that on January 20, 1993, a group of soldiers calling themselves "AMASASU" (bullets) wrote a letter to President Habyarimana warning that the RPF was preparing to violate the cease-fire agreed upon during the Arusha peace negotiations and resume hostilities. The raison d'être of the group, as it said, was to "'detect and destroy' the politicians and others who supported the RPF from within Rwanda."[33] The group claimed that it had identified the enemy within, and it was ready to get rid of it. Although the Prime Minister asked the Minister of Defense to stop such hunts, it was certainly a sign that something was in preparation. Of course, this was a serious threat, as the military had become notorious in different parts of the country, beating, shooting, killing civilians, raping women, and looting.

Since the creation of "Interahamwe" and "Impuzamugambi," the Tutsi and members of the opposition parties lived in a state of perpetual fear fostered by manifold threats of injury, death, loss of property, looting, and destruction. The prefectures of Kigali, Kibungo, Byumba, Ruhengeri, and Kibuye knew most of the human rights abuses. Because the MRND and CDR were not strong in the other prefectures, abuses in those were limited to the leaders of the opposition parties living in Kigali. For example, a certain Emmanuel Gapyisi, a prominent Hutu politician from Gikongoro, head of the political commission of the MDR and president of the party in Gikongoro, was shot on May 18, 1993 in front of his house. Tutsi families in Gisenyi and Ruhengeri were often subjected to nightly attacks that many of them chose to spend the night outside in the bush.

The most conspicuous evidence of the regime of terror is the fact that MRND and CDR militia continued to monitor many road barricades that they erected at their will. The conditions of passage included the presentation of an "appropriate" identity card and political party membership cards. Use of those roads was thus prohibited to the Tutsi and to members of the opposition parties. When they presented themselves, they were beaten, fined, and warned against using the roads again. Given the fact that Habyarimana controlled the two parties, the army and the gendarmerie, this state of unlawfulness could have been easily prevented. On the contrary, these acts of impunity were encouraged, and the rule of law had no place in Rwanda, as long as one was on the side of the repressive ways of Hutu ideology. The opposition parties, the diplomatic representations in Kigali, and different organizations in the country called on Habyarimana and his cronies to stop the practice, but nothing was done. The other parties also had militia, especially in the capital city of Kigali, and they engaged in attacks and counter-attacks with the Interahamwe and Impuzamugambi, but they were neither trained nor equipped, and the Interahamwe and Impuzamugambi, often backed by army soldiers and gendarmes, would always have the upperhand.

As the Arusha peace talks gained momentum in 1992 and 1993, the Hutu power movement became more radical and continued to portray the talks as a betrayal of the 1959 Hutu revolution and accused the opposition parties, which had readily embraced negotiations with the RPF since 1992, as RPF accomplices and thus enemies of Rwanda. Moreover, CDR, the banner-bearer of Hutu Power, was sidelined and would not be included in the transitional government. This exclusion did not just worry the civilians, but also men in uniform who rightly felt that the implementation of the accords would make them jobless, as the new army would have to accommodate RPF soldiers.

The agreement itself comprised four parts signed at different times. The first protocol, the initial ceasefire agreement, was signed on July 12, 1992. The second protocol, a power-sharing protocol for a Broad Based Transitional Government (BBTG), was signed on October 30, 1992 and January 9, 1993. The third protocol, the agreement on the repatriation of refugees, was signed on June 9, 1993. The final protocol, the armed forces agreement, was signed on August 3, 1993. All these elements seriously undermined the grip on power of the northerners (Gisenyi and Ruhengeri) who stood to lose their two-decade long control of the administration (and all the advantages that went with that control) and made up much of the Hutu Power (CDR, much of MRND, and Power factions inside the MDR and PL parties). By the time the final agreement was signed in August 1993, the Hutu Power movement had already established its own institutions. The Interahamwe (MRND) and Impuzamugambi (CDR) militia as well as much of the national army and police, both controlled by MRND, instituted a regime of violence, terror, and intimidation as political tools. A new element in its ideological apparatus was the creation of the extremist media outlet, the infamous Radio-Television Libre des Mille Collines (which openly called for the elimination of the Tutsi and Hutu opposition members). This new medium joined the already effective journal *Kangura* (discussed earlier) and other less known (but no less virulent) papers such as *Umurava Magazine, La Médaille Nyiramacibiri, Echo des Mille Collines,* and *Power-Powa.*[34]

We must keep in mind that the Habyarimana regime that came to power through a coup in 1973 was a military regime whose strength was based on the overwhelming presence of officers and soldiers from Gisenyi and Ruhengeri. Losing this backbone of his power to the power-sharing agreement was unacceptable to the northerners and the Habyarimana administration. In fact, the Arusha agreement so dramatically reduced the power of the President within the BBTG that Habyarimana would be a minor player following the implementation of the accord. He would promulgate laws but would have no veto power. He would lose the power to place civil servants in the central administration (which was a key element, since it dictated the contours of the production, distribution, and consumption of capital as well as the allocation of resources, given the absence of a significant private sector). The BBTG also had the charge to approve the President's speeches to the nation. This was a personal affront to a person who had dictated national politics for two decades. If implemented, the accords would also mean the end of the disproportionate control of the military and of national politics by the *sacred region*.

The assassination of Melchior Ndadaye on October 21, 1993, hardly four months after he took office as the first democratically elected President of Burundi, gave additional ideological ammunition to the Hutu Power movement in Rwanda. When Ndadaye was elected on June 1, 1993, there were celebrations all over Rwanda. A considerable number of Hutu openly celebrated the victory in pubs. His assassination was received with shock by the Hutu Power who used it to convert those who hesitated to join its rank. Now the Hutu Power could say, "We told you so. You cannot trust the Tutsi. They did that in Burundi, and they will not hesitate to do it in Rwanda, if they are part of the government." The assassination happened in a period when the Habyarimana side was using all kinds of political manipulations to avoid the full implementation of the Arusha peace agreement, despite the presence of an UN mission called UNAMIR (United Nations Mission for Rwanda) charged with helping to implement the peace agreement. During political rallies organized by MRND and CDR as well as MDR and PL power factions, the different speakers professed their trust in Hutu unity and power and demanded that the Rwandan government send troops into Burundi to fight for the Hutu of Burundi. Several FRODEBU leaders who survived the Burundi carnage used the RTLM, not to calm the Hutu population, but to encourage it to kill its Tutsi neighbors. As thousands and thousands of Hutu and Tutsi were being killed in Burundi, thousands of Hutu sought refuge in Rwanda and came with tales of violence, terror, and killing by the Tutsi army. Wherever they settled, these refugees would provide some of the most dreadful manpower for the 1994 Rwandan genocide. They used unusual violence and showed no pity in the killing of the Tutsi (see detailed discussion of their Burundi Hutu involvement in the Rwandan genocide in the next chapter).

The militia included the young and the dislocated because they could not find anything better to do. They were unemployed and desperate young people usually roaming the city for jobs and often indulging in violent acts of banditry. A three-dollar pay and an abundance of beer were certainly very attractive to them, and, as a result, they easily abandoned their souls to the mercy of political manipulation.

By the time the comprehensive peace agreement was signed in August 1993, the different players of the 1994 genocide were solidly in place. To understand the dynamics of mass murder in Rwanda, one has to consider the interaction of several elements: the different aspects of the peace accord, the last of which was signed on August 3, 1993 in Arusha Tanzania; the internally displaced persons in Rwanda (especially those in Nyacyonga, at the outskirts of Kigali), the phenomenon of Hutu Power and its tactics to derail the 1993 peace agreement; and the assassination of President Melchior Ndadaye in Burundi in October 1993 and the Burundian Hutu refugees massively fleeing into Rwanda; and the general climate of terror, confusion, and uncertainty engendered by all these elements.

Conclusion

This chapter showed that, in dealing with the RPF attack on October 1, 1990, the Habyarimana government deliberately chose to massacre and encourage its citizens to massacre their Tutsi neighbors in selected regions and, to a lesser extent, Hutu opposed to the regime. In addition to the victims of these killings, thousands were jailed, injured, and their houses burnt and destroyed, their cattle and personal property taken by the assailants. As a witness to the first two years of the Rwandan civil war, I contend that the similarity of strategies and the collaboration observed among different levels of authority testify to the existence of a high command and a network, first operating clandestinely and then openly since 1992 and especially 1993, as peace negotiations were gaining momentum. Those strategies included the use of political speeches (at meetings or on the national radio) encouraging the population to be vigilant, the visit of an important political personality to a region, the presence of a journalist close to the Hutu extremist ideology, the call for community work known as "umuganda" to "clear the bush," the participants (since 1992, the militia and the military assisting the population), and generalized impunity. I would place the beginning of such a network at the end of January 1991 (after the successful RPF attack on Ruhengeri, a stronghold of Hutu extremism). The rallying ideology of the killing was the defense of the republic that came out of the 1959 Hutu revolution. If ever there were any arrests following the attacks, the culprits were released shortly afterward, without any form of prosecution. The repetition of the same scenario from 1990 to 1994 in different regions of the country without any serious legal consequence created a culture of impunity in the country, an ideal framework for a regime of violence, terror, intimidation, and fear. The victims were blamed for their suffering, and future victims of the 1994 extermination were implacably framed as foreigners, invaders, monsters, and vipers that were dangerous to the Hutu social body, and thus had to be driven out, eliminated.

This chapter has also mapped the geography of violence between October 1990 and the beginning of the genocide in April 1994. The fact that the massacres concentrated in the northern prefectures of Gisenyi and Ruhengeri should not come as a surprise, since the hegemony of the military and intellectual elites of the region on the affairs of the country was directly threatened by the civil war and by developments in Rwandan politics. The two prefectures served as experimentation fields for the social engineering necessary for the genocide of the Tutsi of Rwanda and the killings of the Hutu who opposed it. When all is said, it will be clear that the logic behind the planning of the genocide was to keep power in the hands of the "Nordistes."

For those active in killing innocent people and for the onlookers who became so accustomed to seeing death, the continuous presence of massacre and violence resulted in the banalization of evil. In the words of a long-time apt witness, "it's the transformation from 'trivial' to 'normal' and from normal to prescriptive. [...] With a few rare exceptions, the organs of the press [...] became tools for trouble-makers who were serving the interests of regional, ethnic and ideological intolerance."[35]

Chapter Five

From Region to Nation: Ordinary Rwandans and the 1994 Genocide

Monsters exist, but they are too few in number to be truly dangerous. More dangerous are the common men.
--Primo Levi, *Afterword.*

People must be motivated to kill others, or else they would not do so.
--Daniel J. Goldhagen, *Hitler's Willing Executioners*

Cruelty has a human heart,
    And Jealousy a human face,
Terror the human form divine,
    And Secrecy the human dress.
The human dress is forgèd iron,
    The human form a fiery forge,
The human face a furnace seal'd,
    The human heart its hungry gorge.
    --William Blake (1757-1827)

Even though it is difficult to know exactly when the decision to exterminate the Tutsi was made by the Akazu and those at the helms of Hutu Power, I agree with those who put it sometime in 1992 when it became clear to Habyarimana and his supporters within MRND and CDR that the Rwandan civil war would be solved through power-sharing negotiations. For one thing, the common front established by the three most important opposition parties MDR, PSD, and PL (over-whelmingly belonging to the political "south") proved to be a solid block against MRND and CDR. Through popular support and interna-tional pressure, the three parties were given half the ministerial portfo-lios in the government, including the Prime Minister position, which went to MDR. Despite the blocking and intimidation of the former sin-gle party, this new political situation meant that Habyarimana and his northern group were not in total control of the affairs of the country, even though they still controlled the army. In addition, the new block in the administration strongly embraced, and indeed engaged in, direct talks with the RPF. The MRND and CDR leaderships cried foul, argu-ing that the opposition was betraying the 1959 Hutu revolution and was ready to surrender the Hutu republic back to the Tutsi monarchy abol-ished in 1961. Behind the appeal to the revolution, there was, however, the stronger if publicly unacknowledged demise of the Gisenyi-Ruhengeri hegemony over the country. Beyond the talk about "Hutu purs et durs" often heard in Ruhengeri and Gisenyi, there was the greater pride that one of the sons of the region was president of the Re-public, and the two *préfectures* controlled the army, the real power in most African countries (many of which were military dictatorships) in post-colonial Africa.

When the war broke out in 1990, it represented, among other things, a direct attack on the northern hegemony. The final blow came with the signing of the five protocols of the Arusha Peace Agreement, after the city in Tanzania where most of the talks took place. So the only weapon left in their arsenal was to prevent at all costs the imple-mentation of the power-sharing protocol. *Leave None to Tell the Story[1]* carefully traces the chronology of the period between August 1993 and April 1994. Some of the strategies used included organizing massacres throughout the country to convince the Rwandans that this was a fight between the Hutu and the Tutsi, and that by killing the Tutsi the gov-ernment military could push the RPF to violate the peace agreement so that fighting between the government forces and the RPF could resume. Habyarimana and his supporters also figured into their strategy the as-sassination of important political figures, including the Prime-Minister designate Faustin Twagiramungu and the head of the PSD Félicien Ga-tabazi, a vocal and stanch critic of Habyarimana and his northern group. The third strategy was to split the major opposition parties by offering monetary rewards and other advantages to leaders of the opposition parties who joined the Hutu Power movement. This was the case of MDR and PL. For example, Justin Mugenzi, one of the top leaders of PL, was very critical of Habyarimana in 1991 and much of 1992, but when he was guaranteed a ministerial portfolio and other incentives, he introduced Hutu Power ideology into PL and split the party into two ethnic factions. The result was that he was the leader of the Hutu faction, and Landoald Ndasingwa was said to be the leader of the Tutsi faction. Within MDR, leaders like Froduald Karamira, Donat Murego, and Jean Kambanda, unhappy with Twagiramungu's self-nomination to be the Prime Minister of the BBTG and encouraged by Habyarimana's entourage, adopted the extreme ideology of Hutu Power. The only major party that Habyarimana failed to split was PSD. The fourth strategy was to harass the Belgian component of UNAMIR so as to force them out of the country, because the Belgians were viewed by Hutu Power as too close to the RPF and the opposition, but most importantly because they were the only group within UNAMIR that had the military might to hinder the extermination plans, if given the right mandate. In order to achieve their aims without directly involving members of the Rwandan army, MRND and its Power network continued the training of the Interahamwe in the handling of firearms (guns, explosives, grenades, and mines) but also in the tactics and techniques of close combat and assassination.

In the months that followed the signing of the peace agreement, the training and the distribution of weapons were so systematically organized that the head of UNAMIR was told by an inside informant that "the men he had trained, who were scattered in groups of forty throughout Kigali, could kill up to 1,000 Tutsi in twenty minutes. He had distributed 110 guns and had a stockpile of another 135 which he was willing to show to the UNAMIR."[2] Despite Dallaire's plea with New York to allow him to confiscate the weapon caches in Kigali and to expand the UNAMIR mandate, only words urging caution and advising collaboration with the Habyarimana government came back to him. In the meantime, the distribution of weapons to members of Hutu power continued. As an example, on January 16, 1994, "Four thousand to five thousand MRND supporters, many from outside the city, met at the Nyamirambo stadium in Kigali. The meeting looked like a general mobilization, but it was calm, with no indication of why it had been called. In one of the speeches, Justin Mugenzi, leader of the Hutu Power faction of the Liberal Party, played on ethnic divisions. Two days later, UNAMIR officers learned that arms were distributed at this meeting."[3]

On February 17, 1994, at a meeting with senior officers of the gendarmerie, Habyarimana declared, "If the RPF begins the war, we have plans to deal with their accomplices."[4] On February 20, an attempt to assassinate Faustin Twagiramungu failed; the next day, Félicien Gatabazi, PSD leader, was assassinated. Investigation by the civil police of the UNAMIR revealed the involvement of Habyarimana's close associates, including his son-in-law Alphonse Ntirivamunda and Captain Simbikangwa, infamous since 1991 in Kigali for his sadistic tortures of journalists and members of the political opposition. In late March 1994, with the concerted pressure on Habyarimana to implement the Arusha agreement, there was a climate of impending disaster: "The officer in charge of intelligence for the Rwandan army told a group including some Belgian military advisers that 'if Arusha were implemented, they were ready to liquidate the Tutsi'."[5] In the same period, Ferdinand Nahimana, one of the most extremist Hutu Power ideologues (now being tried by the International Tribunal for Rwanda in Arusha) renewed his call for self-defense and invited suggestions for the "final solution" to the "Tutsi problem." It was common knowledge in Kigali that since 1992 hit lists had been drawn and were regularly expanded since then.[6] More chilling, *La Médaille Nyiramacibiri,* one of the voices of Hutu extremism, had a headline that said, "By the way, the Tutsi race could be extinguished."[7] The January 1994 issue of *Kangura (No. 55)* had been even more blatant: "Who will survive the March war? [...] The masses will rise with the help of the army, and blood will flow freely."[8] Habyarimana was not necessarily in full control of his Hutu Power coalition, especially the most extreme CDR. Thus Hassan Ngeze wrote twice in early 1994 that Habyarimana would die in March at the hands of Hutu, not Tutsi, because he had signed the Arusha Peace Agreement, and he was apparently willing to implement it, thus betraying the Hutu Republic. To any well-informed student of Rwandan politics, for anyone, including the editor of the extremist CDR paper *Kangura,* to write that about Habyarimana with impunity, meant that the President's associates had irreversibly given up on him. Three days before Habyarimana's plane was downed over Kigali, the RTLM, the radio station of Hutu extremism, announced: "On the 3rd, 4th and 5th, heads will heat up. On the 6th, there will be a respite, but a little thing might happen. Then on the 7th and 8th and the other days in April, you will see something."[9]

The plane was hit by a missile at 8:30 pm on April 6, 1994, and, within only one hour, the Interahamwe and Impuzamugambi militia as well as the elite Presidential Guard had already erected roadblocks in Kigali and killings had started.[10] Colonel Bagosora, a member of the Akazu and AMASASU and a staunch ideologue of Hutu Power, then Secretary-General in the Ministry of defense (a position he used to justify his authority despite his being a retired soldier), took control of the situation. All things considered, he absolutely had no constitutional authority to take control of the political and military affairs of the country. Even though he declared that what had happened was not a coup, he obviously wanted to assume the Presidency but could not get the backing of the senior officers at the crisis meetings organized during the night of April 6, 1994 and the following days. Nor could he secure the blessing of the UNAMIR head, General Dallaire, or that of the United Nations special representative Jacques-Roger Booh-Booh. The fact that the first killed included the leaders and ministers of the political opposition including those who would assume power under the delayed Broad-Based Transitional Government (under the Arusha Peace Agreement) as well as the President of the Constitutional Court, who in this capacity would swear in any new government, indicated that Bagosora and the Hutu Power wanted to create a political vacuum to fill.   The fact that the killings quickly included the Tutsi and other known Hutu of the political opposition on the lists drawn in advance may well be part of Bagosora's calculation to create an extreme situation and present himself as the only one capable of handling it. After all, he had the backing of the elite troops in Kigali, including the Presidential Guard (which he controlled after the death of Colonel Sagatwa, private secretary to President Habyarimana, who also perished in the plane crash), the elite Para-commando troops (of which he had been commander from 1988 to 1992) based in the Kanombe barracks near the airport and much of the government army, and he could count on the support of the Interahamwe, the Impuzamugambi, and the whole Power movement.

Without a doubt, the military crisis committee was unconstitutional. Among the senior officers present at the meetings were retired Colonel Théoneste Bagosora, General Augustin Ndindiliyimana (Gendarmerie Chief of Staff), Colonel Léonidas Rusatira (Commander of the Ecole Supérieure Militaire), Colonel Murasampongo (G-1 officer) as well as General Romeo Dallaire (UNAMIR Commander) and Colonel Luc Marchal (UNAMIR officer in charge of security in the capital city of Kigali). It is perplexing that the UNAMIR Commander General Dallaire, the UN special representative Roger Booh Booh, and the American and the French ambassadors agreed to meet or talk with the unconstitutional military committee more than once (in most cases) without requiring as a condition the presence or at least the involvement of the Prime Minister. General Dallaire each time suggested the committee get in contact with the Prime Minister, a suggestion that was tenaciously rejected by Bagosora, arguing that the civilian government in general and the Prime Minister in particular had no credibility in the country for having sapped the morale of the army and for being ineffective even before the crisis. I believe that the other Rwandan members of the committee crisis knew exactly the kind of leverage that Bagosora had on all components of the military and on the Interahamwe and Impuzamugambi militia. The fact that they prevented him from heading the committee crisis is probably an indication of their knowledge of his intentions. He angrily reacted to their attitude by telling them that he had created a committee crisis and they were trying to keep him away from it. One wonders why the so called moderate officers including General Ndindiliyimana and Colonel Rusatira did not help General Dallaire press for the inclusion of the civilian government in the management of the crisis. One also wonders why Bagosora's position against the civilian government was not vigorously challenged by anyone. Is it because everybody knew that Bagosora controlled the forces that could launch the killings and thus the power to stop or prevent them?

Bagosora was very shrewd in dealing with his foreign interlocutors. When Roger Booh Booh asked him if what was being done was a military coup, the latter replied that it was not a coup but an attempt to find a political solution in the spirit of Arusha, but again his constitutional competence was not questioned. He seemed to accept all the suggestions from both the UNAMIR Commander and the UN special representative without implementing them (probably to buy time), but Bagosora was adamant in his refusal to get in contact with the civilian government, which should have been the rightful decision-maker of the moment. As he was working in the background, he gave credence to his work by reporting to the crisis committee to foil their suspicion, but the real plans were being drawn somewhere else. The pretense that he was working within the Arusha Accord, assuring his interlocutors that he was not staging a coup, and giving the impression that he was trying to give control to a civilian government allowed Bagosora to act freely in organizing his forces working within another structure. After all, there was no sign that the decisions made by the crisis committee were communicated to the field commanders. If they were, the commanders were asked to ignore them. Strangely enough, knowing his ideological positions and his involvement in the Hutu Power movement, the crisis committee charged Bagosora with contacting the civilian politicians and helping to form a government (Reyntjens 85). He basically ignored the crisis committee in his dealing with the politicians and dealt only with the Power factions of the political parties.

Reyntjens writes that as the crisis was unfolding he contacted an acquaintance in Kigali in an attempt to save some of his friends who were potential targets. His friend was in constant contact with Bagosora who was said to control the "work" of the militia and the army. Another contact of Reyntens' surprised Bagosora on April 7, 1994 telling Lt Colonel Nkundiye (former commander of the Presidential Guard and Commander of the Mutara sector) and Majors Nsanzuwonemeye and Aloys Ntabakunze (commander of the para-commando battalion) instructing them to "Start on the side" (Muhere iruhande), an expression in Kinyarwanda that suggests an operation of extermination so systematic as not to leave anything on the way. The commanders immediately started the "job" (Reyntjens 58). Moreover, several senior Rwandan officers affirmed that in the absence of Elie Sagatwa, private secretary to Habyarimana and commander of the Presidential Guard, Bagosora was the only authority who indeed controlled the best army units, the Presidential Guard and the para-commando battalion.

I believe that Bagosora's contact with the diplomatic representations including the French and American ambassadors was another indication of his ambition. The rejection by his military peers, by General Dallaire, by the UN special representative, and by the western ambassadors left him only the possibility of setting up a government of his own ideological liking, completely made up of Hutu Power ministers and a president, Théodore Sindikubwabo, an aloof and sick relic of the 1960s PARMEHUTU and the MRND years. Sindikubwabo was President of the Rwandan Parliament, not because of his ability but because of his docility. It was common knowledge that he was not elected in the parliamentary elections of 1988 as one of the representatives of Butare prefecture, but since the Habyarimana government wanted him as Speaker, he was declared one of the winners of the elections, an act that caused general outrage in Butare. It was generally known, however, that the "Nordistes" did not like to place outspoken individuals from the south in sensitive positions. Coming from Butare, I know that people used to put Theodore Sindikubwabo, Venant Ntabomvura (minister and later Rector of the National University), Maurice Ntahobari (Speaker of Parliament and later Rector of the National University of Rwanda), General Ndindiliyimana, and a few others in that category of docile individuals from the Butare prefecture who, though certainly qualified, owed their positions more to their docility. Since no member of the inner circle of the Akazu and Hutu Power was at the helms of the Hutu republic, Bagosora and his associates had free reins to carry out their plan of Tutsi extermination—after all, they were not politically responsible, or so they wanted the world to believe.

Perhaps another indication of Bagosora's calculation and the inability of the crisis committee to affect the outcome of the situation was that both the interim President and the Prime Minister hailed from Butare. In his shrewdness, Bagosora and the Power movement knew that Butare had resisted the call to kill since 1990, had massively joined the political opposition (PSD, MDR, and PL), had the largest proportion of Tutsi in the country as well as strong Hutu-Tutsi intermarriage, and had the only Tutsi *préfet* in the whole country. In addition to the two highest positions in the central administration, Butare received two other posts: the Ministry of Family and Women's Affairs that went to Pauline Nyiramasuhuko and the Ministry of Agriculture was entrusted to Dr. Straton Nsabumukunzi. In addition, in the absence of Faustin Munyazesa, the important Ministry of the Interior was run by its Secretary-General, Callixte Karemanzira, who also hailed from Butare. It is mystifying that nobody forcefully opposed this concentration of the highest political power within the interim government in one prefecture. One of the conclusions that can be drawn is that this government was put in place in the perspective of the genocide—Sindikubwabo, Kambanda, and Nyiramasuhuko later galvanized the genocide forces in Butare.

But who exactly was Bagosora? Born in 1941 in Giciye, one of the two communes (the other being Karago, commune of origin of Habyarimana) that make up the Bushiru region, the epicenter of power during the Habyarimana presidency (1973-1994), he took military training at the military academy in Kigali and attended military academies in Belgium and France. He was the commander of the very important military camp of Kanombe in Kigali from 1988 to 1992. After his retirement from the army, Bagosora became Secretary General in the Ministy of Defense. A military man, Bagosora had a better military training than Habyarimana, but both men came from the same region and thus had the same constituency. It was common knowledge in Kigali political circles that Bagosora, who enjoyed the support of the Clan de Madame (the president's wife and her powerful brothers and their associates),[11] entertained presidential ambitions. The other senior officers who were forced into retirement mainly following the insistence of the political opposition in 1992—including the powerful Colonels Rwagafilita and Serubuga (respectfully chiefs of staff of the gendarmerie and the army) (the latter from the Bushiru region and the former from Kibungo, where his family had settled from the North)—had now sneaked back into politics. Bagosora's position as Secretary-General in the Ministry of Defense was due to his closeness with the Clan de Madame and the necessity for the Bushiru region to control the daily operations of this important ministry for the "République des Nordistes."

In exile in Cameroon after the defeat of the genocidal government he had put in place, Bagosora wrote an essay titled "L'assassinat du Président Habyarimana ou l'ultime opération du Tutsi pour sa reconquête du pouvoir par la force au Rwanda"[12] in which he developed the same radical ideas of CDR as propagated in *Kangura* since October 1990 and by RTLM since 1993. In the essay, he argued that the Rwandan question was a question between the Hutu and the Tutsi, not among political parties. Echoing the ideas of Kangura (in its February 1993 edition[13]), he claimed that the Arusha negotiations should have been between the Hutu and the Tutsi--*Kangura* had said between CDR (which it regarded as the true Hutu party or the party of the "Hutu durs et purs") and Kigeli V Ndahindurwa, the Rwandan King deposed by the 1959 Hutu Revolution. Bagosora repeated some of Kayibanda's pronouncements in the 1960s, namely that the central African region (notice Bagosora's expansion from one country, Rwanda, to central Africa, another of *Kangura*'s ideas) belonged to the Hutu, and Tutsi were only "naturalized Nilotic immigrants." Feeding on the old ethnic stereotypes (see Chapter Two), he portrayed the Tutsi as "masters of deceit, dictatorial, cruel, bloody, arrogant, clever, and sneaky" whereas the Hutu were described as "modest, open, loyal, independent and impulsive."[14] Again echoing the ideas of Kayibanda in the early 1960s, Bagosora blamed the Tutsi for their demise, saying that by attacking Rwanda, they knew they would provoke the wrath of the Hutu.

Described by his military colleagues as extremely attached to his Hutu ethnic group and particularly to his fellows from the home region, Bagosora was said to trust only people from Gisenyi. According to General Marcel Gatsinzi, Army Chief of Staff in the first days of the genocide, who opposed the killing frenzy, "he [Bagosora] was always advancing people from his region. Even in his personal relations, he favored people from Gisenyi."[15] In the essay cited above, Bagosora wrote about the Tutsi: "There never were Tutsi people, neither in Rwanda nor in Burundi nor anywhere else. They are immigrants who should moderate their greedy and arrogant behavior."[16]

Further evidence of Bagosora's ethnic and regional extremism comes from different sources. First, there is his association with AMASASU (discussed in Chapter Four). To recall, AMASASU, acronym for "Alliance des Militaires Agacés par les Séculaires Actes Sournois des Unaristes" (Alliance of Soldiers Aggravated by the Age-Old Deceitful Acts of Unarists), was a group of virulent anti-Tutsi soldiers probably organized around Colonel Bagosora and coming proba-

bly exclusively from Gisenyi and Ruhengeri. In January 1993, following the signature of the third protocol of the Arusha Accords, the
AMASASU group sent a letter to President Habyarimana in which they
reiterated some of the ideas developed by Leon Mugesera in his Kabaya speech (analyzed in the previous chapter): 1. "he who wishes
peace must prepare for war"; 2. the Tutsi as a foreign race; 3. the Tutsi
and their accomplices should leave Rwanda before it is too late. As
Mugesera had done in his speech, the group threatened to take justice in
their own hands because the government was not enforcing the law,
that is, did not punish people for helping the enemy. The spokesman of
AMASASU called himself Mike Tango, a pseudonym for either Colonel Bagasora or a close aide, according to *Leave None to Tell the
Story*.[17] Commander Mike advocated the creation and training of civilian self-defense units in each commune and the distribution of weapons
to this popular army, a policy that pitted him against the civilian Minister of Defense James Gasana. Dubbed "Colonel of Death" because of
his "penchant for violence and doomsday rhetoric"[18] against the Tutsi,
Bagosora saw in the death of Habyarimana the opportunity to fulfill the
apocalypse he had announced publicly in Arusha.

As Secretary-General of the Defense Ministry, Colonel
Bagosora also championed the creation of a civilian self-defense force.
I remember that this program was first seriously considered in early
1991 after the RPF's successful attack on and occupation of the town of
Ruhengeri. Firearms were initially distributed to local authorities including the *sous-préfets,* burgomasters, and a few other individuals,
mostly stanch MRND supporters. Small-scale distribution of weapons
continued until 1993 when Bagosora and Ferdinand Nahimana forcefully and successfully promoted the idea of a more structured self-
defense force composed of youth recruited by local authorities and
trained by former soldiers or the local police. Of course, the weapons
went to the Interahamwe and other supporters of Habyarimana, especially in 1993 and 1994. Given the high cost of firearms, the relentless
Bagosora suggested that traditional weapons such as machetes be used
instead. During the genocide, the machete was probably the most used
tool of carnage.

It appears that the initial plan devised by the Akazu to derail
the implementation of the Arusha accords and keep the northerners in
power was to kill Tutsi and Hutu opposition members under the cover
of a coup carried out by colonel Théoneste Bagosora,[19] who was Secretary-General (Director of Administration), the next in line after the
Minister in the Defense ministry. For the first time in the history of independent Rwanda, the minister was a civilian and not directly from

the Akazu, and so Bagosora considered himself as the real minister—one proof of this is that he scared the civilian defense minister James Gasana into exile because of major policy differences, notably regarding the distribution of weapons to civilians. Bagosora, according to the plan, would stage a coup against Habyarimana, with the help of the Armed Forces. He would then use his temporary position to kill the Tutsi and all Hutu political opponents. Then, as Habyarimana had done in July 1973, Bagosora would retake power posing as a savior of the situation. The downing of the plane which carried not only Habyarimana but also the chief of staff (General Deogratias Nsabimana) foiled the plan, and Bagosora could thus dream to be the one in charge in the case of a successful coup.

All in all, Bagosora's ethnic and regional extremism embodied the concerns of the Gisenyi/Ruhengeri axis: CDR member, AMASASU member, virulent anti-Tutsi hardliner, defender of the hegemony of his region, he was the man for the Hutu Power movement and he had the ambition to be president. This is the man who was so irked by negotiations in Arusha that he quit the Tanzanian city prematurely, after stating that he was going back to Rwanda "to prepare for the Apocalypse." After Bagosora's arrest by the International Tribunal for Rwanda, a senior diplomat in Rwanda said, "It's like catching Himmler. Bagosora was at the top. He may not have been the chief theorist [of the genocide], but he was the chief implementer."[20]

Faced with the rejection of his authority by his Rwandan colleagues, the UNAMIR commander, the UN special representative, and the diplomatic missions, Bagosora proceeded to wipe out the civilian leaders that had the constitutional authority to take over after the death of Habyarimana. He probably ordered the military, now in his command, to kill the prime minister Agathe Uwilingiyimana and the opposition ministers in her government and also quickly moved to kill those who had been identified for high offices in the Broad Based Transitional Government, including Felicien Ngago (PSD) and Landoald Ndansingwa (PL), one of whom would be chosen Speaker of Parliament according to the Arusha accords and in the current situation would be sworn in as President of the Republic. He also had Joseph Kavaruganda, President of the Constitutional Court, killed because he would be swearing in any new President and Speaker. Also, men under Bagosora's command killed ten Belgian soldiers, members of the UNAMIR forces, on April 7, to push the Belgians into withdrawing all their peacekeeping forces from Rwanda, another calculation by Bagosora. The fact that these killings occurred within the 24 hours that followed the death of Habyarimana shows, among other things, that it was a military coup that aimed at placing Bagosora at the Presidency. I am strongly convinced that the only gesture that could have saved the hundreds of thousands of Tutsi in 1994 was for the crisis committee, the UNAMIR commander, the UN special representative, and the major diplomatic missions to hand power over to Bagosora, but this would have put an end to the Arusha Accords.

The Presidential Guard and other elite troops as well as Interahamwe and Impuzamugambi carried out most of the initial killings (April 6-12, 1994) based on lists of victims drawn in advance, but later thousands and thousands of ordinary Hutu citizens answered their government's call to kill their Tutsi neighbors and sometimes relatives, people with whom they shared language, culture, religion, and all aspects of a hard life on the hills of Rwanda. How did a personal and regional crusade to maintain power transform itself into a national agenda? What made people who had resisted for three years joining the anti-Tutsi campaign spearheaded by northern forces (Akazu, Kangura, CDR, MRND, a good part of the military, Amasasu, and other death squads) join the killing frenzy?

Given the widespread violence that led to the Rwandan genocide in 1994, one must ask the level of participation by the Hutu. After all, this was the group that was called upon by the authorities to eliminate their Tutsi neighbors and any Hutu who opposed Tutsi extermination. This issue is not a simple one, as some have suggested in their writing that affirmed, certainly following a Manichean logic, that all Hutu were killers and all Tutsi were victims. No one can refute the proposition that there was indeed extensive participation of many ordinary Hutu in the attempt to exterminate the Tutsi of Rwanda and even an incredibly high degree of voluntarism and initiative on the part of many Hutu from all walks of life. It is true that the massacres that started on the night of April 6 and continued for the next several days targeted a priority list—Hutu politicians who belonged to the opposition (leaders of MDR, PL, PSD and PDC) and did not join the Hutu Power movement as well as prominent Tutsi (politicians, professionals, and businessmen), human rights activists, journalists, clergy, and civil servants who, because of past political positions, were known to the Hutu Power. These killings were carried out by the Presidential Guard assisted by regular army soldiers and by the MRND and CDR militia— all these were professional killers, all of whom had received some sort of military training and had acquired skills and tactics of killing. Also, the same were dispatched to the rest of the country to kill and encourage or force the population to kill wherever there was resistance to join in the extermination of the Tutsi.[21] The organizers of the Rwandan "final solution" knew that killing the Tutsi would take much more than the few thousand presidential guard troops and militia men—they wanted the participation of the Hutu. "The work had to be every Hutu's job," as a Hutu Power authority Froduald Karamira (of MDR Power) stated in an April 12 radio speech.[22] Indeed, ordinary people quickly became the executioners of their Tutsi neighbors. How does one explain this massive participation in the ultimate evil? Explanations have ranged from tribal conflict,[23] ethnic strife, manipulation of the population, intrinsic hatred between the Hutu and the Tutsi, revenge of the Hutu on the Tutsi,[24] and a threshold of acceptability of Tutsi exclusion by the Hutu,[25] among other accounts.

One cannot possibly begin to probe the involvement of ordinary people in mass murder in the post-Holocaust period without invoking the classic if controversial book by Daniel Goldhagen, *Hitler's Willing Executioners: Ordinary Germans and the Holocaust*, in which he deliberately omitted to discuss the manifold nature of ordinary Germans' participation in the Shoah. In fact, he forcefully asserted that "with regard to the motivational cause of the Holocaust, for the vast majority of the perpetrators, a monocausal explanation does suffice."[26] For him, the Germans were prewired, so to speak, to kill the Jews because of their "demonological anti-Semitism" that underlied "the common structure of the perpetrators' cognition and of German society in general."[27] In this truncated logic, all Hitler needed to do was to push on the right switch to trigger the Holocaust. This line of argumentation was reviewed and criticized extensively by able pens.[28] Suffice it to mention some of the counterarguments presented: (1) anti-Semitism is a necessary but not sufficient element for the Holocaust to take place; (2) even though Goldhagen is right to point out hat "Jews were systematically treated worse than other terribly abused victims of the Nazis,"[29] he also explains this fact by pointing to the same anti-Semitism of ordinary Germans. In suggesting that they could not have acted so lethally toward other groups, Goldhagen omits to mention equally lethal killings that the Nazis organized against other groups (for the example, the Poles, the Gypsies, and the Slavic populations, among others); and (3) Goldhagen rejects the universal human traits that may render a group genocidal, as we witnessed more recently with the Serbs (in Bosnia in 1992-1994 and in Kosovo in 1998/99), the Kmers Rouges in Cambodia 1975-1978, the Hutu in Rwanda in 1994, and the Tutsi in Burundi in 1972.

Christopher R. Browning accuses Daniel Goldhagen of practicing "keyhole history," a single and narrow-minded approach that selects only convenient historical facts and ignores contradictory testimony simply to lead to the conclusion that a pervasive anti-Semitism cognitively structured the Germans civil society.[30] It follows from this view of German history that Hitler and Nazism not only represented the ordinary Germans but also reflected pre-Nazi German culture. While C. R. Browning agrees that anti-Semitism certainly shaped German culture in the nineteenth century and certainly more than any other Western European country and helped the advent of National Socialism, he also argues that Goldhagen goes beyond this point by asserting that "virulent, lethal anti-Semitism is the veritable leitmotiv not only of Hitler's ideology but also of 150 years of German history."[31] Goldhagen is also guilty of "methodological determinism"[32] because in his forceful attempt to prove the Germans' ready embrace of the Final Solution, he chooses to exclude "any uncorroborated perpetrator testimony that he deemed self-exculpatory."[33] Since this is a serious methodological shortfall, I shall quote Browning's argument verbatim:

> Goldhagen effectively ignores the possibility that a historian might judiciously accept some self-exonerating testimony that is uncorroborated by other testimony as having occurred on occasion. Goldhagen's approach likewise prohibits the historian from selective use of unusually detailed and vivid testimony that has a "feel" about it, especially in comparison to the formulaic and transparently dishonest testimony so often encountered.[34]

Goldhagen's one-dimensional perspective with a predetermined conclusion painfully rejects the multiple factors that could have led ordinary Germans to be, in fact, Hitler's unwilling executioners, notably the Nazi reign of terror and violence,[35] dictatorship, conformity, and peer pressure, among other processes. Suggesting that "if indeed Germans had disapproved of the mass slaughter, then peer pressure would not have induced people to kill against their will"[36]reflects total, deliberate ignorance of the nature of dictatorship. How can Goldhagen acknowledge the authoritarian and dictatorial nature of Hitler and Nazism and yet develop his argument as if German reaction was free of the dictatorial environment and as if ordinary Germans enjoyed unlimited freedom of speech? "One of the hallmarks of modern dictatorship," Christopher R. Browning counters, "is the epidemic of hypocrisy in virtually all public discourse and the corruption of sincerity in public behavior and that it engenders."[37] Browning gives an example of real repression: "students of the White Rose, who passed out leaflets condemning the mass murders of the regime, were arrested, tortured, and beheaded."[38] The point here is that Hitler's Germany was a severely repressive dictatorship that did not tolerate any dissension.

Nobody in his or her right mind would even try to deny the uniqueness of the Holocaust or the fact that horrendous, inhumane, unprecedented German State-sanctioned extermination of the Jews took place. Indeed the Jews were targeted simply because they were Jews and were born Jews, seen by Hitler and his cronies as an inferior race, a gangrene of which Europe had to be gotten rid of (as with the Gypsies, the handicapped, and other undesirable). As the post World War II era has shown, however, extreme cruelty is not unique to the Germans. Our contemporary world has shown us that with the "right" factors the Kmers rouges, the Tutsi of Burundi, the Hutu of Rwanda, the Serbs, and the Chinese, to cite a few examples, can be genocidal murderers. The idea of a cognitive model is probably not the best idea that can be advanced in trying to explain violence and human behavior.

Goldhagen's merit, however, was to try to explain what is fundamentally difficult for us human beings to understand--the unspeakable cruelty of the Holocaust and of mass murder in general. From the point of view of the victims, the murderer is necessarily seen in a Manichean logic. Goldhagen's argument makes sense from this vintage point. In addition, any attempt to "speak the unspeakable," to explain how anti-Semitism developed a complex machine for the final solution, from the rudimentary means to the industrialization of killing, from one man (Hitler) and his ideological entourage to the involvement of the whole administration and the ordinary Germans as well as the non-Germans in occupied countries—any attempt to explain extreme evil, I say, is worth the intellectual effort. Unfortunately, Goldhagen's laudable effort is thwarted by an argument based on the doctrine of collective guilt rooted in ethnocultural determinism, fixated on a monocausal, cognitive explanation of the unspeakable still not fully spoken.

Christopher R. Browning proposes to correct Goldhagen's one-dimensional approach by advocating Primo Levi's concept of the "Gray Zone."[39] Browning defines it as "that murky world of mixed motives, conflicting emotions and priorities, reluctant choices, and self-serving opportunism and accommodation wedded to self-deception and denial—a world that is all too human and all too universal"[40] that, to my mind, has nothing to do with any innate, cognitive inclination. For a more complete appreciation of the gray zone, let us turn to Primo Levi's work for a moment.

In describing the Nazi concentration camps, Levi, a survivor, seeks to avoid the Manichean logic and its oversimplification of the categories involved to suggest that, in fact, all kinds of opposites constantly collided. While the roles or plight of the camp management, the SS (Special Squads), and the prisoners were certainly well regimented and understood by those concerned, its internal structure was less permanent: "It is a gray zone, poorly defined, where the two camps [prisoners and functionaries] of masters and servants both diverge and converge. This gray zone possesses an incredibly complicated internal structure and contains within itself enough to confuse our need to judge."[41] First of all, its "occupants" came from multiple sources. The power structure and its auxiliaries (the functionaries) from Germany and the occupied countries (former enemies) were at the top of the hierarchy. The non-Germans could not be trusted; therefore they had to be overwhelmed by blood and guilt to bind them in complicity with the power structure that conceived the humiliation, exploitation, and murder of the Jews and other undesirable groups. Overwhelmed by brutality, broken by humiliation, guided by the instinct of survival, the prisoners drifted towards collaboration.

Levi's description of prisoners' collaboration with the concentration camp authorities does not aim to issue "moral judgment on such human cases"[42] and only those "who found themselves in similar circumstances and had the opportunity to test for themselves what it means to act in a state of coercion,"[43] only those, Levi insists, are entitled to judge both "big and small collaborators."[44] Levi is not suggesting that they are not guilty; he simply means that no human tribunal is morally qualified to pass the judgment. The ultimate, greatest guilt falls on the Nazi totalitarian regime, but the rest is not always easy to grasp and categorize. Levi writes:

> Around us, prisoners with rank, swarmed low-ranking functionaries, a picturesque fauna: sweepers, kettle washers, night watchmen, bed smoothers (who exploited to their minuscule advantage the German fixation about bunks made up flat and square), checkers of lice and scabies, messengers, interpreters, assistants' assistants. In general, they were poor devils like ourselves, who worked full time like everyone else but who for an extra half-liter of soup were willing to carry out these and other tertiary functions: innocuous, sometimes useful, often invented out of the whole cloth.[45]

Also included in the rest were the "chiefs (kapos)... of squads, the barracks chiefs, the clerks, all the way to the word (whose existence at that time I did not even suspect) of the prisoners who performed diverse, at times most delicate duties in the camps' administrative offices, the political section (actually a section of the Gestapo), the Labor Service, and the punishment cells."[46] Carefully chosen by the Lager commander or his delegates, the collaborators comprised "common criminals, taken from prisons, for whom a career as a torturer offered an excellent alternative to detention," political prisoners "broken by five or ten years of sufferings, or in any case morally debilitated", and later on Jews themselves in concentration camps "who saw in the particle of authority being offered them the only possible escape from the 'final solution.'"[47] All the above aspired to the trap of power with its attendant benefits. Unfortunately, their affirmation of power took the form of fear, "inflicting suffering and humiliation on those below them,"[48] and this is why they were chosen after all.

The totalitarian structure of the Lager also attracted the frustrated as long as they were willing to "pay homage to hierarchic authority,"[49] and the oppressed who thus were mimicking "their oppressors and unconsciously [striving] to identify with them."[50] The power thus acquired was usually transient, as with the SS who operated for a few months before they were suppressed and replaced by others and so on. All in all, the power structure of the concentration camp—a space designed to break resistance, to humiliate and eventually to kill—makes it impossible to describe in any binary, Manichean fashion. It was a space characterized by ambiguity, fear, corruption, collaboration, guilt, terror, and obsequiousness.... Needless to say, the aim of including those already doomed because they were Jews or undesirable, those who were condemned to die anyway, was to deprive them of "even the solace of innocence."[51]

Perfidious was this enlisting of complicity in the final solution. Levi gives the example of a work pause that consisted of a soccer game between the SS and the SK (Sonderkommando):

> Nothing of this kind ever took place, nor would it have been conceivable, with other categories of prisoners; but with them, with the "crematorium ravens," the SS could enter the field on an equal footing, or almost. Behind this armistice one hears satanic laughter: it is consummated, we have succeeded, you no longer are the other race, the anti-race, the prime enemy of the millennial Reich; you are no longer the people who reject idols. We have embraced you, corrupted you, dragged you to the bottom with us. You are like us, you proud people: dirtied with your own blood, as we are. You too, like us and Cain, have killed the brother.[52]

Levi discusses the case of Chaim Rumkowski as an eloquent example of the gray zone. For four years (1940-1944), Rumkowski was the president of the Lodg concentration camp. Even though the position of a ghetto president was terrible, Chaim Rumkowski enjoyed the authority it conferred upon him. A dictator, he had "megalomaniac dream, barbaric vitality, and real diplomatic and organizational skill."[53] He duplicated the totalitarian regime in the camp. He wanted obedience, respect, and love, and wanted his subjects to idolize him as "one beloved and providential president."[54] He established a power structure similar to that of any dictator. Primo Levi writes that Rumkowski even imitated "the oratorical technique of Mussolini and Hitler, the style of inspired recitation, the pseudo-colloquy with the crowd, the creation of consent through subjugation and plaudit."[55] But in all his dupery, he was an ambiguous figure and a corrupt collaborator (who thus had to identify with the Nazi oppressor), and he viewed himself as a savior of his people (the Jews) (or at least he must have so desired).

The obvious irony of the gray zone was that Rumkowski could not survive because "there was only one fate for Jews in German hands, whether they were cowards or heroes, humble or proud. Neither the letter nor the special carriage were able to save Chaim Rumkowski, the King of Jews, from the gas chamber."[56] He definitely embodied the paradoxical reality of the gray zone. In the final assessment, however, Levi asserts that Rumkowski cannot be exonerated by the totalitarian state.

In trying to explain the 1994 Rwandan genocide, a number of scholars have adopted Goldhagen's monocausal and cognitive perspective, supplemented by a sense of ethnic determinism. One such scholar is Josias Semujanga who forcefully explains the Rwandan genocide using the same line of argumentation that Daniel Goldhagen uses in his explanation of the Shoah.[57] Semujanga does an excellent job of showing how ethnocentric colonial narratives dramatically changed the Rwandan culture especially in their use of the Hamitic Hypothesis to explain the social, cultural, and political structure that explorers, colonialists, and missionaries found in the Kingdom of Rwanda at the end of the nineteenth century. He also does a judicious analysis of how the Hutu leaders appropriated the Hamitic myth, manipulated it for ethnic mobilization, and later on used it as the founding ideology of Hutu extremism. Whereas the European Hamitic myth made of the Tutsi the civilizing agent of the Hutu, the Hutu extremism's variation of the Hamitic myth made of the Tutsi a colonizing race, of "dangerous type," the "absolute enemy of the Hutu." In the face of cruelty and mass murder, it is the duty of humanity to try to make sense of the absolute evil that led the Hutu to kill their Tutsi neighbors and the Hutu who opposed the pogrom. As the task is daunting, any attempt to explain how

Hutu extremism developed into a machine capable of killing around one million people within a record time of three months at a pace of at least five times that of Nazi concentration camps is indeed a great service to Rwanda and its people, especially the survivors of the genocide and of course to humanity in general, for despite the inadequate (to say the least) response of the international community, any genocide is a call and a warning to humanity as a whole, because what is killed is ultimately humanity. In 1972, the Hutu of Burundi were killed because they were Hutu. In Rwanda in 1994, Tutsi were humiliated and killed simply because they were born Tutsi. The Jews were humiliated and killed because they were born Jews, Bosnians in 1992 were killed by the Serbs because they were born (Muslim) Bosnians, and Kosovars were killed and forced into exile in 1998/99 because they were born (Muslim) Kosovars.

What is problematic about Semujanga's book is the cornerstone of his argument that posits the existence of the "threshold of acceptability" of the Tutsi exclusion within the Hutu population.[58] It is true that leaders of independent Rwanda solidly established an anti-Tutsi ideology to the point of making it an institution of the new Republic born on July 1, 1962. It is also true that at periods of difficulty, in 1957-1963 when the Hutu movement worked at reversing the historical power structure, in 1963 when "Inyenzi" attacked in Bugesera, in 1973 when the northerners wanted to prepare a coup, and in 1990-1994 when the government experienced great difficulty in containing the Rwandan Patriotic Front, the government propaganda machine worked hard to polarize Hutu and Tutsi. It is indeed also true that thousands of ordinary Hutu participated in the killing of their Tutsi neighbors with whom they shared almost everything (country, language, religion, culture etc). Nonetheless, it is not right to ignore the political and economic reality of Rwanda in order to impose a monocausal explanation to the unspeakable extermination of the Tutsi of Rwanda in 1994. Semujanga's argument then becomes a narrative of demonization whereby the doctrine of Hutu collective guilt becomes a motif repeated over and over in the book. Even though he does not cite Goldhagen's work, Semujanga certainly applies the "ethnocultural determinism" found in *Hitler's Willing Executioners* by fixating the archaeology of the Rwandan genocide on a monocausal explanation. In fact, all the excellent discussions he does of different social, cultural, and political realities from the Hamitic Hypothesis to its colonial application, to the myths of origin, and other texts and social phenomena, all point to the doctrine of collective guilt that is embodied in his affirmation of the existence of a threshold of Tutsi exclusion in the collective memory of ordinary Hutu in Rwanda. However, the many aspects of the genocide—organization, patterns of killings, perpetrators, resistance, etc.—question the validity of any monocausal perspective.

Semujanga mentions the explanations advanced by several authors who offered their own views on the Rwandan genocide. Some accuse the lethargy of the international community that watched as the worst genocide after the Shoah was committed and as the world pompously celebrated the fiftieth anniversary of the Allies' landing in Normandy.[59] Other books point the finger to the French government of François Mitterrand, which supported the Rwandan government that prepared the genocide and the interim government of April 6 to July 19 that actually implemented the genocide—two governments that were obviously applying Nazi methods. Despite the intense obsession with the memory of World War II and the Holocaust in France, the French government did not make a wiser assessment of the Rwandan situation in 1990-1994, but again memory and politics often have different agendas. Other books deplore the failure of the Catholic Church, from the simple parishioner to the Holy See--here Semujanga cites *Golias,* a Catholic journal, No. 48/49--*Rwanda: l'honneur perdu des missionaires,* summer 1996.

Semujanga points out that these explanations center on the transformation of Rwandan memory from without[60] and then proceeds, for much of the book, to show how external agents succeeded in inducing an internal agent that he calls "parmehutu-cederism," an extremist ideology that Semujanga then uses to develop his monocausal argument. In his own words, "CDR (acronym in French for Coalition pour la Défense de la République) [Coalition for the Defense of the Republic] is the extremist Hutu party responsible for the ideology of the Tutsi genocide in 1994. Its ideology is an adaptation of the program of the popular party, the Parti pour l'Emancipation Hutu (Parmehutu) [Party for the Emancipation of the Hutu] (...) To be more precise, it is appropriate to use 'parmehutu-cederism' that considers itself as the only defense of the Republic and accuses the other parties of conspiring with the enemy."[61] This ideology of genocide is also known as *Hutu Power* in other books. Semujanga subsequently uses one for the other though he admits to favoring the term "parmehutu-cederism" when discussing the ethnic ideology that led to the 1994 genocide. Thousands of ordinary people who ended up participating in the genocide were not necessarily CDR members nor were they necessarily members of the Power factions of the other parties. So Hutu Power is a necessary condition, but it does not adequately and fully explain the participation of the masses.

On the level of political discourse, "parmehutu" is a term of Hutu mobilization and Tutsi exclusion, altogether a gross misrepresentation of the social, cultural, economic, and political reality in such a homogenous situation as that observed in Rwanda. In 1960, the Parmehutu promoted the idea that "Rwanda was a Hutu nation" ("Le Rwanda est un pays des Hutu"); in other words, the Republic is Hutu. This is the element that syntactically, CDR recuperated in "Coalition pour la Defense de la Republique." One should also note the dramatic, belligerent nature of that party's name, a call to arms, as it were, to defend the republic against the attack by the Rwandan Patriotic Front (RPF), described as monarchists and feodalists who wanted to reestablish monarchy, with all the negative connotations associated with it in Hutu Power propaganda. CDR was founded by extremist elements from the MRND, and especially by people from Gisenyi and Ruhengeri. Despite all appearances, it was nothing but a faction of the MRND. With its 1970s and 1980s rhetoric of unity among the ethnic groups in Rwanda, MRND could not abruptly and easily recuperate all the extremist elements from the MDR-Parmehutu of the 1960s. By recuperating Kayibanda's ideas, CDR sought to question the legitimacy of MDR to replace the 1960s MDR-PARMEHUTU and thus push it to the extreme right of ethnic divide and alienate it from the electorate in the South. CDR was there to do the dirty job for MRND for the ultimate goal of keeping power in the control of Gisenyi and Ruhengeri. CDR's adoption of an extreme Hutu ideology also aimed at covering the thorny issue of regionalism by presenting the Rwandan problem as a problem between the Hutu and the Tutsi, not between the North and the South. Finally, CDR's extreme hutuism focused on blaming the war and all the attendant problems (internal displacements for thousands of people from Byumba and Ruhengeri and poor economic performance) on the RPF and its Tutsi and Hutu accomplices inside the country. The objective sought in this case was to reclaim the (southern) Hutu, advance Hutu solidarity, help the Hutu military protect and reinforce Habyarimana's regime, but, as Christopher Taylor aptly puts it, "to many southern Hutu, neither the RPF nor Tutsi in general were the principal enemy; northern Hutu supporters of Habyarimana were."[62]

MDR had been resuscitated without the "parmehutu" attached and indeed was very strong in the region of the first president of the Republic of Rwanda, that is, in the central/southern prefecture of Gitarama. From 1991 to October 1993, extremist elements did not show themselves. It is after internal splits caused by the thwarted individual ambitions, different approaches to the Arusha peace talks, the maneuvering of Habyarimana and his party, and the death of Melchior

Ndadaye, assassinated by the Tutsi military of Burundi, that the Hutu power movement vocally appeared not only in MRND and MDR but also in PL and to a very minimal extent in PSD (the only major party that resisted Habyarimana's repeated attempts to divide it). Hutu power embraced the CDR extremist ideology. Before then, CDR was a rather negligible party confined to Gisenyi and Ruhengeri (where, interestingly enough, also MRND was the strongest). It was generally disliked outside those two prefectures and was actually used as an insult in many milieus—"Uri igisederi" and "Genda wa gisederi we" ([I despise you because] "you are a CDR member, "get lost, you dirty CDR member") were common disparaging insults heard in the south.

The Arusha Peace Accords of August 1993 and the assassination of President Melchior Ndadaye of Burundi on October 21, 1993 were the determining elements in the vocalization of the Hutu Power. With the implementation of the Peace Accord, Gisenyi and Ruhengeri were now clearly facing the ultimate loss of the control of the administration and thus were ready to use all means necessary to sabotage any power-sharing arrangement.[63] The assassination of Ndadaye, who had studied and worked in Rwanda as a Hutu exile from Burundi, came as a blessing to the Hutu Power movement, for CDR and the other Power groups had unsuccessfully tried to force their extremist propaganda onto the rest of the country since 1991.

An incident that not only tested the resolve of Hutu extremism but also showed the resistance to the CDR ideology in the south was the assassination of the PSD Secretary General, Félicien Gatabazi, a native of Butare, on February 21, 1994, by the MRND and CDR forces working with the inner circle of President Habyarimana. The next day, the CDR president was killed in Butare, as he was returning from Cyangugu. The situation remained tense in Kigali for several days, as the PSD youth militia and their supporters wanted to avenge the death of their leader. They knew that the responsible party was CDR and MRND. All things considered, there was considerable resistance against CDR and its ideology until April 6, 1994—in fact, the prefectures of Butare and Gitarama remained free of violence for two weeks after massacres began in the capital city and elsewhere in the country. Thus does it not come as a surprise that Bagosora appointed two men from Butare to occupy the top two positions in the land—President and Prime Minister—to help shake what was perceived as Butare's lethargy.

The sudden shift that occurred begs the question: What broke that resistance previously embodied in the opposition parties of the South? What convinced the "resisters" to cease resistance and join the killing spree? I believe that a judicious understanding of the genocide needs to trace the different stages of development that eventually turned to daily mass murder. A monocausal explanation à la Goldhagen does not do the job. Instead, one needs to look at a more plausible notion, the "gray zone" that would include, in the context of the Tutsi genocide, certainly deep hatred of the Tutsi among extremists, especially in the northwestern prefectures of Gisenyi and Ruhengeri; a considerable number of diehard, nostalgic parmehutists throughout the country; the totalitarian state; blind obedience to authority; the culture of impunity created by repeated human rights violations; the economic crisis of the second half of the 1980s; an underlying competition model that pitted north against south for the control of the limited resources of the country; manipulations of all kinds; but certainly not a generalized existence of a threshold of acceptability of Tutsi exclusion. The gray zone thus defined reflects a variety of motives and a sophisticated social engineering that used notions historically defined by the Hamitic Hypothesis, the 1959 Hutu revolution, and the so-called moral revolution of 1973 that brought Gisenyi and Ruhengeri to power.

    The existence of a threshold of acceptability of Tutsi exclusion permeates Semujanga's definition of genocide in his book, especially in his effort to undermine the role of the government and to focus more on the involvement of the ordinary people. If mass murder is the work of ordinary people, it starts as a State project that shapes its historical, ideological, and psychological contours. But what is the relationship between the government and the governed in a non-democratic country such as Rwanda? In the introduction to his book, Semujanga mentions the necessity to study three elements of the act of communication: the sender, the message, and the receiver. He argues that one cannot separate the CDR, MRND, MDR-Power, and the people because the latter play an important role in the act of communication. But this is no normal act of communication, where roles are negotiated freely. In this non-democratic situation, the receiver may resist it, but in Rwanda in 1990-1994, it was repeated over and over on the national radio and on the RTLM and in extremist newspapers and in the many political rallies that took place between 1991 and 1994, all these sometimes complemented by bomb attacks to instill fear. The message was imposed and helped by elements external to the message sent to people used to hearing only one perspective imposed as the truth. Thus, one must at least question the statement that "de fait, dans le discours du génocide, les énoncés sur le rejet du Tutsi sont partagés aussi bien par le meneur que par le peuple ("in reality, in the genocidal discourse, the discourse on the exclusion of the Tutsi are shared by both the leader and the ordinary people").[64] This argument totally ignored the immediate developments and factors that preceded the genocide in the time span of 1990-1994, and most important the repressive, dictatorial nature of the totalitarian regime.[65] As I was in Rwanda until July 1992, I observed several instances when people were coerced (both Hutu and Tutsi) to participate in public demonstrations of support for the Rwandan government military and the condemnation of the Rwandan Patriotic Front. Simply put, there was no choice. Actually, some of the people who participated in those demonstrations were themselves humiliated, but they would go back to the next one anyway. In 1990-1992, everybody was asked to contribute to the "war effort." It was supposed to be a voluntary contribution, but money was taken from everybody's pay. I never heard anybody going to court over that, even though there were many among the Hutu and the Tutsi who were unhappy about that forced contribution. There were many examples that showed clearly the coercive nature of a dictatorial regime.

Ignoring the immediate history that precedes the genocide, the multiple motivations of those who participated in the massacres, and the different levels of involvement can lead to bizarre and even dangerous generalizations, for example: "Car la haine antitutsi existait à l'état latent dans la mémoire collective des Hutu au Rwanda moderne" (For anti-Tutsi hatred existed in a latent state in the collective memory of the Hutu in modern Rwanda"[66]). It is true that for a genocide to succeed in the manner in which it succeeded in Rwanda, the first criminal (the government) needs the help of ordinary men, who then become accomplices to the crime, but it is necessary to add that this happens at the very moment of the crime and does not necessarily presuppose the existence of a threshold of acceptability of Tutsi hatred and exclusion.

Semujanga's book forces the bipolarization wrought by the colonialist and the missionary onto his threshold of acceptability. He does an excellent job of analyzing the cultural transformation that negated existing values to replace them with the paradigms of European civilization, for it is true that both worked for the triumph of European civilization, well embodied in the philosophy of the Enlightenment, which created the modern state in western Europe and North America. The book traces an interesting linguistic trajectory in the discussion of such dichotomies as "bakirisitu-bapagani/bashenzi," (Christians versus pagans) "amazina ya gipagani" (pagan names) versus "amazina ya gikirisitu" (Christian names) and "Catholics versus Protestants." But these categories were also created in other colonies of the world, and they simplified the colonized subjects by annihilating them and portraying them using European values, which consequently led to inadequate portrayals of "inferior to (European) Whites," "savages," "cannibals," "uncivilized," "heathens," and more. It did not follow that people in those colonies ended up committing genocide.

As discussed in Chapter Two, these ideas obviously exclude the non-Europeans from the Enlightenment ideas of man and its characteristic features among which reason, arts, sciences, liberty, civilization, progress, brotherhood, tolerance, and the other *grands récits* that undergirded European colonial ventures for centuries. In the eyes of the colonizer the indigenous people of Africa, Asia, and Latin America lacked those elements, and thus they were viewed as savages on whom the good enlightenment values had to be imposed, and, perhaps, the new ideas would help the natives climb the Big Chain of Being. It is this kind of binary society that Europeans were looking for in Rwanda and that they established by destroying the existing social, cultural, economic, and political structures. They set up a colonial, Christian culture that was founded on a dichotomized racial ideology that they set out to teach in Christian schools and churches.

In describing the complex mechanism of the Rwandan genocide, we must resist the temptation to reduce it to one or a few binary oppositions of the kind seen in 1994 in the Western media that tended to describe the massacres as Hutu and Tutsi tribesmen butchering each other. It was, instead, a carefully planned attempt to exterminate the Tutsi, with known genocide ideologues, direct and indirect beneficiaries, sponsors, willing and unwilling executioners, and even people who resisted and challenged the genocide. Levi's concept of the "gray zone" indeed offers a critical framework that can be useful in circumscribing the motivations and involvement of different players in the Rwandan genocide.

No investigation has been carried out to determine who shot the Mystère Falcon carrying the Presidents of Rwanda and Burundi on April 6, 1994 at 8:30 in the evening. Whoever shot the plane gave the Hutu Power an opportunity to implement what its proponents called the "final solution" of the Tutsi problem in Rwanda. Rather than focus on who might have done it, I will focus on what forces came to bear after the event, i.e. who stood to gain, who killed, and what motivated the executioners?

First, there are those who stood to gain politically from Habyarimana's death. Akazu members, the Gisenyi/Ruhengeri-dominated army, the Hutu Power movement, and politicians all over the country who would probably lose their positions after the implementation of the Peace Accords could not forgive the President for signing the Arusha accords. Now that the agreement was signed, the only possibility left for them was to prevent, at all costs, its implementation. Habyarimana himself had signed the accords under pressure from the international community and later on, feeling the heat from his Hutu power supporters, had called the agreement just a scrap of paper. Indeed, from August 1993 until the President's death on April 6, 1994, MRND, CDR, the military, and other Hutu Power forces succeeded in blocking all attempts to implement the agreement. When Habyarimana went to Dar-es-Salaam, Tanzania, to attend a meeting with regional presidents, the Hutu power saw that as his final capitulation. What followed the shooting constituted a coup, as the main players subverted the power-sharing arrangement in place and the one waiting to happen with the BBTG by killing the Prime Minister and the other political leaders of the opposition, by replacing in all levels of government those leaders who had opposed or resisted Hutu extremism or those who had not shown real enthusiasm in killing. No provision in the Rwandan power hierarchy allowed Théoneste Bagosora, a retired army officer from the region of Habyarimana, only secretary general in the ministry of defense, to take control of the situation and form a crisis committee. The leverage he had was the support of the Presidential Guard and other elite troops in Kigali as well as the vast majority of the Rwandan army, generally recruited from Gisenyi and Ruhengeri, the two prefectures that stood to lose the tremendous influence they had in the country's affairs if the Arusha accords were implemented. Bagosora wanted to be President, but his ambitions were thwarted by the rejection of his colleagues of the crisis committee and the lack of support from the UNAMIR commander General Dallaire, the UN special representative Roger Booh-Booh, and the diplomatic missions that he contacted in the night of April 6, 1994. We must entertain the possibility that the swift political killings of April 6-12, 1994 were used to raise the stakes for those around Bagosora to see the extent of his power. He may have executed the plan of killing the opposition leaders and the other people on pre-established lists as a way of forcing his colleagues to recognize his authority, but did not see any interest in stopping the violence once he realized that he would not be accepted as president. Also, if he could not fill the power vacuum created by Habyarimana's death, then he would stuff the administration with Hutu power leaders who would do his bidding. Even though the killings followed three years of planning and sustained anti-Tutsi propaganda, it is not farfetched to posit that Bagosora's inability to secure the presidency the first few days after the death of Habyarimana fueled his desire to fully implement what he had called the "apocalypse."

Bagosora represented the interests of the Akazu, the "sacred region" of Gisenyi and Ruhengeri, the military, and Hutu Power in general—all these forces were adamant to keep the military, political, and economic power in the hands of the northern region. If Rwanda was a Hutu republic, then it should be entrusted to the "unsullied and rough" Hutu of the north, not the Hutu of the south, who the northerners liked to think were not distinguishable from the Tutsi. We must also keep in mind that the 1973 so called moral revolution (coup) led by Habyarimana replaced a Gitarama-based republic with a Gisenyi-Ruhengeri-based Hutu republic, a change of historical significance since the northern part of the country was not incorporated in the kingdom of Rwanda until 1912 with the help of the Germans. Thus the 1973 coup was something of a historical reversal whereby power was concentrated in the hands of northerners. They were not going to let it slip away from them and give it to southerners and Tutsi without a serious fight.

Probably because of the historical grudge of being forcibly drawn into the Kingdom of Rwanda in 1912 and being ruled by chiefs sent by the royal palace in Nyanza until the 1959 Hutu revolution, the north was a bastion of anti-Tutsi sentiment. Schoolteachers were known to spend time in their classrooms talking about the Tutsi as "evil." As a result, it was not surprising that there were more people in the north (more than anywhere else in the country) who believed that the Tutsi were a different race that did not belong to Rwanda.

From 1992 to 1994, the Akazu and Hutu power supporters financed the operations of Interahamwe, Impuzamugambi, and the death squads called "Network Zero" and "Amasasu" (Bullets), the latter being composed on extremist elements in the military and coming from Gisenyi and Ruhengeri. "Network Zero," composed of trusted allies of Habyarimana and his wife's relatives carried out its first operation in the killing of the Bagogwe in January 1991, helped by the local commune government and the military. During the genocide, a group of wealthy and influential businessmen, including Félicien Kabuga, a parent by marriage to the Habyarimana family who was instrumental in the creation of the RTLM, continued to advise the government and to provide financial support. They are the ones, for example, who advised the Hutu Power government to send delegations abroad to give their version of what was happening in the country—of course, they did not call it genocide, but spontaneous outbursts of anger from a people attacked by the RPF and intent on avenging their beloved President. Kabuga also started a fund to support the war effort and asked Rwandans inside and abroad to contribute money.

The government put in place by Colonel Bagosora positioned him to control the organization of the genocide and operate as the real head of the Rwandan army, mainly because in the tradition of militaristic regimes in postcolonial Africa, he had the support of the Presidential Guard and its Commanders, as well as the elite troops, most of whom came from Gisenyi and Ruhengeri. According to Protocol # 4 of the Arusha Accords, the RPF and the Rwandan Army would be integrated into a smaller unified army. The RPF got a pretty good deal out of the negotiations: it would get forty percent of the ranks and fifty percent of senior officers in both the army and the national police (gendarmerie). The Presidential Guard would be replaced by a smaller Republican Guard including RPF elements. Understandably, this provision irked the Presidential Guard and the elite troops, who were used to huge privileges and who committed abuses with impunity. In addition, the army was the real force behind northern hegemony. The northern coalition of MRND, CDR, Akazu, most of the military, and many from the Hutu Power movement wanted to keep it that way, in the name of the 1959 revolution; in reality, it was to safeguard the regional entitlements of July 5, 1973. It should not be surprising then that the army played a pivotal role in the organization of the genocide and intervened in all large-scale operations, especially in cities. Military skills, weapons, vehicles, and communication systems provided effective means of carrying out the genocide.

Once the Hutu power government was in place, it could count on the legendary Rwandan administrative structure known for its tight top-down ability to force obedience on the masses. Traditionally, authority was not contingent; it was real and tended to be absolute at all levels to the point that even low-level administrator likes the sector's councilor had the power to inflict severe punishment without recourse to any due judicial procedure. As an example, in 1992 the councilor of my native sector cut the hands of a young man wrongly accused of stealing a goat by his neighbors; he lost proper use of two fingers, but the councilor suffered no consequences whatsoever for his illegal action. The absolute power of leaders meant that authority often rested on blind obedience for fear of undeserved punishment.

The Hutu Power government put in place on April 8, 1994 provided the ideology, motivation, rallying force, and administrative and financial support needed for the success of the genocide apparatus. The new president, the ministers, and other top authorities traveled to their home regions to organize the local militia and encourage the local population to participate in the killings of their Tutsi neighbors and anyone opposing the massacres. They were heard on national radio and

on the RTLM promoting Hutu solidarity, justifying the killings as a patriotic duty of self-defense, calling the masses to dislodge the "enemy"
from wherever he might be, and forcefully claiming that if the killing of
the Tutsi was not done, the Tutsi would exterminate the Hutu and take
all their land and property. As a consequence of this, killing the Tutsi
became both a personal and patriotic duty. Local administrators used
their power to force their communes, sectors, and cells to carry out the
actions demanded by the extremists on the radios. In most cases, they
were assisted by the commune police, the local militia, and, if need be,
the military would be called in to help. Local authorities would call the
population for "umuganda" and direct it in house-to-house hunts or to
public sites such as churches, schools, and stadiums where the victims
would have fled at the encouragement of the same local authorities.
Local leaders also made sure that roadblocks were manned to check
identity cards and kill the Tutsi on the spot. They would also arrange
for teams to search hiding places such as ceilings for survivors. Indeed,
the Rwandan genocide was an administrative process in which the
State's administration structure played the most important organizational role.

The Hutu Power government also could count on the support
of the directors of parastatals, a group overwhelmingly dominated by
men from Gisenyi and Ruhengeri and some of whom were members of
Akazu. Some had already openly supported the militia and promoted
Hutu ideology in their companies. Others knew that to keep their jobs
they had to support the persons who had placed them in the position.
For example, they used their companies' trucks to transport Interahamwe to places of attack and provided them with refreshments (usually beer). According to the report filed by an International Panel of
Eminent Personalities (IPEP) appointed by the Organization of African
Unity to investigate the genocide in Rwanda, "whether out of fear, opportunism, conviction, or some combination, the private sector re-
sponded to the genocide campaign by contributing money, transport,
weapons, alcohol, petrol, and other needed goods."[67]

Various motivations, including hatred for the Tutsi, fear, regionalism, and opportunism also explain the intellectuals' involvement
in the genocide. Some of the stanch ideologues of the genocide were
former university professors, for example Léon Mugesera (whose
speech we looked at before) and the historian Ferdinand Nahimana
whose scholarship had focused on exalting the independence of northern Hutu kingdoms before the Germans helped King Musinga bring
them under the control of the central government. In showing their zeal
in denouncing and killing their Tutsi colleagues and actively participat-

ing in the genocide (writing and speaking for the genocide, manning
roadblocks, organizing killers, and guiding attacks), some university
professors and high schools teachers calculated to be rewarded with
good government positions after the war or scholarships abroad. Some
others participated simply because they hated the Tutsi and wanted
them exterminated. A considerable number of university professors
came from the same region as Habyarimana and had already enjoyed
the advantages of being from the "sacred region," and like the Akazu
members and the military described above, they took it personally to
kill the Tutsi (and Hutu dissidents) to defend their "northern rule."
Others took advantage of the situation to settle personal scores against
Tutsi or Hutu colleagues (accusing the latter of being RPF sympathizers). Others got involved because they feared for their lives and the
lives of their family members.

        A case that notoriously reflects Primo Levi's concept of the
"gray zone" is that of known Tutsi who became killers of other Tutsi.
Some had succeeded in changing their identity from Tutsi to Hutu to be
able to go to school and enjoy the advantages of being Hutu in a Hutu
republic. The more they were suspected of being Tutsi, the more they
showed zeal during the genocide. This situation necessitates more investigation, but one cannot miss the ironic twist that made a Tutsi the
head of the infamous Hutu militia known as "Interahamwe." On the
surface, nothing in this name necessarily reflects the brutality of the organization, but the word was probably chosen for its misleading
polysemy. It may mean "those who sing the same tune," "those who
have a common goal," "those who stand together," or "those who attack together." Robert Kajuga, however, cannot be said to have been
tricked by this semantic complexity. He made a deliberate choice to
join and lead the Interahamwe. But who was he exactly? Robert Jerry
Kajuga had a Tutsi father and a Hutu mother, which made him a Tutsi,
but his father had changed his identity from Tutsi to Hutu in 1959, in
the heat of the Hutu revolution. In the late 1950s and early 1960s, this
change of identity was still common and relatively easy. Extreme brutality was a way for him to show Hutu credentials. One of his brothers,
who lost many family members during the genocide, told *African
Rights*:

> Robert is the only member of the family who is a member of
> MRND. Wilberforce and I are members of the Liberal Party.
> Another brother had no political affiliation. Robert got to
> know the President because he was the manager of a football
> team which two of the President's children joined. That was
> the connection. Since the President already knew and liked

Robert, he was chosen when they were looking for somebody
to head the Interahamwe. The President was very fond of
Robert and he owed his position to that. We talked to him
constantly about the dangers, but he made it clear that it was
his choice and his life and we were not to interfere.[68]

Reminiscent of Chaim Rumkowski, Kajuga was known as "Le
Président" (The President), and he seemed to be enjoying his position.
Asked by journalist Jean Hélène of Radio France Internationale if the
killings were organized, he replied: "They are not organized—no way,
no way, no way. You have to see the situation: the President died, and
after three hours, the population really did not understand what was going on. They saw their neighbours next door who had guns to kill everyone, --well, they just defended themselves."[69] To the question
whether his militia collaborated with the army, he lied, saying: "...We
just exchange advice. Otherwise there are really no regular contacts
with the army. We are doing our best not to disturb the army. If the
army asks us to leave a spot, we leave it, but we help the army to defend the country."[70] Speaking to another journalist, he blamed the RPF
for the killings taking place in Rwanda and justified the massacres as
self-defense. As for the bodies of women and children (including
eleven-year olds) found at the roadblocks, he blamed the victims calling them RPF fighters.[71] Kajuga did not do anything to prevent deaths
in his own family, including his own father. His brother interviewed by
African Rights said,

> According to a nephew who survived, [on the first day of the
> killings] three gendarmes went to the home of my brother
> Hus on the [sic] Thursday. They took twelve people out onto
> the lawn and shot them including Hus, our seventy-two-year
> old father, Hus's Belgian wife and the wife and children of
> Wilberforce. Hus's wife put her arms around my twenty-year
> old nephew which seems to have saved him. They even
> killed one of the people who worked in the house.[72]

Why Kajuga did not show any concern about his family begs a
few questions: Was it a good occasion to sever any association with his
Tutsiness hung around his neck like an albatross? Did he fear disap-
proval if he tried to save his family? Or had his position as president of
the Interahamwe militia made him insensitive to the death of close
ones? Whatever the case, he had real power. If people in very low positions could openly save Tutsi, why did he not try to save his immediate

family? When Kajuga and a group of Interahamwe moved to Butare in
early May 1994,

> they installed themselves at Hotel Ibis, where they spent a
> great deal of time drinking with soldiers. (...) But they [the
> Interahamwe who accompanied Kajuga] displayed also the
> assurance that came from being associated with the most im-
> portant national leaders of the militia as they looted widely in
> town among Hutu as well as Tutsi. Several young Tutsi
> women who were part of Kajuga's entourage moved freely
> about town and the market, their safety guaranteed by their
> protector. Kajuga also provided protection to some Tutsi of
> Butare, alerting their Hutu hosts whenever Shalom's militia
> was planning an attack on them.[73]

Shalom Anselme Ntahobari was the most known militia leader
in Butare during the genocide. He was a mediocre student who had
failed at the National University of Rwanda. His father was Rector of
this university, and his mother was minister of Family and Women's
Affairs before and during the genocide. Nyiramasuhuko had been a
high school classmate of President Habyarimana's wife, and most people in Rwandan believed that her family's prominence was due to the
friendship she continued to entertain with Agathe Kanziga Habyarimana. During the genocide, she and her son Shalom were instrumental
in the most devastating killings in Butare. After Bagosora put the government in place, Nyiramasuhuko was sent to Butare to inflame the
killing frenzy. Using loudspeakers mounted on pick-up trucks, she went
through the city of Butare, announcing that the Red Cross was distrib-
uting food and offering a safe haven at the Huye soccer stadium. The
thousands who gathered there were massacred under the supervision of
Nyiramasuhuko, who also encouraged the Interahamwe to rape humiliate Tutsi girls and women before killing them. She referred to the Tutsi
women as dirt that needed to be taken away. Her son Shalom became
notorious for raping women and using extreme cruelty in his killing.
Son of a university rector and a minister and armed with a gun and grenades, he is said to have enjoyed a strong sense of power over other Interahamwe and even military officers. Mother and son thus became accomplices of evil. On the surface, the story of Nyiramasuhuko and her
son was similar to that of other officials who used their influence to
gather the Tutsi at places of slaughter and transport killers and provide
them with weapons (such as guns, machetes, and grenades) and other
tools (such as gas to burn the victims). In an article published in the
New York Times of Sunday, September 15, 2002, Peter Landesman es-

tablishes that Pauline Nyiramasuhuko is a Tutsi. Through a social process described in Chapter Two, her great-grandfather, a Tutsi, became poor and lost his "Tutsiness." Also, in the wake of the Hutu revolution, her whole family changed from Tutsi to Hutu. Nyiramasuhuko was not the only high official of Tutsi descent who acted so cruelly against fellow Tutsi. They are scores of other such individuals who displayed unusual cruelty and "useless violence" to show that they were true Hutu. Some of them had been previously investigated by the Habyarimana's government but were allowed to stay in their positions for lack of records to prove they were Tutsi. When the genocide started, they had to protect the property and fortune they had amassed, but also inside them they developed that hatred of the Tutsi inside them after seeing the manifold ways in which the Tutsi were humiliated and butchered.

By the time the genocide started, the Interahamwe and Impuzamugambi militia had at least a two-year experience in military training and mass killings—Bugesera in March 1992 and the multiple attacks after the signing of the Arusha Agreement in the effort to derail its implementation. Locally organized, they knew their Tutsi neighbors, and thus could easily plan, organize, and carry out massacres with the help of the local population and the military. They could also be sent to other places where they were needed to assist soldiers already on location. The militia were recruited among the many unemployed and helpless young men, especially in cities. They received a little money, primus or Miitzig beer, and were encouraged to loot, which gave them a sense of power. In April 1994, they could be heard saying that they were just doing their job.

A February 1993 RPF attack displaced thousands and thousands of people from the prefectures of Byumba and Ruhengeri, who from then until the genocide lived in precarious condition at the outskirts of Kigali in a place called Nyacyonga. Many of the young men in this camp for the internally displaced were recruited into the militia. The Hutu Power did not waste any time to blame the RPF and the Tutsi for the plight of the displaced. In April 1994, after more than a year of misery, those recruited from the camps probably did not need any more propaganda to kill the Tutsi. The same applies to high school students who came from Byumba and Ruhengeri. During vacations (Easter, Summer, and Christmas 1993 and Easter 1994), they stayed in their school dorms, while the rest of their classmates went home to their families in regions not directly affected by the conflict. The students who stayed in school dorms were the first to kill when the genocide started. Informants who were in the town of Nyanza (in the prefecture of Butare) told me that students from Byumba and Ruhengeri who had stayed at Nyanza schools during the Easter vacation were the first ones to go after their Tutsi teachers and classmates. They knew where they lived. Like the Burundi refugees, they showed the most determination and cruelty in killing the Tutsi inside houses and at roadblocks.

Interahamwe also recruited among the Burundian refugees, who had sought refuge in Rwanda in the aftermath of the October 21, 1993 assassination of Melchior Ndadaye. These refugees, many of whom had probably participated in the killings in Burundi, acquired notoriety for their extreme cruelty during the Rwandan genocide. They were active in the prefectures in which their camps were situated, especially Butare, Gitarama, and Kigali (Bugesera region), but they were also sent to Kigali (Nyamirambo), Gisenyi, Cyangugu, and Gikongoro. An informant who was a student at the National University in Butare in 1994 told me that even before the genocide, anybody remotely resembling a Tutsi who passed near the Burundi refugee camps did so at his or her own expense. Another informant who lived in Nyanza through much of the genocide told me Burundian refugees were among the leaders of the killings of Tutsi, eating of cows belonging to Tutsi victims, and looting. They showed unqualified brutality, especially towards women and children. I was told of one example of a certain Burundian refugee named Jagasi. At a roadblock in Nyanza, he saw a woman for whom everybody else seemed to have mercy. She had a baby in her hands. The Burundian went to the woman, took the baby from her, and swung it toward a wall nearby. The baby hit the war and died instantly. He then proceeded to taunt the woman and then killed her with machete blows.

This kind of "useless violence" was not uncommon during the Rwandan genocide. The intent was not only to kill the Tutsi but also to humiliate them, to inflict maximum suffering and psychological trauma, and to annihilate their humanity. This was particularly true of the use of rape as an instrument of genocide. Rape systematically occurred as part of the implementation of the genocide since April 7 to mid July 1999, and in the whole country. As the Interahamwe militia and the Hutu power as well as government soldiers arrested and massacred Tutsi families, women were targeted for being Tutsi, or for belonging to the political opposition, or simply for their enviable social status. The militia raped the women before killing them off, or women were spared to be the sexual servants of those whom they had watched killing their husbands, children, and other family members. Their bodies became the property of the killers who used them in whatever manner they chose. Survivors of rape were hidden in ceilings for the whole duration of the war by those whom Bonnet refers to as "violeurs sauveurs"(rapist saviors).[74] As a result, rape survivors were referred to after the genocide as "femmes de plafond" (ceiling women) or "femmes de miliciens" (wives of militia men). It must be stressed that these women were forced into being sex objects, bounty for the "victorious" killers, often in the presence of their husbands and their children. The use of the expressions cited above was also a way of avoiding the utterance of "rape," a taboo word in the Rwandan society because it brings ostracization to the victim. As a result, the rape victim would not willingly report or make her plight known to avoid being victimized by societal judgment. After witnessing the massacre of their family, they demanded death for themselves but instead were forced into daily rape.

Even before the war, Tutsi women were commonly said to be more beautiful, more charming, and better in bed than their Hutu counterparts. On top of these stereotypes, it was added that they were arrogant and they despised Hutu men. For the Hutu militia to usurp the youth and beauty of Tutsi women was a way of gaining access to what was previously almost impossible. Because of this, the Hutu militia gained a sense of power because they had subdued and now owned those who were previously supposed to be superior to them.

Both Hutu and Tutsi girls could be raped as part of what the militia and the soldiers called the contribution to the "war effort." This practice had been rehearsed, by the way, long before the genocide itself. For example, in 1991 and 1992 in the city of Ruhengeri, which was one of the major concentrations of government soldiers, young girls and women, Hutu and the few Tutsi who stayed in that particularly anti-Tutsi region, were regularly raped in the name of the "war effort."[75]

Hutu women were raped particularly during the exodus that preceded the defeat of the government army in July 1994. The Interahamwe militia and the government soldiers repeatedly raped women and young girls, and any resistance was discouraged by the threat to kill the victims' children or cut them into pieces. Women were made available to soldiers and militia to boost their morale. It was reported that many women were also taken to camps outside the country as the defeated government soldiers fled to Zaire, which in 1997 became the Democratic Republic of the Congo. Rape was often collective. Squads of militia or soldiers raped one person or more at houses where killings had taken place, or women were permanently available at army headquarters. There were also many cases of individual rape.

The sadism displayed in the rape of Tutsi women went beyond anything humanly comprehensible. Human Rights Watch/FIDH reports that even a two-year old baby was raped.[76] Rape was, of course, part of the overall plan to exterminate the Tutsi, as some rapists were also driven by the stereotypes about Tutsi women, in addition to the fact that the Hutu extremists in the media had highlighted the myth that Tutsi women were actively pursuing the interests of the Rwandan Patriotic Front and of Tutsi men in general, notably by sexually corrupting leaders in the Hutu administration. To exemplify the "useless" violence and humiliation involved in the rape of Tutsi women, I will quote what Alison Des Forges wrote in *Leave None to Tell the Story:*

> Assailants sometimes mutilated women in the course of a rape or before killing them. They cut off breasts, punctured the vagina with spears, arrows, or pointed sticks, or cut off or disfigured body parts that looked particularly "Tutsi," such as long fingers or thin noses. They also humiliated the women. One witness from Musambira commune was taken with some 200 other women after a massacre. They were forced to bury their husbands and then walk "naked like a group of cattle" some ten miles to Kabgayi. When the group passed roadblocks, militia there shouted that the women should be killed. As they marched, the women were obliged to sing the songs of the militia. When the group stopped at nightfall, some of the women were raped repeatedly.[77]

There are no words to convey the gravity of this type of humiliation. For a Rwandan woman to be seen naked by anyone is the peak of degradation. Some survivors of rape have committed suicide or had suicidal thoughts because of guilt felt for submitting to rape, as if they had any choice at all. In some cases, the psychopathology reached the level where the militia raped women after these had given birth, and in some places the militia raped dead bodies of Tutsi women.

It needs to be said that Hutu women, probably driven by an inferiority complex because of the stereotypes about the beauty and sexuality of Tutsi women, encouraged the soldiers and the militia to rape them. Some Hutu women also participated in the disfiguration of Tutsi women, using pointed sticks.

Consequences of these rapes included, in addition to death or suicide, the dissemination of HIV, a way of killing slowly (a considerable number of militia and soldiers were known to have AIDS), prostitution, destruction of family cohesion (especially in cases where there were survivors in the rape victim's family), self-recrimination, the social stigma of having been raped (when this is somehow known, because victims of rape normally did not venture this dreadful information), alcoholism, complication on subsequent pregnancies, suicidal thoughts, and unwanted pregnancies. Catherine Bonnet, who studied the phenomenon of "war pregnancies" and "the children of bad memory" ("enfants mauvais souvenirs") wrote that these pregnancies were often psychologically "refused and dissimulated, denied and discovered tardively."[78] Forced abortion, infanticide, and suicidal thoughts become part of the rape victim's life. At birth, the child is, of course, associated with the rapist, or even regarded as a criminal in the womb.[79] Bonnet discusses two approaches toward this severe social problem: (1) to give the victim the right to abort the child; (2) the Catholic Church's view that the child was a gift from God, a challenge from Heaven, who needed to be loved even if conceived in violence. The clergy maintained that victims must be helped toward this goal.

One must conclude from this discussion of rape during the 1994 Rwandan genocide that it was used as a tool of humiliation and extermination accompanied by "useless violence." It annihilated Tutsi women's dignity and affected their reproductive system as well as their family and community life.

Explaining the Extreme: Todorov's Theory

Having described the multiplicity of historical, political, social, and economic processes that led to mass murder in Rwanda, we also need to inscribe them in a superordinate framework if we want to capture the extreme evil that genocide is. As in the Nazi concentration camp, "evil is," to use Tzvetan Todorov's words, "the main character"[80] in the Rwandan genocide. Todorov offers a non-conventional description of evil in the concentration camp.[81] In his discussion of the structure that broke, humiliated, and exterminated the Jews and the other groups in concentration camps, Todorov rejects the qualification of the auxiliaries of the Nazi power structure as monsters or pathological beings. They were "neither monsters nor beasts," as the title of the second part of Todorov's book indicates.[82] There was only a small minority of guards that were perceived by witnesses as sadists (thus abnormal and pathological), but the vast majority of camp functionaries were just functionaries, paid or given a little power to do their job without displaying the pathological tendency of abuse and torture.[83] The five or four percent that took pleasure in torture were the Volksdeutcher (Germans born outside Germany, who were eager to prove that they were true Germans), not the Reichsdeutcher (Germans born in Germany). In addition, those five or ten percent were mostly "individuals scared by physical defect, grave psychological handicap, or simply vicious fate,"[84] in other words, people who had some personal "misery" to expurgate, or those who were part Jews and needed to prove otherwise through their overzealous acts of barbarity. The final solution, as we all know, was the affair of millions, not the exceptional, sadistic few. It is those millions whose behavior needs to be understood. Invoking collective pathology oversimplifies the question, blurs the comprehension of the processes involved in mass murders, and ultimately exonerates those responsible for the Holocaust. Likewise, in the case of the Rwandan genocide, we know about the passionate hatred that CDR and Hutu Power members had against the Tutsi, but we need to explain the behavior of thousands and thousands of peasants and civil servants who did not necessarily share the extremist ideology of Hutu Power.

If the few monsters offer little help in understanding the participation of the common Germans in the final solution, then the answer is somewhere else. What led the millions of Germans and citizens of occupied nations to obey Nazi rule? We have concluded that it could not be innate sadism, collective monstrousness, bestiality, primitiveness, or ideological fanaticism. At this point, Tzvetan Todorov invokes non-conventional explanations including Hannah Arendt's "banality of evil" and the structure of the totalitarian regime.

Hannah Arendt sat at the Adolph Eichmann trial in Jerusalem in 1961and noted that "the trouble with Eichmann was precisely that so many were like him, and that the many were neither perverted nor sadistic, that they were and still are, terribly and terrifyingly normal."[85] As a consequence, the evil in Eichmann is "banal," "common," all too human, too dangerous because it is too easy, "no exceptional human equalities were required for it to come into being. The wind had only to blow in the right direction, and the evil spread like wild fire."[86] This evil is ordinary, Todorov agrees, exceptional and extreme, but not radical. But then, how does it spread to a whole society to drive millions of people to mass murder? Todorov suggests we look beyond the individual and the psychological and instead posit a superordinate structure: the political and the social. What made the Germans, the Russians, and others who committed mass murder, Todorov argues, is the political structure—totalitarianism—that ruled those societies. He distinguishes three characteristics of the totalitarian regime that alter the individual's moral behavior.

First, the totalitarian regime defines a clear enemy or "who is not with me." This principle has terrible consequences in the totalitarian state: the enemy must be destroyed, annihilated. The enemy is internal to the regime, a group inside the borders of the state. Todorov gives the examples of Nazi Germany and the Soviet Union who applied imperialist policies when dealing with their neighbors but used warfare drama on the *enemy* within. He cites one Eicke saying: "The obligation to destroy an internal enemy of the State is in no way different from the obligation to kill your adversary on the battlefield."[87] The totalitarian regime works with a very simple dichotomy, a simple binary logic: "US" and "THEM"—the latter being the undesirable other, the enemy that must perish. "Them" do not have any rights. For Nazi Germany, the "them" are the Jews, the Gypsies, the homosexuals, political prisoners and others, described as "dogs," "parasites," "subhumans," and "vermin." They constituted a gangrene in the body of society and thus had to be extricated.

Second, the totalitarian State suppresses individual aims and makes itself the originator and end of the "society's ultimate aims":

> The supreme values that are supposed to govern the individual's conduct are no longer accessible to him; the individual can no longer think of himself as one of the humanity's many representatives and consult his conscience to determine which goals to pursue and according to which criteria to judge the actions of others.[88]

Society thus becomes the moral compass of judgment, of the distinction between good and evil. In this system, power means that one gains the moral position bestowed by the State. Authority cannot be questioned; it demands absolute allegiance. Unlike a democratic regime, the totalitarian State usurps power: it is not rule by, for, of the people; it is simply rule on the people. Rauschning reports that Hitler spoke determinedly of "the nothingness and insignificance of the individual human being and of his confirmed existence in the visible immortality of the nation." [89]

Third, the totalitarian regime controls the totality of its subjects' social and moral existence and behavior. It goes beyond the suppression of the political opposition and the total control of the administration. It controls the "entire public sphere of each person's life and encroaches substantially on his private life as well. It controls what work the individual does, where he lives, what he owns, his children's education and leisure, even his family life and his love affairs."[90] Obedience and submission are obtained through total control accompanied by "direct threat of physical violence and death. In more 'relaxed' times, the totalitarian state is content to deport its subjects, deny them work, prevent them from traveling abroad or owning property, keeping their children out of the university, and so on."[91]

Consequences of the totalitarian regime include the establishing of a culture of impunity for those who follow its edicts. The regime
encourages brutal action against the enemy, for the law does not punish
those who attack the internal enemy. Those who follow this principle
enjoy power over the state enemy. In the totalitarian state, the individual, acting from the state's injunction, has no personal responsibility for
his or her decisions, since these are the domains of the State. Ordinary
people become executioners because the totalitarian regime appropri-
ates social goals and succeeds in making people do whatever is assigned by the superordinate decider. This state of affairs, Todorov
maintains, does not "disturb the individual's moral structure at all.
[Nazi] guards who committed atrocities never stopped distinguishing
between good and evil."[92] Because their behavior was dictated by the
totalitarian regime, then it was good, not evil. This is the new moral
yardstick of their actions. The totalitarian regime inoculates the individual against any sense of guilt and responsibility. Individuals become
docile followers of the State's will. That is what made ordinary German
citizens Hitler's executioners. This situation can lead to social schizo-
phrenia, Todorov contends. The regime is

> quite satisfied with 'merely' public docility, because it needs
> no more than that to remain firmly in power. At the same
> time, its subjects live in the comforting illusion that in 'in
> their innermost selves" they remain honorable and pure. So-
> cial schizophrenia thus becomes a weapon in the hands of
> those in power; it lulls to sleep the conscience of the totalitar-
> ian subject, reassures him, and lets him underestimate the se-
> riousness of his public deeds. Master of his heart of hearts,
> the subject no longer pays much attention to what he does in
> the world.[93]

Since the enemy within is a domestic entity, it is also regulated by national laws. The overwhelming control and power of the
State make it impossible for the enemy to organize a sustainable resistance because of the fear of violence and death. The enemy within is
indeed under the constant watch of the policing system put in place by
the regime and is constantly depersonalized and humiliated by the State
propaganda machine.

Through its coercive structure, the totalitarian State makes its
subjects accomplices of its crime—just plain, common, ordinary people. Years of this political ideology make it easy for common people to
become executioners, but it does not exonerate them from their crimes.
They are guilty and if ultimately judged for their crime against human-

ity, it is not by the totalitarian regime itself that created them (because it would be a contradiction of itself as a system of government). Real courts judge individuals, not collectivities.

After this discussion, we must therefore refute any idea of any nationality's innate inclination to hatred and extermination. Goldhagen's idea of some type of innate, cognitive antisemitism is simply untenable because it does not take into account the Nazi totalitarian regime and its effects on the ordinary German people's social psychology. Again, those millions who became Hitler's executioners were individually guilty of their individual acts. Morally and judicially, it is important to remember those who suffered and individually try those who made them suffer—after all, this is our democratic, contemporary view of justice: in a court of justice, an individual responds to his or her individuals acts.

The twenty-one years of Habyarimana rule that preceded the Rwandan genocide read like a perfect textbook case of the totalitarian regime, and this reality became quite conspicuous when the war broke out in 1990.

The Enemy Within/Without

Immediately after the RPF invasion from Uganda on October 1, 1990, the Rwandan government did not waste any time to define the enemy: the Tutsi who were defeated by the 1959 revolution and their "ibyitso" (accomplices), which meant the Tutsi of the interior but also the Hutu who had shown dissent with the regime. The administration, the press, and the army enthusiastically spread this characterization of the enemy in rallies in official releases and speeches, at the many popular meetings that were called throughout the country in the weeks that followed the attack, and on the national radio as well as *Imvaho* and *La Relève*, two weeklies (the first in Kinyarwanda and the second in French) run by the government. The army, composed of many from the same region as Habyarimana, encouraged and often assisted the local Hutu population to kill the Tutsi or commit acts of intimidation against them and against those Hutu opposed to the politics of Habyarimana. Hatred of the Tutsi became the ideology that inspired many among the military, who killed hundreds of innocent civilians on the operation fields (particularly in Byumba and Ruhengeri in 1990 and 1991). On the role of the military in this campaign of hatred, fear, and violence, *Leave None to Tell the Story* writes that

in early December 1991, the high command of the Rwandan
army issued two press releases that proclaimed in a pro forma
way their support for democratization and neutrality towards
all political parties. But the military leaders then went on to
condemn Rwandans who 'knowingly or unknowingly, aided
the enemy under the cover of political party activities.' They
declared that newspapers critical of the president were subsi-
dized by the RPF. They blamed RPF infiltrators and their
'acolytes' for the increase in crime and acts of random violence and they concluded one press release by asking the secret police to 'neutralize all collaborators identified with the
enemy.'[94]

It took another year before a more formal definition of the enemy
was circulated, the result of a military commission headed by Colonel
Déogratias Nsabimana, Chief of Staff of the Rwandan army. In this capacity he sent the document to his commanders ordering them to "dis-
tribute this document widely, insisting especially on the sections relat-
ing to the enemy, identification of the enemy, as well as the group
within which the enemy is recruited."[95] The document went on to define the enemy in unequivocal terms: (1) The principal enemy: "the
Tutsi inside or outside the country, extremist and nostalgic for power,
who have NEVER recognized and will NEVER recognize the realities
of the 1959 social revolution and who wish to reconquer power by all
means necessary, including arms"[96]; (2) Political partisans of the enemy, that is Hutu and Tutsi politically opposed to Habyarimana and the
MRND. More than once, "enemy" and "Tutsi" were used inter-
changeably. The document also condemned what it termed "Tutsi hegemony," appealed to debris of the 1959 Hutu revolution, called for
Hutu solidarity as an antidote, and deplored the enemy's infiltration of
political parties to manipulate them into supporting the RPF. It was no
secret in Rwanda then that the MRND and CDR parties promoted the
idea that the PL party was a branch of the RPF inside Rwanda, because
it counted more Tutsi in its leadership and membership than any other
opposition party. The document cast the problem at hand as an ethnic
problem (Hutu versus Tutsi), not a regional one (North versus South),
but the definition of the enemy within obviously applied to members of
MDR, PL, PSD, and PDC, whose members were overwhelmingly from
the south. Any informed observer could not miss the fact that these parties had formed an alliance with the RPF and thus had politically isolated the north.

Between 1990 and 1994, the enemy thus defined suffered reprisals from the Habyarimana regime and its associates, the MRND and

the CDR parties. The thousands rounded up in the first few days of the conflict (especially in Kigali) (both Tutsi and Hutu of the political opposition), the Bagogwe (Tutsi group) of Ruhengeri (in 1991), the Tutsi of Bugesera in March 1992, the many victims of different attacks, as we saw in the previous chapter, and, of course, the genocide victims, were part of the enemy that had to be destroyed.

The Totalitarian State

Despite the presence of the political opposition in the Rwandan government between 1992 and 1994, the administration continued to function within the structure and management style put in place by the single party (MRND) in 1975. Under the presidency and the interior ministry, the country comprised 10 préfectures administered by préfets (roughly the equivalent of governors) appointed by the President of the Republic. The prefectures were subdivided into sous-préfectures, each combining 4-5 communes and run by sous-préfet. Below the sous-préfecture, there were 145 communes (counties) (with a population of approximately 40 to 50 thousand persons), each run by a burgomaster, also appointed by the President of the Republic. The commune was divided into sectors ("secteurs"), each with a population of about 5 thousand persons and run by an elected councilor. Below the sector was the final administrative structure called "cellule" (cell), with a population of approximately one thousand persons. The cell was run by a group of five "cell members," one of whom was called the "responsible to cellule" (the head of the cell).

In a country as tiny as Rwanda, the existence of these many administrative structures reflected the State's obsession with control. The "cell members" and the sector councilors' role was to implement the burgomaster's decisions; the burgomaster, the sous-préfet, and the préfet reported to their hierarchical superiors. According to the statutes of MRND, every leader at all levels was a representative of the President (not the people). This structure was almost a textbook for administrative efficiency. Much of it predated the colonial times, and in the wake of the 1990 civil war, the administration added one more level below the "cell" called "nyumbakumi" (Swahili for "ten houses"), which grouped ten households and was headed by a person also called "nyumbakumi" (the head of ten households). This tight administrative structure ensured total control of the whereabouts of every person and mercilessly tracked down any newcomer in any neighborhood (in fact, a host had to immediately inform the nyumbakumi of the presence of guests in his household), and the nyumbakumi had to verify the guests' identity, record the information, and report to a superior in case of doubt. Identity cards also bore the ethnic group and the place of residence. While people could travel freely before the war, changing residence was discouraged and needed the burgomaster's authorization. Civil servants, who in most cases had to move to cities or to places away from their communes, were required, upon arrival, to register with the new commune of residence by applying for a residence permit at the burgomaster's office. The burgomaster was required to inform the government's ubiquitous secret service of any newcomers in the commune.

       To apply for any job or to enlist in the military (in fact doing anything outside the commune), everybody was required to submit a number of forms duly signed by the burgomaster. They included a birth certificate; a certificate of complete identity specifying the date of birth, place of birth, and residence (cell, commune, and prefecture), parents, ethnic group, marital status, and employment position, if any; certificate of good conduct, life, and morals (this in a country where many burgmasters were openly corrupt); and a marriage certificate (even for unmarried folks, to ascertain that they were really single). As long as one had never irked the burgomaster, these documents were easy to obtain, but there were instances of people who for political dissent or for personal problems with the burgomaster stood no chance of getting the forms and so could not apply for anything, unless they were well connected in the higher levels of administration.

       For the few who passed the national exams for admission into high school, the State chose their orientation and their schools. Those who finished high school and applied for jobs with the government heard about their hiring and the place of their new jobs on the national radio, without any interview, and without any choice of job location. The State had the same power over those who applied for higher education. Even though students put their choices on their application forms, the education ministry often followed arbitrary lines in the assignment of the majors, according to the needs of the country, it was said. There were few complaints, however, because it was a huge privilege to get admission to higher education because of very limited places. It was even more difficult to get a scholarship to study abroad, mostly in Belgium, France, and other Western countries. In most cases, these scholarships were the most coveted and were usually reserved to the well connected. Those who finished their BA and Licence (roughly the equivalent of MA) in June of every year did not need to apply for jobs; many of them were sent by the education ministry to teach high schools. Their assignments were read on the national radio sometime at the end of August. Refusal to report to the place of assignment was tantamount to political dissent and was not tolerated.

As discussed earlier, every Rwandan was a member of MRND. Dissent was not tolerated and was deterred by known cases of arrest, torture, and long imprisonment without indictment, let alone trial with due process. The "maneko" (spy for the secret service) was omnipresent, especially in towns, where the majority of the educated resided. In my last year of high school (in the southern city of Nyanza), all my classmates knew that one of us, a student from Gisenyi, regularly fooled the tight vigilance of the priests at this all-boys' catholic boarding school to go downtown to file reports with the town's secret service representative. We were often amused because we wondered what on earth he could possible report about high schools students!

Although the constitution stipulated that there was separation of power (executive, legislative, and judiciary), this was only nominally, since the President's services controlled all the three branches. Any civil servant in any of the three branches who strayed away from government policy faced disciplinary measures, including being fired, jailed, or passed over for promotions. That there were few dissenters is certainly a measure of the success of the system. Freedom of speech and press, also guaranteed by the constitution, was inexistent. Before 1990, there were only a few known regular newspapers. The government owned *Imvaho* and *La Relève* (the first in Kinyarwanda and the second in French). The Catholic Church published *Kinyamateka*, the only independent paper and often the sole voice of dissent.

The only trade union known as CESTRAR (Central des Syndicats des Travailleurs du Rwanda) (Association of Rwandan Workers' Unions), launched in the 1980s, was an organ of the single party MRND and was expected to promote the MRND ideology. Local human rights organizations were only created in the wake of the multiparty system that started in the last quarter of 1990 following the outbreak of the 1990 civil war. They simply did not have any room in the dictatorial frame of 1975-1990 politics.

This totalitarian state was legitimated by the all-powerful Catholic Church and by the international community (in the form of foreign aid). We already saw how the Catholic clergy shaped identity and power politics during the colonial period and the turbulent 1950s. After independence, the Hutu leaders continued to enjoy the strong support of the Catholic Church. In many ways, Kayibanda (the first President) was a creation of Mgr André Perraudin of the Diocese of Kabgayi, and after he became President, Mgr Perraudin continued to be his mentor. Under both Kayibanda, Habyarimana, and even today, many elementary schools and the best high schools in the county belong to the Catholic Church, so that the state and the church have depended on each in the domain of education since the colonial period. Thus, the constitutional separation of state and church in Rwanda has been largely a myth. It is not surprising then that though the Tutsi dominated the Catholic clergy, only two bishops were Tutsi in the Habyarimana years. State and Church leaders worked closely together, and some Church leaders were indeed very active in the single party politics. The most known example is that of Mgr Vincent Nsengiyumva, the Archbishop of Kigali, a native of Ruhengeri, who was a member of the central committee of MRND until the Vatican pressured him to resign from that very important position in 1989. I must note here that a member of the central committee was politically more important than a minister—some ministers were also members of the central committee of MRND, which greatly increased their influence. A close ally of Habyarimana and personal confessor of his wife, Mgr Vincent Nsengiyumva was known to wear Habyarimana's portrait pin on his cassock as he celebrated mass. A practicing Catholic (he had a chapel in his Kanombe residence), Habyarimana enjoyed the unequivocal support of the Church. One can easily argue that Mgr Vincent Nsengiyumva played the same role of mentor that Mgr Perraudin had played for Kayibanda during the first Republic. According to a 1991 population census, 62 percent said they were Catholic, 18 percent Protestants (of different denominations), 19 percent practitioners of traditional religion, and 1 percent Muslims. None of the Protestant leaders were as influential as Mgr Vincent Nsengiyumva, but the Anglican and Baptist leaders readily supported the Habyarimana regime. The President of Rwanda's Presbyterian Church, based in Kibuye, was a member of the MRND committee at the level of prefecture.

Both Kayibanda's first republic and Habyarimana's second republic legitimated their power by what I would like to call a "demographic or ethnic democracy." Since the Hutu made up about 80 percent of the Rwandan population, then it was the country of the Hutu, and the Hutu had to be its leaders. As a result, Hutuism, Christian morality, and hard work became the cornerstones of the two Presidents, instead of the ideas of socialism and revolution, popular elsewhere in the postcolonial world (for example, "ujamaa" or African socialism in neighboring Tanzania under Mwalimu Julius Nyerere, and the "Theology of Liberation" popular in South America in the 1970s and 1980s). Both Kayibanda and Habyarimana promoted a rural ethics: hard working poor, Catholic (or at least Christian) peasants in the countryside, content to stay there.

Both the State and the Church instilled these values of Christian morality, hard work, obedience, and dependence on the Church and State power structures, thus ensuring the regulation of people's behavior in all aspects of life. As an example, despite the high birth rate, the government's hands were tied by its ally's adamant opposition to birth control; no new policy on this issue could pass without the blessing of the Catholic Church. Abortion was illegal and contraceptive methods anathema until the 1980s when the National Population Office was created, probably after some kind of behind-the-scene understanding between the State and the Church—afterwards, abortion continued to be illegal, and the Church occasionally spoke against contraceptive methods. Paradoxically, in the 1970s and 1980s, Habyarimana used the argument of overpopulation to refuse the return of refugees until the Arusha talks of 1992-1993 forced a change on the issue.

The third form of legitimating came from international assistance programs. Unlike the insular Kayibanda, Habyarimana tried to open Rwanda to the outside world, establishing good relations with Rwanda's neighboring countries, traveling quite extensively to other countries, and attending international meetings. The major backer, however, became France, successively under President Valery Giscard d'Estaing in the 1970s and especially the socialist President François Mitterrand, with whom he entertained a very close relationship. Under Habyarimana, Rwanda became, in the eyes of international assistance, an African economic success story. Reliable roads, electricity, water, and telephone systems were built. It became the country of a thousand assistance projects (mostly in the agricultural sector) and a thousand aid workers. The volume of foreign aid to Rwanda increased from less than 5 percent in 1973 to 22 percent by 1991, a clear sign of confidence that the international community had in the performance of Rwanda. Blinded by the veneer of Christian morality publicly exhibited by Habyarimana, even Christian NGOs, including the European Christian Democratic Circles (especially the Belgian and German sections), turned a blind eye on human rights violations. One German missionary (Herbert Keiner) summarized this attitude when he qualified the Habyarimana government as "ein Entwicklungsdiktatur" (a development dictatorship),[97] an expression that betrayed the international community's lack of foresight. How can sustained development occur without basic democracy and respect for human rights? International donors were certainly aware of the politics of ethnic and regional quotas, identity cards bearing one's ethnic group, repeated human rights abuses, absence of democracy and freedom of speech, and a corrupt judiciary system.

Another form that Habyarimana used to legitimate his power was the organization of capricious presidential elections, which, according to the single party constitution, allowed only one candidate—himself. In the December 1988 election, for example, he received 99.98 percent of the vote. The exercise, far from being a democratic one, was indeed intended for the consumption of the international community, but it was a total waste of government money and people's time. In my native commune of Muyira (prefecture of Butare), on the day of such presidential elections in December 1988, the burgomaster of the commune (Adalbert Muhutu) left in the commune's truck a little before noon to report to his superiors that Habyarimana had received 100 percent of the vote in the commune. By the time he left, it was obviously too early for the polls to have closed. A corrupt opportunist who had enriched himself through bribery and embezzlement of public funds, he wanted his commune mentioned during the 12:45 pm news in Kinyarwanda (and the French news at 1:15 pm) to score political points with the MRND hierarchy. During the tarring, the ballots of the naysayers were probably never counted.

During the genocide, the same administrative structure and mentality prevailed in the country, and many MRND operatives were still in place, despite the political in-roads made by the political opposition. The MRND associates throughout the country saw in the killing frenzy the occasion to reclaim political ground and fully embraced the genocide ideology of Hutu Power. Moreover, those who did not agree with the genocide ideology were removed as quickly as it became clear that they would block the implementation of the "final solution" to what was referred to as the Tutsi problem.

How exactly did the totalitarian regime in place before and after April 6, 1994 lead perfectly normal people to join in the killing frenzy? It has been already established that since October 1990, the government had sought to galvanize the Rwandan civil war as a conflict between two distinct groups (the Hutu against the Tutsi), but this strategy failed. When it came to the genocide in 1994, the government in place, the Akazu, the military, and the Hutu Power supporters increased their effort to make killing the Tutsi every Hutu's responsibility. The RTLM and the national public radio played a critical role in the new propaganda effort of encouraging the killing of the Tutsi and every Hutu opposed to Hutu extreme ideology. The control of the national radio on April 6, 1994 by hardliners was very important in that it could be heard over the whole country, unlike RTLM which was well heard only around Kigali. Before this date, the Hutu Power had accused Radio Rwanda of sympathizing with the RPF, but now both radios worked in concert, even though Radio Rwanda was a little ambiguous and not as blatant as RTLM—an unnecessary distinction because everybody understood what was meant anyway. They constantly played on already known ideology, including the definition of the enemy within. "The enemy is that one from far away," one broadcast from Radio Rwanda said, "that one who harbors him, that one who hides his weapons. That is why you should watch those who pass and arrest them. RPF is the enemy for as long as they fight. We know where their supporters are in every commune."[98]

A listener to both radios told *African Rights* that the public radio would have a message like "the enemy—we know him. We only have one enemy; it is he who has never accepted the fact of the republic [i.e. those who favored the Tutsi monarch] and his allies. The enemy is he who operates from outside the country and who wants to put the country under foreign domination. The majority of the population [rubanda nyamwinshi] who have benefited from the 1959 revolution, rise up and make sure that the enemy and his accomplices are not around you."[99] RTLM was direct in its repeated calls to kill the Tutsi and attack the RPF sympathizers. It encouraged people to kill, for example, challenging people to fill the half-full mass graves; it directed killers to certain neighborhoods of Kigali where Tutsi were known to be hiding; it celebrated successful operations by the Interahamwe and spread rumors and lies about the success of the government forces against the RPF; and it promised rewards to those who did a good job of killing. "Those helping on roadblocks will be rewarded after the war is finished," RTLM journalist Kantano Habimana announced on May 23, 1994. "Those very active within the government and the army and who really 'work' [i.e. kill] are well known. They will get very nice rewards. Those who do not 'work' will receive no reward at all. This is not the time to fall ill."[100]

The two radios were the main source of information during the period of the genocide, and many people tuned to them to listen to inflammatory calls to murder and justifications of the killings by the ideologues of Hutu Power. Like the other strategies of indoctrination, radio broadcasts aimed to establish two camps, the killers (Hutu) and the killed (the Tutsi and any Hutu showing dissent). The formation of this new Hutu identity and solidarity without any regional consideration would thus be achieved through a common struggle and solidarity in the defense of the Hutu republic. In short, the message heard was: if you are a Hutu, kill the Tutsi or be killed. The ideal situation sought was to engage the collective responsibility of all the Hutu for the ultimate creation of a pure Hutu republic.

Government ministers and Hutu Power leaders used their appearance on the two radios to repeat what they were saying in public meetings, namely that killing the Tutsi and any Hutu sympathizers was a patriotic duty. They would also formulate their encouragement in a language that suggested normalcy, for example, calling the killing "umuganda," public work required of every adult Rwandan during the Habyarimana regime. On the waves and on the hills, they would encourage collective attacks to play on peer pressure. In using this language of normalcy, they aimed to create a new code of morality—if everybody is doing it, then it is not wrong.

The President and Prime Minister picked by Colonel Bagosora and the Hutu Power on April 8, 1994 were both from Butare, a region the extremists knew would not easily be drawn into the killing frenzy because of the strong bond between the Hutu and Tutsi (through strong intermarriage, among other things) and because it was the stronghold of the PSD opposition party and other parties opposed to the Hutu Power ideology. The préfet of Butare was the only Tutsi préfet in the country. A combination of these factors made Butare immune to the genocide for two weeks until the préfet was removed and replaced by another one who would do the bidding of the Hutu Power government. The President and the Prime Minister made several rounds in the prefecture haranguing and chastising people of Butare for their lack of concern about what was going on in the rest of the country. Sindikubwabo gave a new definition of the enemy, saying in a speech delivered in Butare on April 19, 1994, that the enemy was the FPR and all those who thought that what he called the "national problem" did not concern them. According to informants who were present, he was visibly angry and he insisted that those individuals be eliminated.

At the multiple meetings he held in Butare and other parts of the country during the months of April, May, and June, Prime Minister Kambanda proclaimed that indifference had to be forcefully condemned and everybody should choose his or her side, either the government or the RPF. After Sindikubwabo's and Kambanda's interventions in Butare, following a pattern used elsewhere, elite troops moved in to start the massacres and terrorize those who resisted the call to kill. Killings soon started in Butare on a large scale, involving the notorious Interahamwe and Hutu professionals of all walks. Massacres in Butare proved to be most devastating because there was a concentration of Tutsi who had fled from other parts of the country thinking that the massacres would never reach the region. Afterwards, people would justify their involvement in the killing saying, "If I had not killed, my family and I would have been killed," "an order is an order," or "an order is heavier than stone."

Wherever propaganda failed, a combination of terror and incentives was used. Many Hutu in such prefectures as Butare and Gitarama refused to heed the call to kill for at least two weeks. In these instances, the Presidential Guard and Interahamwe were brought in to force the local population to kill. Many Rwandans had heard about the cruelty of Interahamwe, so their appearance in a region sufficed to sway a number of people and thus make them unwilling executioners, even though they became quite willing after the first killings and rewards in the form of looting. Killers would kill wealthy Tutsi or Hutu of the opposition and take their property; sometimes people were wrongly accused of siding with the enemy so their property could be taken. In few instances, those who paid huge sums of money to the attackers were left alone. In a country stricken with chronic poverty, looting was indeed a great incentive. It allowed the poor to have things they had seen the salaried Rwandans consume or possess; they could drink Primus or Miitzig beer, they could drive a car, own or sell a Television set, a computer, furniture, and other materials that they could not otherwise afford. A few weeks into the genocide, looting became the main preoccupation in some areas that even Hutu could become victims of fellow Hutu attackers who wanted their possessions.

Another form of looting was killing Tutsi's cows and collectively eating them. I asked an informant who now lives in France and whom I knew had participated in this activity why and if he felt compelled to eat the meat. He lived in the town of Nyanza in the prefecture of Butare and helped man one of the roadblocks in his neighborhood. He told me that if he had not eaten the meat he was given, his family and himself could have paid with their lives. Since the collective eating of Tutsi's cows was tantamount to participating in the massacres of the Tutsi, refusal to participate in this collective act would attract attention to him. I did not buy his claims. He certainly had the choice of not eating the meat. He could have taken the raw meat inside the house and refrain from cooking and eating it with his wife and children. Though he probably was not one of the sadistic killers, he was known, even before the genocide, to be an opportunistic employee who was always seeking favors from his supervisor by telling on other employees. Anyway, when you get the "I had no choice" excuse from everybody, you want to say, "what if all of you had made the right choice?" My informant replied, "You had to be there to understand. There was suspicion all around; so people did not want to take any chances."

An aspect that renders the concept of Primo Levi's "gray zone" even more valid in the case of the Rwandan genocide is the opposition to the ultimate evil. In spite of all the terror, violence, incentives, and propaganda, there were still people who courageously refused to join the killing and instead hid the Tutsi. As in other acts of mass murder in the history of humanity, there were many Rwandans and expatriates who risked their lives despite generalized moral bankruptcy and the betrayal of human values. There are documented reports of Hutu who assisted, hid, or protected Tutsi (friends, relatives, and complete strangers), and some of them died as a result of their refusal to be involved in the genocidal madness.[101] In parts of Gitarama and Butare, leaders (such as the prefect of Butare and the burgomasters of Ntyazo and Nyabisindu) refused to obey the order to kill, and Hutu and Tutsi in Muyira, Ntyazo, and Nyabisindu, among other communes, fought interahamwe attackers together until military attacks and political action weakened their resolve and thus the killers could complete their work.[102]

Conclusion

The discussion of the different players in the Rwandan genocide as well as the multiple and complex motivations of the thousands of ordinary Rwandans who became executioners has shown that what I have called the Gisenyi-Ruhengeri axis was the sine qua non of the unfolding of the catastrophic killings of April-July 1994. Confronted with losing the power they had conquered on July 5, 1973, the military and intellectual elites saw in the protocols of the 1993 Arusha peace accord the end of the privileges that they had enjoyed for only 20 years. They were not going to let go without a serious fight, especially because they dominated the army. They used the 1990-1994 period to promote extreme Hutu ideology, commonly known as Hutu Power, which eventually attracted a considerable number of Hutu from the rest of the country. So what was essentially a political struggle carefully exploited the flawed Rwandan historiography to turn the Hutu against the Tutsi and the Hutu who opposed the genocidal ideology. In other words, the main motive of the killings was power, but the ideological instruments had been created by the Hamitic Hypothesis and the appropriation of that myth by both the Hutu and the Tutsi elites, who imposed it on the Rwandan collective consciousness since the 1950s.

Conclusion

Remembering the Rwandan Genocide

Memory is life, always embodied in living societies and as such in permanent evolution, subject to the dialectic of remembering and forgetting, unconscious of the distortions to which it is subject, vulnerable in various ways to appropriation and manipulation, and capable of lying dormant for long periods only to be suddenly reawakened. History, on the other hand, is the reconstruction, always problematic and incomplete, of what is no longer. Memory is always a phenomenon of the present, a bond of tying us to the eternal present; history is a representation of the past. Memory, being a phenomenon of emotion and magic, accommodates only those facts that suit it. It thrives on vague, telescoping reminiscences, on hazy general impressions or specific symbolic details. It is vulnerable to transferences, screen memories, censorings, and projections of all kinds. History, being an intellectual, nonreligious activity, calls for analysis and critical discourse. Memory situates remembrance in a sacred context. History ferrets it out; it turns whatever it touches into prose.
--Pierre Nora, "General Introduction: *Between Memory and History*"

Towards a Taxonomy of Memory: A Comparative Perspective

Discussing the history and memory of the Holocaust, LaCapra posits two reasons pertaining to the relevance of memory: "the importance of trauma" and the interest in "memory sites" (lieux de mémoire).[1] It goes without saying that people who survive horrendous acts of dehumanization and all types of humiliation will experience trauma. In the case of genocide, for example, trauma will have a national dimension. In addition to touching the targeted race or ethnic group, it will necessarily enter the collective conscience, thus generating collective responsibility.

In post-World War II West Germany, leaders affirmed time and again German national responsibility even though the atrocities were committed mainly because of one man, Adolf Hitler, in the name of and involving the German people. In an address during the ceremony commemorating the 40th anniversary of the liberation of concentration camps at the site of the former Bergen-Belsen concentration camp, April 21, 1985, Chancellor Helmut Kohl asserted that "reconciliation with the survivors and descendants of the victims is only possible if we accept our history as it really was, if we Germans acknowledge our shame and our historical responsibility, and if we perceive the need to act against any efforts aimed at undermining human freedom and dignity."[2] Chancellor Kohl talked about the Holocaust as "the darkest, most painful chapter in German history."[3] Before invoking the presence of survivors at the Bergen-Belsen concentration camp, the Chancellor said, "A nation that abandons its history forsakes itself."[4]

Likewise, on May 8, 1985, in a speech in the Bundestag during the ceremony commemorating the 40th anniversary of the end of the war in Europe and of National Socialist tyranny, Richard von Weizsäker, President of the Federal Republic of Germany, reiterated Chancellor Kohl's point in asserting that

> The vast majority of today's population were either children then or had not been born. They cannot profess a guilt of their own for crimes that they did not commit. No discerning person can expect them to wear a penitential robe simply because they are Germans. But their forefathers have left them a grave legacy. All of us, whether guilty or not, whether old or young, must accept the past. We are all affected by its consequences and liable for it. The young and old generations must and can help each other to understand why it is vital to keep alive the memory.[5]

This "grave legacy" that Chancellor Kohl repeatedly affirmed must be assumed by the German nation: "Germany bears historical responsibility for the crimes of the Nazi tyranny. This responsibility is reflected not least in never-ending shame."[6] In his speech, he repeated "historical liability" and "dark era of our history."[7] Since there could possibly be no reparation to "suffering and death, pain and tears, the only answer," he concluded, "can be collective commemoration, collective mourning, and a collective resolve to live together in a peaceful world."[8]

In his book about how the Nazi past was manipulated by the two Germanys after World War II, Jeffrey Herf showed how political choices conveniently affected the memory of the Holocaust for political purposes and certainly poses a crucial question as to how a now re-united Germany is going to reconcile two opposing political views of the Nazi past.[9]

A second example of how trauma enters the collective conscience in the form of memory or the duty of memory is that of the French obsession with the Vichy regime that collaborated with the Germans in the repression, deportation, and extermination of the Jews as well as the shame of the regime itself, embodied in the French conscience. The French obsession with the Vichy past translates in many aspects including the importance of history in contemporary French society, the regular, annual commemorations of events of the 1940s, and the many memory sites found all over the country. During my summer 1999 visit to France, for example, I could observe on the Paris metro station walls as well as on streets panels that said "Ceux qui ont dit NON" (Those who said NO) with the names and pictures of Charles de Gaulle, Jean Moulin, Guy Moquet, and Leclerc. These names evoke, as they celebrate resistance, a permanent representation of the Vichy regime in the French historical conscience.

A perspicuous historian of contemporary France, Henry Rousso has termed this French trauma the *Vichy Syndrome.*[10] He posits three main reasons to explain the traumatic nature of memories of Nazi Germany's occupation of France (1940-1944). First, Germany defeated and humiliated France; ninety thousand French soldiers were killed and newly 2 million taken prisoners, and German troops occupied France. A "civil war" broke out among and between the collaborators and the Resistance during the occupation and the period of "epuration" that followed the liberation of France. Charles de Gaulle's "resistancialism," among other factors, did not allow the French to properly mourn their national tragedy.[11] Instead, the "epuration" helped the

French gauge the whole extent of their defeat under the Vichy regime of Marechal Pétain.[12]

Second, the defeat of France in 1940 destroyed national institutions (the military and the administration) and disrupted the flow of goods and people. This sudden and seemingly easy shattering of the nation seriously "undermined" the imperial standing of France as a modern state. The Vichy government, Rousso argues, was founded on a dangerous paradox: on the one hand, the belief that it could replace the institutions left vacant in June 1940, and, on the other hand, the proposition that it could do so in collaboration with the occupying forces in spite of the civil war. Moreover, the forces of resistance that opposed Pétain and his regime and combated the German occupation were not unified, so that the result within France was a "civil war" with multiple facets: the Vichy regime and its collaboration, various groups of resistance, and certainly diverse forms and degrees of collaboration. This "guerre franco-française" was not a nouveauté, Rousso cautions, since already in the 1930s the issue of the internal enemy was problematized by the presence of several ideological constituencies: fascism, nazism, the Popular Front, or communism, depending on who was pointing to the "enemy within."[13] Added to these internal conflicts was the question of French anti-Semitism that antedated the current troubles. The difference was that Vichy's anti-Semitism, in the collaborationist spirit, was codified in law and justice.[14]

The third reason that prevented the French from properly dealing with the difficult past of the 1940-1944 Vichy regime and other attendant problems is the French experience of "mass terror, concentration camps, the systematic use of death as a political weapon.[15]

Henry Rousso argues that in addition to the "ubiquitous state, technology, and organized violence," the French understanding of the 1940s was complicated by the "globalization of trade, the unification of the marketplace, and the convergence of the people's outlooks over a large portion of the planet."[16] The fact that these changes on the global arena took place before the French had adequately dealt with their difficult past rendered this task more traumatic. It is important to note that Henry Rousso arranges his argument along the lines of collective memory, or rather national pain, alienation, and division. This hypothesis is centered around a government that accepted the defeat of the French people:

> The civil war, and particularly the inception, influence, and acts
> of the Vichy regime, played an essential if not primary role in
> the difficulties that the people of France have faced in reconcil-

ing themselves to their history—a greater role than the foreign occupation, the war, and the defeat, all things that, though they have not vanished from people's minds, are generally perceived through the prism of Vichy.[17]

In mapping the history and memory of World War II in France since 1944, Henry Rousso distinguishes four distinct periods that make up what he calls the "Vichy Syndrome," a linguistic and psychological (Freudian) construct that aims at capturing the collective trauma, anxiety, and obsession of a nation vis-à-vis its past. It is a syndrome, Rousso asserts, precisely because the end of the war, instead of putting an end to the trauma, "perpetuated and at times exacerbated it through its permanent presence in political, social, and cultural life" (10). The four periods are: (1) the unfinished mourning (1944-1954); (2) Repressions (1954-1971); (3) The broken mirror (1971-1974); and (4) Obsession (1970s-1980s).

Talking about the Vichy syndrome, Henry Rousso asserted, "to speak of the memory of Vichy is first to speak of 1999."[18] He quoted Saint Augustine's definition of time, "la mémoire, c'est la présence du passé" (memory is the presence of the past). This presence belongs to the collective domain. It is, so to speak, the historicity of the present. History and memory are thus shaped by the moment of locution. It is the moment of writing or (re)telling the story that is the origin of memory. As George Poulet suggested, "to apprehend the present as the generative act of time in its concrete reality is ... without a doubt, the tendency of our epoch."[19] This view of history concurs with what developments in information technologies make available to us, as we have now the possibility of experiencing news and events as they happen. Lynn Higgins calls this new reality "the historicity of the present," that is, "the media give us a present tense that is already historical."[20]

This historiographical perspective creates tension between history and the idea of collective memory which is, after all, a set of experiences told by political groups (political parties, for example), racial or ethnic groups (victims), religious groups (for example, Bosnians are Muslims and were targeted by the Serbs for ethnic cleansing in 1992, because of their religious affiliation, among other things), or even nations. Above all, collective memory is national memory. From this point of view, collective memory consists of a series of representations and actions of a public nature wrought upon the past. As such, it carries ideological import because it is an integral part of national identity. To call oneself American, Rwandan, or French is necessarily to commit oneself at least to a certain extent to American, Rwanda, or French history.

It is in this historiographical context that the speeches by Chancellor Kohl and President Richard von Weizsäcker of the Federal Republic of Germany (quoted a few pages before) find their full meaning in their commemoration of an event that reminds the German people of a national crime committed by an individual acting on behalf of the nation.

An interesting aspect of French collective memory is what historian Henry Rousso call the *resistancialist myth* constructed by General Charles de Gaulle during the period that Rousso terms *the repression of Vichy memory* (1954-1971).[20] He defines resistancialism as follows:

> This term, first coined after the liberation by adversaries of the purge, is used here in a rather different sense. By resistancialism, I mean, first, a process that sought to minimize the importance of the Vichy regime and its impact on French society, including its most negative aspects; second, the construction of an object memory, the "Resistance," whose significance transcended by far the sum of its active parts (the small groups of guerrilla partisans who did the actual fighting) and whose existence was embodied chiefly in certain sites and groups, such as the Gaullists and Communists, associated with fully elaborated ideologies; and, third, the identification of this "Resistance with the nation as a whole, a characteristic feature of the Gaullist version of the myth.[21]

This myth has to be interpreted for what it is: a political myth or discourse whose primary goal was to construct a strong sense of national identity imposed through a certain idea of collective memorialization of the past. General Charles de Gaulle was basically projecting an epic vision of history. An epic, let us recall, is a narrative (thus a construct) that tells the heroic deeds of (a) legendary figure(s) whose goal is the creation, invention, or narration of national history and identity. In resisting the idea that the Republic had ceased to exist during the Occupation, Charles de Gaulle nevertheless dexterously projected the myth of a new beginning, a new national history and identity of which he was the center as the legendary hero. De Gaulle's proposition that France as a nation had participated in the liberation of France, Rousso argues, does not mean that all the French participated in the Resistance—in fact not many Frenchmen were active in the resistance movement—but there was a consensus in the whole nation regarding the goals of the resistance movement.[21] The French were not particularly heroic since they were run over and humiliated, but they sustained the blow as a nation and stayed as a nation despite the humiliation, and France retained its place as a major power in world affairs.

Another aspect of resistancialism is that, according to de Gaulle, resistance was a national movement, a position he held since 1940, thus denying supremacy to resistance movements—the communists liked to call themselves the Resistance Party.[22] All things considered then, the resistancialist myth aimed at preserving and recreating a sense of national identity, incarnating the idea of resistance, creating a new legitimacy for de Gaulle (to replace Vichy's own claim of legitimacy), and establishing a sense of continuity for the Republic. Thus, resistancialism was an epic projection of the past on the present and the future of the French nation and de Gaulle's own positioning of himself as the heroic protagonist against the Occupation and mostly as the main political actor in post-World War II France.

The contradictions and conflicts of the 1940s will resurface after the death of de Gaulle. May 1968 and the new social ideologies it inspired as well as the publication of new books about the 1940's and the emergence of cases such as the Touvier Affair in July 1972, the Claus Barbie trial in 1987, and the trial of Maurice Papon in 1997-99: all these events summoned the past and marked the period of the return of the repressed memory. Rousso has recently revised the period he previously referred to as *obsession.*[24] Instead of talking about obsession, he now prefers to divide the period into two parts: (1) The 1970s to the 1980s, during which the issue of Vichy and collaboration was reevaluated, for example in cinematic representations. This reevaluation was justified by the fact that Vichy was part of the "Gaullian exorcism," a discourse of denial that did not give voice to anything that did not advance the resistancialist myth. (2) The 1980s and 1990s during which the question of resistance was re-reexamined. Most importantly, however, the question of anti-Semitism was seriously posed for the first time. It was previously absent from the public discourse. Since the 1980s, the issue of anti-Semitism has become the problem through which the memory of the 1940s is approached. The question of the spoliation of Jewish property has been asked and is being asked again. Along with the return of the question of resistance and the centrality of anti-Semitism, there is also the return of the memory of Vichy, notably via the trials of Claus Barbie and Maurice Papon. In 1987, the Barbie trial was dubbed the trial of memory. After his presidential election in 1995, President Jacques Chirac acknowledged the responsibility of France in the deportation of Jews.

Since the liberation, France has erected many memorials to commemorate the memory of occupied France—memory sites ("lieux de mémoire") that memorialize, and reflect on, the Vichy era. An authority on the subject, Pierre Nora defined a memory site (lieu de mémoire) as "any significant entity, whether material or non-material in nature, which by dint of human will or the work of time has become a symbolic element of the memorial heritage of any community (in this case, the French community)."[25] Memory sites loosely correspond to what Henry Rousso calls classic vectors of memory. Vectors of memory consist of processes that allow the present to position its discourses *on* the past. Classic vectors of memory include commemorations, memorials, monuments, official speeches, and accounts of witnesses whereas particular vectors of memory include associations of veterans, survivors, laws, and the judicial dispositions that came about as a result of what was remembered. Genocide judges, historians, defense attorneys, and witnesses are all particular vectors of memory.

Particular vectors of memory somehow take me back to a more personalized experience of trauma associated with a difficult past, in our case with the Holocaust and Nazism in Germany and the Nazi Occupation of France. I would like to discuss one example of a particular vector of memory, especially for its relevance to the taxonomy of memorialization that I seek to develop about Rwanda. My discussion here centers on the remarks that Elie Wiesel made on the occasion of the ceremony for Jewish Heritage Week and the presentation of the Congressional Gold Medal at the White House, on April 19, 1985, roughly two weeks before the controversial visit of President Ronald Reagan to West Germany. As part of the visit, Chancellor Kohl had invited President Reagan to visit the Bitburg Cemetery, where it was later revealed that 25 SS were also buried.

Elie Wiesel's remarks were very emotional, for as a concentration camp survivor he is still very much invested with the unimaginable, inhuman conditions of survival in a concentration camp. His speech, though by one individual, speaks for the millions who perished because of Nazism. He first talked of his own reconciliation with President Reagan: "But then, we were never on two sides. We were on the same side. We were always on the side of justice, always on the side of memory, against the SS and against what they represent."[26] Through his own memory of suffering, he viewed the medal as not his alone but as belonging "to all those who remember what SS killers have done to their victims. (...) When I write, I feel my invisible teachers standing over my shoulders, reading my words, and judging their veracity. And while I feel responsible for the living, I feel equally responsible to the dead. Their memory dwells in my memory."[27] It is because of this internalized memory that Wiesel could not keep silent about the gravity of the trip that Ronald Reagan was about to make to Bitburg. " I have learned the perils of language and those of silence," Wiesel said. "I learned that in extreme situations when human lives and dignity are at stake, neutrality is a sin. It helps the killers, not the victims."[28] He then went on to talk about the "solitude" of those who were in concentration camps, those who were alone in their suffering, while the world was totally indifferent. After invoking the uniqueness of the Holocaust, he pointed to the "danger of indifference, the crime of indifference. For the opposite of love, I have learned, is not hate, but indifference."[29] The point that Elie Wiesel wanted to get to President Reagan was that there is one way to redeem the indifference and be-trayal of the world in the face of the Holocaust, and that is to remem-ber: "And I believe, we believe, that memory is the answer—perhaps the only answer."[30] Remembering gave Wiesel the strength "to speak truth to power" and ask President Reagan not to go to Bitburg Ceme-tery because it also had SS graves. He suggested that Reagan "do something else, (to) find another way, another place."[31] He then in-voked a moral and ethical argument, saying: "The issue here is not politics, but good and evil. And we must never confuse them, for I have seen the SS at work, and I have seen their victims."[32] At this point, Wiesel came back to the emotional appeal, by mentioning the "suffer-ing and loneliness" of the concentration camps and retelling the story of loneliness, the hunger, "the terror, fear, isolation, torture, gas cham-bers, flames, flames rising to the heavens."[33]

All in all, Wiesel's address to President Reagan can be readily inscribed in the line of prescriptive memory, that is, the kind of mem-ory that seeks to influence political practices as well as social and cul-tural policies. The opposite of prescriptive memory is descriptive memory. Even thought it shares the elements of the former, the latter seeks to describe, document, erect, and record elements of memory.

Ethnicity and Memory

It took the international community a long time to call the butchery in Rwanda in 1994 by its right name: genocide. Even today, it is not difficult to find politicians in both Africa and Europe (especially in France and Belgium), journalists, university researchers in social sciences, genocide suspects in Rwandan prisons, and diverse groups within and without Rwanda who, are intent on trivializing the 1994 carnage, notably by advancing the theory of a double genocide, calling the killers the real victims, and generally invoking the civil war context

to justify the massacres as acts of self-defense. Early signs of the failure of the international community came in the way the genocide was
presented in the media as just another episode of entrenched, centuries-
long tribal conflict or at best as savage acts of barbarity regularly seen
on the African continent, thus failing to make any connection to what
happened during World War II when Hitler and his cronies unleashed
their annihilation apparatus against the Jews and other undesirable
groups.

      This simplistic view of the Rwandan strife was mainly based
on long held stereotypes about Africa in general. The international
community failed the memory of "never again!" forcefully voiced at
the end of World War II. It is as if history and the instruments of justice and memory established after World War II (the Nuremberg Stat-
ute, the United Nations Convention against Genocide, and the Universal Declaration of Human Rights) were just dead letters on pieces of
paper. These international instruments should be interpreted in the
sense that a government that plans and implements the extermination of
a part of its population because of race, ethnicity, religion, and political
opinion no longer qualifies as a government and thus renders nil the
concept of non-interference. This is no mere complaint, as the different
diplomatic representations in the capital city of Rwanda (Kigali) and
indeed the United Nations were fully aware of what was going on since
1990 and particularly after the signing of the Arusha Peace Agreement
in August 1993.

      The greatest challenge of the post-genocide Rwandan gov-
ernment and of the Rwandan people in general is to remember, never to
forget, by establishing mechanics and vectors of memory such as
memory sites (memorials, monuments, documentation centers on the
genocide, research, and annual commemorations), associations of survivors, and impartial trials of those who conceived and those who executed the orders. If the question of memory is neglected, or indeed if it
serves the convenient purpose of just changing actors, as many journalists and observers have noted since 1994, then Rwanda is doomed not
to recover from the annihilation of 1994. In the months that followed
the end of the genocide, some groups, instead of serving the memory of
the victims, turned themselves into associations of accusers intent on
settling old scores, or appropriating property. While the vast majority
of inmates certainly participated in the genocide, there is also a sizeable
percentage of prisoners who have been in prison since 1994 because
they are Hutu, or because someone coveted their property or their job.

      It is imperative that, whatever vectors of memory (both classic
and particular) are put in place, choices and decisions are not made *au*

rabais but are well thought out for the best benefit of the nation. The challenge is most daunting, for beneficial and profound changes will not occur without a comprehensive reinvention of such notions as authority, power, education, justice, law, family, gender, religion, and more. Somehow an epic vision of a new Rwandan society needs to be projected in the collective mind through public and official discourses, and should be complemented by dramatic changes or revisions of societal institutions. But will the Tutsi believe that they can peacefully live with those that belong to the ethnic group that exterminated three-quarters of Rwandan Tutsi in 1994?

As I argued throughout this book, the genocide in Rwanda was not and could not be the result of some "tribal" conflict tilting to one side, nor was it committed by a group harboring innate cognitive hatred of the Tutsi. Instead, it was the result of a well planned, rehearsed, and executed plan whose major ideologues came from the region of Gisenyi and Ruhengeri, who stood to lose their tight control of the country if the power-sharing arrangement known as the Arusha Peace Accord were implemented. There is not doubt that those who planned the genocide shared a profound hatred of the Tutsi, but they were also aware the ethnic card had been a very convenient way in the past for those who wanted to conquer power. Since the situation involved higher stakes in 1994, the ethnic game was elevated to apocalyptic proportions.

The Rwandan government has embarked on a program of national unity and reconciliation. In remembering the 1994 genocide in Rwanda, however, one must take care not to mix apples and oranges just for short-term political dividends. There is a grave issue of responsibility that must be shouldered by everyone in Rwanda. The idea of collective guilt is counter-productive in all instances, but it must be remembered that the genocide was planned by a small group of people in the name of all the Hutu, and it was mostly carried out by ordinary Hutu. The majority of Hutu did not share the genocide ideology, but they were eventually convinced or forced to kill. This disastrous reality has ominous consequences for the future of Rwanda. No matter what ideologies prevail within Rwanda now and in the future, the 1994 genocide constitutes a "historical liability" and a "dark era of our history," to use Helmut Kohl's expressions cited earlier in this conclusion. One can try to deny that genocide ever took place or even advance the theory of a double genocide, but no one can deny the weight of the legacy of 1994.

It is important to remember and celebrate the many Hutu who resisted the call to kill, those who fought with the Tutsi in some places to stop the Interahamwe from entering their towns or villages, and those who died because they had hidden Tutsi in their homes. Jean-Philippe Schreiber, however, cautions us to distinguish between the ethnic victims and the Hutu and the Tutsi political victims. He writes:

> The Tutsi victims of genocide and the Hutu and Tutsi victims of political assassinations did not die for the same reasons. Just as under Nazi yoke, the Jews—and non-Jews—were not persecuted for the same reasons. On the one hand, there were Jews deported for political reasons, and, on the other hand, Jews deported for racial reasons. Genocide pedagogy and historical rigor require us at present to distinguish between the victims so that facts are correctly understood and interpreted in the future. The reconciliation among Rwandans requires consideration of historical evidence, even if the weight of history is not always easy to accept.[34]

It would be a dangerous feat if Rwandan identity, especially Tutsi Rwandan identity after 1994, was solely defined by the 1994 genocide. Invoking the Shoah, Jean-Philippe Schreiber advises that, as the Jews strived not to define themselves solely with regard to the Shoah but also in consideration of what defined them through centuries, namely the message of Moses and other prophets, likewise Rwandans must be careful not to define memory only from the perspective of 1994. As Rwandans, the Tutsi have a long history before 1994.[35] As the Rwandans unlearn the fallacious historiography that placed a major role in the anti-Tutsi propaganda of the last fifty years or so, they should resist the temptation to replace it with another erroneous history tailored to the masters of the present. This is probably an ideal time for Rwandans to reinvent their social, cultural, and political institutions and imagine narratives of a Rwandan nation, not a Hutu or Tutsi country.

The ideal relationship between history and memory should be of constant dialogue and complementarity to cancel out shortcomings of each other. History can correct the potential *débordements* of memory, and memory can help minimize history's tendency to trivialize through its critical investigations. Even though it can hardly harness the plurality of historical interpretations, memory can beneficially serve as a reminder of the human emotions that come human tragedies.

The complementarity advocated between history and memory has severe limitations that can hardly be surmounted. There are aspects of memory that are close to the realm of history. The unspeakable horror of genocide, the humiliation, the torture and all means of annihilation render lived memory unspeakable and many times unspoken. Death puts an end to memory, and those who survive do not necessarily have the words to talk about their ordeal. In this sense, memory is non-existent, even though it can be recreated with the help of witnesses. Moreover, the testimony of a survivor comes from a biased perspective shaped by one's experience of a traumatic event. This presents no problem for memory (since it is primarily individual), but it complicates the role of history in its application of critical tools.

Because of the extreme suffering endured by the survivor, silence may be another major problem for memory and history. With time, different factors may color the original memory. These may include politics, new social realities, and new achievements that may altogether lead to a new sense of identity.

The oral nature of the survivor's testimony, especially in a country like Rwanda where the manipulation of truth is often an art, makes it urgent to record witness accounts sooner rather than later. It is well known that the Nazis were effective in destroying evidence of their horrendous deeds. Jean-Philippe Schreiber cites Itzh'ak Niborski and Annette Wievorka" to underscore the paramount importance of the survivor's story:[36] "témoigner est un acte de résistance en ce qu'il s'oppose au projet nazi d'effacer toutes les traces de l'existence des Juifs, et conserver de l'extermination les images servant leur dessein"[37] ("to testify is an act of resistance because it fights the Nazi project of erasing all traces of Jewish existence and saves from extermination the images of their scheme") (my translation).

Elie Wiesel has said that there cannot be justice for the dead. I would add that there cannot be justice for the survivors: the humiliation that the Jews endured in concentration camps and even before as their businesses were sacked, as they had to deal with racial laws in several countries of Europe, the deportations, the labeling with the Star of David, the Sarah and Samuel names given as middle names to female and male Jews respectively, and more, cannot possibly be reversed by any form of justice. So, Wiesel concluded, only memory is possible. The same applies to the Tutsi of Rwanda and those Hutu who opposed the 1994 carnage or paid of their lives for defending the Tutsi. As I have shown, the Tutsi served as scapegoats for Rwandan political and economic problems. They were humiliated and deceived in multiple ways; tortured; murdered in their houses, at roadblocks, and in churches and stadiums; and raped. Only memory is possible.

How do people who have lost most of their family members, who had limbs cut off during the genocide, who bear visible and hidden machete scars on their bodies, who were publicly humiliated, who were repeatedly gang-raped, who were infected with HIV/AIDS through rape, who were sex slaves during the three months of the genocide, who raise children given to them in violence, and who live in poverty, begin to take unity and reconciliation among the Tutsi and the Hutu seriously? What can memorials and other vectors of memory possibly mean to them?

The question of memory is further complicated by the negation and/or revision of genocide. In all known cases of genocide, killers tried to deny their responsibility for mass murder by accusing the victims of causing their own demise. For example, the Ottoman regime invoked Armenian provocation. The Kmers Rouges have never admitted their responsibility in the Cambodian killing fields. Many Hutu politicians and military officers who planned and implemented the genocide in Rwanda, such as Colonel Bagosora, have written and argued that the Tutsi brought it on themselves before of their greed and arrogance. Others have defended the position that the Rwandan Patriotic Front (RPF) attack on Rwanda on October 1, 1990 caused the 1994 genocide, as if genocide was a corollary of war. Because of its close ties with the Habyarimana regime, the International Christian Democracy has denied that a genocide ever occurred in Rwanda in 1994 and has claimed instead that that the Hutu were the real victims. The same opinion is widely shared by Hutu exile communities in Africa, Europe, and North America. There are historians and social scientists who have somewhat defended the same logic. Mahmood Mamdani's unfortunate choice of *When Victims Become Killers* as the title of his book on Rwanda suggests that the genocide was an instance of Hutu revenge on the Tutsi, a gross misrepresentation of Rwandan history since the Tutsi never organized genocide against the Hutu. Political domination in precolonial and during the colonial period should not constitute ground for equivalence with genocide.

Another obstacle to memory, unity, and reconciliation among the Rwandans is the state of fear and suspicion between the two major ethnic groups in Rwanda. While it might be politically incorrect to display these psychological states inside Rwanda, they are visibly displayed in the exile communities. For examples, Hutu and Tutsi communities in cities like Brussels and Montreal are so ethnically divided that they have bars for the Hutu and bars for the Tutsi. On a visit to Brussels in July 1999 doing research for this book, I was speaking with a Rwandan refugee when he suddenly turned mute. When he recovered his speech a few moments later, I asked him about the reason of his abrupt silence, and he pointed to a black man who had passed by us in the hotel lobby. My interlocutor had stopped talking because he thought that the man could be Rwandan. Even though we were speaking Kinyarwanda, we were not talking about Rwanda at all, but about life in Brussels in general. "What's the problem with you?" I asked. "You never know with Rwandans," he replied. "The man is not even Rwandan," I said. His logic was that the man could be not only a Rwandan but also a Hutu. Later on, I heard about a highly educated Rwandan living in exile in the Canadian province of Québec who has vowed not to shake the hands of any Rwandan he does not know, lest he should shake the hands of a Tutsi. In the past few years, I have heard many similar stories of ethnic animosity, but the two should suffice to express the bizarre relationship that the Hamitic Hypothesis has wrought on the consciousness of Rwandans. Wherever I have gone in the past four years, I have seen unambiguous signs that Rwandans have transported their lethal ethnic identities into exile. What is more, Hutu groups in the United States, Canada, and possibly in Europe, regularly collect money to send to the Interahamwe and former Rwandan soldiers operating in the Democratic Republic of Congo with the aim to reconquer power in Rwanda.

For the record, my interlocutor in Brussels was a Tutsi. He was not in Rwanda during the genocide, but much of his family was wiped out. The Rwandan fellow in Quebec was a Hutu from Ruhengeri. He had received a scholarship to do doctoral studies. He was not in Rwanda during the genocide either. If the political landscape had not changed in Rwanda in 1994, he would have gone back to be at least a director-general in a ministry or even a minister. This assertion might seem outrageous, but some people from Gisenyi and Ruhengeri went to school knowing what they were going to be after graduation. The Brussels acquaintance lost most of his family in Rwanda, and the Quebec fellow lost his opportunity to be a government minister. The two stories perhaps express in a bizarre way the challenge facing Rwandan for the foreseeable future. On the other hand, there are the Tutsi who faced extermination in 1994 and will continue to bear the physical and psychological scars of genocide. On the other hand, there are Hutu within and without Rwanda who are convinced that demographic majority should be the only basis for political exercise. If ethnic and regional politics in Rwanda is not replaced by political ideologies, the dreadful history of 1994 may well repeat itself. In the past, ethnic and regional politics decided who belonged to Rwanda, who could go into politics, who could be enlisted in the military, who would to school, and who would get good jobs. If Rwanda is to survive as a nation, there is urgent need to construct narratives of political majority, not ethnic majority. To me, the best form of memory for the victims of the 1994 genocide is one that discourages ethnic polarizations, empowers Rwandans to question the herd mentality, promotes multiple centers of power (not the deification of leaders), establishes cross-ethnic political formations, and develops a powerful and independent judicial system at the service of the nation, not at the mercy of powerful individuals or groups of individuals. If the 1994 genocide was the result of a variety of factors and motivations, minimizing its long term effects on the Rwandan society will also depend on the successful tackling of what made those motivations operational. The involvement of thousands of ordinary Hutu citizens in the execution of their Tutsi neighbors is probably the most troubling aspect of the 1994 genocide in Rwanda. The State project of genocide became a social project because of the use of well-defined social, historical, geographical (regional), ideological, and psychological strategies that enticed ordinary people to join the annihilation frenzy. It is these processes that need to be addressed in the short and long run.

Appendix

Some Important Dates in the History of Rwanda

1884-1885
The Berlin Conference divides Africa among European powers.

1894
Rwandan Mwami Kigeli IV Rwabugili receives von Götzen, a German captain.

1895
Rwanda becomes part of German East Africa protectorate along with Urundi and Tanganyika.

1896
Mwami Musinga Yuhi V succeeds Mibambwe IV Rutalindwa following the "Coup d'Etat" of Rucunshu.

1900
The *"Pères Blancs" or White Fathers* arrive in Rwanda. Musinga receives them, but he sends them to Save, thought to be an unfriendly place.

1917

Following the German defeat in Rwanda in 1916, Belgium rules the kingdom through indirect rule. The Mwami is no longer the absolute monarch, as he has to accommodate Belgian colonial authority, represented by a Belgian resident.

1923

The League of Nations mandates Belgium to administer both Rwanda and Burundi under the name of Ruanda-Urundi.

1925

Ruanda-Urundi becomes part of a larger Belgian Colonial entity: Ruanda-Urundi and Belgian Congo.

1931

Not well liked by the Belgians, King Musinga is forced to abdicate his throne. He is then exiled in Kamembe (current province of Cyangugu). The Belgian colonial administration enthrones Musinga's son, Rudahigwa, who received the throne name of Mutara III Rudahigwa

1935

The Belgian colonial administration initiates the distribution of identity cards that categorize Rwandans as "Hutu," "Tutsi," or "Twa," depending on how many cows they own. Using the functional logic discussed in Chapter Two, owners of ten or more cows are classified as "Tutsi," those with less than ten are given the category of "Hutu." This rigid classification freezes social categories and creates three supposedly discreet ethnic groups, thus sowing the seeds for future discord.

1943

Mutara III Rudahigwa is Christianized (he takes the name of Charles), resulting in a massive Christianization of Rwanda. Three years later, the Kingdom of Rwanda is dedicated to Christ the King.

The Belgian colonial administration in league with the Catholic Church initiates a series of administrative reforms that systematically replace Hutu chiefs with Tutsi chiefs appointed by the Mwami.

1946

Following the creation of the United Nations (UN) in 1945, Rwanda becomes a UN trustee territory in 1946. The UN mandates the Kingdom of Belgium to administer the territory.

1954

"Ubuhake," a clientship arrangement that mostly placed the Hutu at the service of Tutsi cattle owners, is abolished. Not surprisingly, King Rudahigwa's move angers those who benefited from the system.

1955
Jean-Paul Harroy becomes Governor of Ruanda-Urundi.

1956
In a bold but risky move, King Rudahigwa demands total independence from Belgium.

Mgr. Perraudin, a Swiss priest, becomes the head of the Roman Catholic Church in Rwanda. He would later play a pivotal role in the development of a new Hutu elite.

1957
With the guidance of his mentors (Governor Jean-Paul Harroy and Mgr. André Perraudin), Grégoire Kayibanda, a Hutu catechist and editor of the Catholic newspaper *Kinyamateka*, along with other Hutu intellectuals, publishes the "Hutu Manifesto" demanding the end to the monopoly of the Tutsi. The Catholic Church and the Belgian colonial administration encourage Grégoire Kayibanda and his associates to form political parties. Joseph Gitera launches APROSOMA (L'Association pour la Promotion Sociale des Masses) (Assocation for the Social Promotion of the Masses), initially favoring a rapprochement between the Hutu and the "petits" (little) Tutsi. Encouraged by the colonial administration whose aim is to sabotage the King and his supporters, Tutsi Chief Bwanakweri launches RADER (Le Rassemblement Démocratique Rwandais) (Rwandan Democratic Union) to attract both Tutsi   and   Hutu   and   thus   undermine   Tutsi   solidarity.

1959
King Rudahigwa dies in Bujumbura, Urundi, in mysterious circumstances. Many Rwandans still believe that the Belgian colonial administration was involved in his death.

Rudahigwa's half-brother succeeds him and adopts the name of Mwami Kigeli V Ndahindurwa. Both the Belgian colonials administrators and the emerging Hutu elite are unhappy with the way in which the succession takes place. They refer to it as a coup d'Etat.

UNAR (Union Nationale Rwandaise) (Rwandan National Union) and PARMEHUTU (Le Parti du Mouvement de l'Emancipation Hutu) (Party of the Movement for Hutu Emancipation). The former party, comprising the supporters of the King, demand immediate independence under a constitutional monarchy. As its name suggests, the latter appeals to the Hutu masses and aims to put an end to what it calls Tutsi colonization. To avoid alienating the Catholic Church and the colonial administration, it refrains from demanding immediate independence. In its name and ideology, PARMEHUTU is openly anti-Tutsi.

With the help of the Belgian Colonel G. Logiest and his Commandos, Hutu mobs burn Tutsi houses, kill Tutsi, and force thousands into exile in the Congo, Uganda, Burundi, and Tanzania. Mwami Kigeli V Ndahindurwa himself leaves his kingdom.

1960

The Belgian colonial administration organizes communal elections, which are easily won by PARMEHUTU under Grégoire Kayibanda, who then becomes Prime Minister of a provisional government.

1961

A referendum on the monarchy is organized under the auspices of the United Nations. With the state of civil war and terror, the referendum overwhelmingly rejects the monarchy.

1962

July 1: Rwanda officially becomes an independent country. Grégoire Kayibanda becomes the first President of independent Rwanda.

1963

Tutsi exiles, called *"inyenzi"(cockroaches),* launch attacks against Rwanda. Officials organize the massacre of more than 10 thousand Tutsi in Gikongoro.

1969

An MDR-PARMEHUTU party convention renames it MDR (Mouvement Démocratique Républicain) (Democratic Republican Movement), dropping PARMEHUTU. There is a North vs. South tension within the party, as Kayibanda favors Hutu from Gitarama, his region of origin.

1973

There are massacres of Tutsi throughout the country. They are expelled from high schools, from the National University of Rwanda, and from the civil service. Many go into exile. There is general unrest in the country. General Juvenal Habyarimana, defense minister in the Kayibanda government, stages a military coup with the help of other senior officers, the majority of whom are from Gisenyi and Ruhengeri.

1975

President Habyarimana launches MRND (Mouvement Révolutionaire National pour le Déloppement) (National Revolutionary Movement for Development). Every Rwandan is automatically a member of the party. The party structure coincides with that of the State.

1978

President Habyarimana organizes a referendum on a new constitution that sanctifies MRND as the only political party in Rwanda.

1979

A group of Rwandan exiles in Kenya and Uganda establish RANU (Rwandese Alliance for National Unity) in Nairobi (capital city of Kenya) in order to find a solution to the problem of Rwandan refugees.

1982

The Ugandan government of Milton Obote expels thousands of Rwandans. The Habyarimana government reluctantly accepts entry to some whom it detains in refugee camps inside Rwanda; others are killed, and others enter Tanzania.

1987

RANU is renamed RPF (Rwandese Patriotic Front).

1990

October 1: RPF launches a military attack against Rwanda. October 4: the Rwandan government stages a dramatic attack on Kigali and lies to the Rwandan people that it is an RPF attack. The drama is used to gain help from the French, Belgian, and Zairian governments. Also, thousands of Tutsi and southern Hutu are jailed, accused of complicity with the RPF.

Massacres of Tutsi occur in different parts of Gisenyi and Ruhengeri and in other parts of the country between 1990 and 1994.

1991

New political parties are established. The three major parties have their strongholds in the political south—MDR, PSD, and PL.

1992

The opposition parties control half of the ministerial portfolios and vow to start direct negotiations with the RPF. This new front directly threatens the hegemony of the military and political elite of Gisenyi and Ruhengeri.

March 1992: President Habyarimana's party and his extremist supporters stage the first significant attack outside Gisenyi-Ruhengeri, in the Bugesera region. Hundreds of Tutsi die.

1993

August: The Rwandan Government, under national and international pressure, signs a comprehensive peace agreement with the RPF—it consists of several protocols collectively called "The Arusha Peace

The Debris of Ham

Agreement."

August 1993-April 1994:

Through a series of derailing techniques, the Habyarimana government resists the implementation of the peace agreement and the establishment of the Broad Based Transitional Government.

1994
April 6: President Habyarimana's plane is hit by a missile as it prepares to land in Kigali, after a peace summit in Dar-es-Salam, Tanzania. President Habyarimana and his Burundian colleague, President Ntaryamira, die.

The genocide starts.

The RPF launches a military campaign that will lead to the capture of Kigali, the capital city in early July and the establishment of a government of national unity.

1996/1997
Rwanda attacks refugee camps in eastern Zaire in an effort to thwart military incursions from soldiers of the former Rwandan army (ex-FAR) and Interahamwe. The operation also leads to the toppling of Marechal Mobutu Sese Seko, who is replaced by Joseph Kabila.

1998
Following insecurity caused by the Ex-FAR and Interahamwe in several prefectures, particularly Gisenyi, Ruhengeri, Kibuye, and Gitarama, Rwandan forces again enter Zaire (which Joseph Kabila has renamed the Democratic Republic of the Congo in 1997).

Notes

Introduction: From Auschwitz to Rwanda

1. Elie Wiesel, *Night* (New York: Bantam Books, 1982), 43.
2. Elie Wiesel, "Does the Holocaust Lie Beyond the Reach of Art?" *New York Times*, 17 April 1983.
3. *The Drowned and the Saved*. Levi chose the epigraph to his book from Samuel Taylor Coleridge, *The Rime of the Ancient Mariner*:

> Since then, at an uncertain hour,
> That agony returns,
> And till my ghastly tale is told
> This heart within me burns.
> (vv. 582-85)

4. Ibid., 86-87.
5. For a more detailed discussion of the regional element in the Hutu movement under the First Republic, see René Lemarchand, *Rwanda and Burundi* (New York: Praeger Publishers, 1970), 228-263.
6. Expression used by Primo Levi, *The Drowned and the Saved*, 105-126.
7. Aimé Césaire, *"Discourse on Colonialism." Colonial Discourse and Post-colonial Theory: A Reader, ed.* Williams Patrick and Laura Chrisman (New York: Columbia University Press, 1994), 177.
8. *Au revoir les enfants*, film by Louis Malle, 1987.9. Lynn Higgins, *New Novel, New Wave, New Politics* (Lincoln and London: University of Nebraska Press, 1996), 27.

10. Daniel J. Goldhagen, *Hitler's Willing Executioners: Ordinary Germans and the Holocaust* (New York: Alfred A. Knopf, 1996).

Chapter One: Framing Rwanda: Ethnic and Nationalist Conflicts in the Post-Cold War Era

1. Irving Massey, *Identity and Community: Reflections on English, Yiddish, and French Literature in Canada* (Detroit: Wayne State University Press, 1994), 18.
2. H. R. Isaacs, *Idols of the Tribe* (New York: Harper & Row, 1975), 3.
3. Brian Du Toit, ed., *Ethnicity in Modern Africa* (Boulder, Colorado: Westview Press, 1978), 3.
4. Ibid., 2.
5. Julian Huxley & A.C. Haddon, *We Europeans: A Survey of "Racial" Problems* (London: Penguin Books Ltd., 1939), 91-92.
6. Du Toit, 2.
7. Gunnar Myrdal, *An American Dilemma: The Negro Problem and Modern Democracy* (New York: Harper & Brothers, 1944).
8. M. Lloyd Warner & Leo Srole, *The Social System of American Ethnic Groups* (New Haven: Yale University Press, 1965), 28.
9. Paul A. F. Walter, *Race and Culture Relations* (New York: McGraw-Hill Book Co., 1952), 21.
10. Frederick C. Gamst & Edward Norbeck. eds., *Ideas of Culture, Sources and Uses* (New York: Holt, Rinehart & Winston, 1976), 240.
11. Du Toit, 5.
12. Ibid.
13. Seligman, quoted in Du Toit, 6.
14. Siefried F. Nadel, *The Nuba: an Anthropological Study of the Hill Tribes in Kordofan* (London: Oxford University Press, 1947), 13.
15. Susan Olzak and Joane Nagel, eds., *Competitive Ethnic Relations* (Orlando: Academic Press, 1986), 1-14.
16. Suzan Olzak & Joane Nagel. eds., *Competitive Ethnic Relations* (Orlando: Academic Press, 1986), 1-2.
17. Ibid., 2.
18. Ibid.
19. Ibid.
20. Ibid.
21. See also Joane Nagel and Susan Olzak, "Ethnic Mobilization in New and Old States: An Extension of the Competition Model" *Social Problems* 30, 127-142.
22. Susan Olzak, "A Competition Model" *Competitive Ethnic Relations*, ed. Susan Olzak and Joanne Nagel (Orlando: Academic Press, Inc., Orlando, 1986), 17-46.
23. Joane Nagel, "The Political Construction of Ethnicity" *Competitive Ethnic Relations*, ed. Susan Olzak and Joanne Nagel (Orlando: Academic Press, Inc., Orlando, 1986), 93-112.

24. The colonial construction of ethnicity in Rwanda is discussed in detail in the next chapter.

25. See also Geertz (1963, 120). He argues that the central government in such cases is "a valuable new prize over which to fight and a frightening new force with which to contend."

26. Joanne Nagel "The Political Construction of Ethnicity" *Competitive Ethnic Relations*, ed. Susan Olzak and Joanne Nagel (Orlando: Academic Press, Inc., 1986), 93-112,98.

27. Ibid.

28. J.- C. Willame, *Aux sources de l'hécatombe rwandaise* (Bruxelles & Paris : Cahiers Africains/L'Harmattan, 1995). See also by the same author *Les Belges au Rwanda* (Bruxelles : Editions Complexe/GRIP, 1997).

29. Ibid., 61.

30. Human Rights Watch /Africa, *Emptying the Hills: Regroupement in Burundi* (New York, 2000).

31. Ibid.

32. Joanne Nagel, "The Political Construction of Ethnicity" *Competitive Ethnic Relations*, ed. Susan Olzak and Joanne Nagel (Orlando: Academic Press, Inc., 1986), 93-112, 101.

33. Ibid.

24. Ibid.

35. For a detailed discussion of this issue, see Jean-Pierre Chrétien, *Le défi de l'ethnisme: Rwanda et Burundi 1990-1996* (Paris: Karthala, 1996), 160-163.

Chapter Two: The Hamitic Hypothesis and Rwandan Historiography

1. Donald L. Horowitz, *Ethnic Groups in Conflict* (Berkeley, Los Angeles, and London: University of California Press, 1985), 74.

2. Ibid.

3. Emmanuel Ntezimana, "Histoire, culture et conscience nationale: le cas du Rwanda des origines à 1900" *Etudes Rwandaises*, juillet 1977, 488-489, quoted by Jean-Pierre Chrétien, *Le défi de l'ethnisme*: Rwanda et Burundi 1990-1996 (Paris: Karthala, 1997), 21.

4. Mahmood Mamdani, *When Victims Become Killers: Colonialism, Nativism, and the Genocide in Rwanda* (Princeton, NJ: Princeton University Press, 2001) uses this assertion as its premise, claiming historical dispensation for the thousands of Hutu who participated in the killing of their Tutsi neighbors in 1994. The argument runs as follows: the Hutu were victims of Tutsi and Belgian colonial oppression in the past; they became killers in 1994 because they did not want to be victims again. This line of argumentation ignores the complexity involved in the social engineering that took about three years.

5. Bronislaw Malinowski, *Magic, Science and Religion and Other Essays* (New York: Doubleday Anchor Books, 1954), 146.

6. René Lemarchand, *Rwanda and Burundi* (New York, Washington, and London: Praeger Publishers, 1970), 33.

7. Pierre Smith, "Origine de l'inégalité" *Le récit populaire au Rwanda*, ed. Pierre Smith (Paris: Armand Colin, 1975), 140-147.

8. Pierre Smith, *Le récit populaire au Rwanda*, 39.

9. Ibid., 39-40.

10. Pierre Smith, *Le récit populaire au Rwanda* (Paris: Armand Colin, 1975), 40 (My translation)

11. Cited in Alexis Kagame, " La poésie du Rwanda" *Compte-rendu des travaux du séminaire d'anthropologie sociale* (Astrida: IRSAC, 1952), 20.

12. Myth cited by M. d'Hertefelt, "Myth and Political Acculturation in Rwanda," paper presented at the XIVth conference of the Rhodes-Livingstone Institute for Social Research, Lusaka (Zambia), Armch, 1960.

13. Helene Codere, "Power in Rwanda" *Anthropologica*, Volume IV, No.1, 45-87. Quoted in Rene Lemarchand (1970).

14. Jacques Maquet, *The Premise of Inequality* (London/New York: Oxford University Press, 1961).

15. For a different reading of the Rwandan myths of origin, see Josias Semujanga, *Récits fondateurs du drame rwandais: discours social, ideologies et stéréotypes* (Paris: L'Harmattan, 1998), 68-73. Semujanga argues that the three ethnic labels are in fact symbols of a tripolar representation of Umunyarwanda (the Rwandan)—an interesting reading, even though he uses elements outside the Rwandan mythic realm; he borrows the Biblical notion of the Holy Trinity, a cultural sphere (Christianity) that his book otherwise faults for the destruction of the tripolar sense of Rwandan identity.

16. Malinowski, 101.

17. Aimé Césaire, "Discourse on Colonialism" *Colonial Discourse and Postcolonial Theory*, ed. Patrick Williams and Laura Chrisman (New York: Columbia University Press, 1994), 172-181.

18. Ibid., 178.

19. Morgan Goodwyn, quoted by Henry Louis Gates, Jr. and Nellie Y. McKay, eds., *The Norton Anthology of African American Literature* (New York: Norton, 1997), xxix.

20. David Hume, "Of National Characters" quoted by Henry Louis Gates, Jr and Nellie Y. McKay, eds. *The Norton Anthology of African American Literature* (New York: Norton, 1997), xxx.

21. Immanuel Kant, quoted in *The Norton Anthology of African American Literature*, xxx-xxxi

22. Immanuel Kant, quoted in *The Norton Anthology of African American Literature*, xxxi.

23. Adolphys Frederick Mecklenburg, *In the Heart of Africa* (London: Cassell, 1910), 54.

24. Hans Meyer, *Die Barundi* (Leipzig: Otto Spamer, 1916), 14.

25. Ibid., 15.

26. Minstère des colonies, *Rapport de l'administration belge du Ruanda-Urundi, 1925*, 34. Quoted in Gérard Prunier, *The Rwanda Crisis: History of a Genocide* (New York: Columbia University Press, 1995), 6.

27. Meyer, 15.

28. Quoted in Prunier, 6.

29. *Rapport annuel du Territoire de Nyanza* (1925). Quoted in G. Prunier, 6.

30. Edith R. Sanders, "The Hamitic Hypothesis; its origins and functions" *Time Perspective, Journal of African History*, 1969, X-4: 521-532.

31. John Hanning Speke, *Journal of the Discovery of the Source of the Nile* (London, 1863). See Chapter IX "History of the Wahuma."

32. R.Pagès, *Un Royaume Hamite au Centre de l'Afrique* (Brussels : IRCB, 1933). Translation : *A Hamitic Kingdom in Central Africa.*

33. Louis de Lacger, *Le Ruanda* (Kabgayi, Rwanda, 1959).

34. Father van den Burgt, *Dictionnaire Français-Kirundi*, LXXV. Quoted in G. Prunier, 7.

35. Mgr Le Roy in J. B. Piollet, *Les missions catholiques françaises au XIXème siècle* (Paris : les Missions d'Afrique, 1902), 376-377. Quoted in G. Prunier, 7-8. Prunier rightly mocks Le Roy's use of the expression "love of money" as proof of Tutsi's Semitic origin. Le Roy's invocation hardly veils another centuries-long racial bias: Anti-Semitism.

36. Prunier, 8.

37. Dominique Franche, "Généalogie du genocide rwandais—Hutu et Tutsi: Gaulois et Francs" *Les Temps Modernes*, No. 582, 1995, 1-58, 12.

38. Sir Harry Johnston, *The Uganda Protectorate*, vol. 2 (London: Hutchinson, 1902), 486-610.

39. Pierre Ryckmans, *Dominer pour servir* (Brussels, 1931), 26. Quoted in Prunier, 11. See also Jean-Pierre Chrétien, "Hutu et Tutsi au Rwanda et au Burundi" *Au Coeur de l'ethnie*, ed. J.L. Anselle et E. M'Bokolo (Paris : La découverte, 1985), 138.

40. Louis de Lacger, 522-23.

41. Louis de Lacger, 512.

42. Quoted in Josias Semujanga, *Récits fondateurs du drame rwandais : discours social et idéologies* (Paris: L'Harmattan, 1998), 129.

43. Prunier, 30.

44. "Kubandwa" was a form of initiation whose goal was to bring young adults under the spiritual protection of imandwa, chief among them Ryangombe. Previous graduates of the initiation, called cult fathers or cult mothers, served as the role models of the new initiates and taught them the secret language and songs honoring the ancient heroes (Ryangombe and other imandwa). Painted in white clay and acting quite wildly, the initiates called each other Ryangombe, were beaten and made to swear obscenities against their mothers as a way of showing that they had grown up. They drank a sour, red potion, symbolizing blood and suggesting that all the initiates shared the same blood and became members of the category of all adults. Toward the end of the ceremony, the new initiates lay besides their cult mothers or fathers for a few minutes to take on the heroic qualities of imandwa and begin a new life as adults.

45. For a more detailed discussion of this cultural transformation, see Josias Semujanga, 74-82.

46. Charles Gabriel Seligman, *Races of Africa*, 4th ed. (London: Oxford University Press, 1966).

47. Serge Tornay, "Pour mémoire: l'hypothèse hamitique" *Rwanda: un génocide du XXè siècle*, ed. Raymond Verdier, Emmanel Decaux & Jean-Pierre Chrétien (Paris: L'Harmattan, 1995), 57-6, 60.
48. Jacques Maquet, "Societal and Cultural Incorporation in Rwanda" in Ronald Cohen (1970), 201-216, 204.
49. Ibid.
50. Ibid.
51. Ibid., 205.
52. Ibid., 206.
53. Tharcisse Gatwa, *The Churches and Ethnic Ideology in Rwandan Crises (1900-1994)* (Ph.D. dissertation, University of Edinburgh, 1998), 84; Mahmood Mamdani, *When Victims Become Killers: Colonialism, Nativism, and the Genocide in Rwanda* (Princeton, NY: Princeton University Press, 2001), 98-99.
54. Maquet, 213-214.
55. Ibid., 214.
56. Pierre del Perugia, *Les derniers rois mages* (Paris: Phoebus, 1978), 35.

Chapter Three: The Debris of Ham : From the 1959 Hutu Revolution to the Institutions of Ethnic and Regional Otherness

1. Jean-Jacques Maquet and Marcel d'Hertefelt, *les élections en société féodale* (Brussels: ARSOM, 1959), 26. Quoted in Gérard Prunier, *The Rwanda Crisis: History of a Genocide* (New York: Columbia University Press, 1995), 43.
2. Gérard Prunier, *The Rwanda Crisis: History of a Genocide* (New York: Columbia University Press, 1995), 45.
3. The best account of these social, political, and economic transformations that significantly affected the clientship system is probably in Catherine Newbury's *The Cohesion of Oppression: Clientship and Ethnicity in Rwanda, 1860-1960* (New York: Columbia University Press, 1988).
4. Ibid.. 42.
5. Reference to Josias Semujanga, *Récits fondateurs du drame rwandais : discours social idéologies et stéréotypes* (Paris : L'Harmattan, 1998).
6. F. Nkundabagenzi, ed., *Rwanda Politique* (Bruxelles : CRISP, 1962), 22-23. (My translation)
7. Ibid., 23. (My translation)
8. Ibid., 28. (My translation)
9. Ibid., 35-36. (My translation)
10. *Rwanda Politique*, 88.
11. Ibid., 244-246 and 247-253.
12. Ibid., 248.
13. Ibid., (My translation). Note the close similarity of this discourse with the one that accompanied the 1994 genocide of the Tutsi described as foreigners and actually thrown into the Nyabarongo River, a shortcut to Ethiopia, according to the genocide ideologues. See detailed discussion in Chapter 6.
14. Jean-Pierre Chrétien, *Le défi de l'ethnisme : Rwanda et Burundi, 1990-1996* (Paris : Karthala, 1997), 37.

15. The Belgian vice-governor general later wrote in his memoirs that "the Tutsi wanted independence and were trying to get it as quickly as possible by sabotaging Belgian actions, whether technical or political. (...) The administration was forced to toughen its attitude when faced with such obstruction and hostility coming from chiefs and sub-chiefs with whom we had collaborated for so many years" (Jean-Paul Harroy, *Rwanda: du féodalisme à la démocratie 1955-1962*, Bruxelles: Hayez, 1984), 241.

16. Gérard Prunier, *The Rwanda Crisis: History of a Genocide* (New York: Columbia University Press, 1995), 50.

17. Colonel Guy Logiest, *Mission au Rwanda* (Bruxelles: Didier-Hatier, 1988), 135. Quoted Gérard Prunier, 49. (Translation by Prunier).

18. Donald L. Horowitz, *Ethnic Groups in Conflict* (Berkeley, CA: University of California Press, 1985), 291.

19. *The Old Regime and the French Revolution*, vii.

20. *Rwanda Politique*, 245.

21. *Rwanda Politique*, 245 and 247. (My translation)

22. Gérard Prunier, *The Rwanda Crisis*, 56.

23. Quoted by René Lemarchand, *Ruanda-Urundi*, p. 224; Josias Semujanga, *Récits fondateurs du drame rwandais*, 180-181.

24. See Jean-Pierre-Chrétien, *Le défi de l'ethnisme : Rwanda et Burundi, 1990-1996* (Paris : Karthala, 1997); Reyntjens, Filip, *L'Afrique des Grands Lacs en Crise, Rwanda-Burundi 1990-1994*.

25. The statutes of the single party stipulated that every Rwandan was automatically a member of the party. A zealous Secretary-General of the party publicly said that even the unborn children were members of the party.

26. One must note the change of vocabulary under the Habyarimana regime (1973-1994). Hutu, Tutsi and Twa were now referred to as "ethnic groups," not "races," as it had been the case during the colonial period and in the Kayibanda years (1962-1973). This change may have been for international consumption, however, since the two words are rendered by one word in Kinyarwanda: ubwoko. Whatever terminology may be used, however, undermined the linguistic, cultural, and religious unity of the Rwandan people, attributes that the three groups have shared for centuries. I deliberately avoided delving into the arguments (historical and otherwise) for the distinction between the three groups. Interested readers will find useful and not so useful discussions about this issue in numerous works cited in the bibliography.

Chapter Four: The Path to Genocide: Human Rights Violations as Genocide Rehearsals

1. A relatively detailed discussion of the refugee problem between 1959 and 1994 can be found in Gérard Prunier, *The Rwanda Crisis: History of a Genocide* (New York: Columbia University Press, 1995), 61-74; Mahmood Mamdani, *When Victims Become Killers: Colonialism, Nativism, and the Genocide in Rwanda* (Princeton: Princeton University Press, 2001), 159-184.

2. Gérard Prunier, *The Rwanda Crisis: History of a Genocide* (New York: Columbia University Press, 1995), 66.

3. Ibid., 66-67.

4. Ibid., 67.

5. Ibid., 72-73.

6. It was consistently rumored that Lizinde killed a few men whose wives he coveted.

7. André Sibomana, *Hope for Rwanda: Conversations with Laure Guilbert and Hervé Deguine*, trans. Carina Tertsakian (London: Pluto Press, 1999), 20-21. Father André Sibomana describes the circumstances of his colleague's work and death as follows: "Father Silvio had a lot of information about the abuses of the regime. He was talented and passionate. His investigations hit their target every time. He was made to resign on December 1985. He narrowly escaped several assassination attempts, including one in the offices of *Kinyamateka*. Finally, on November 7, 1989, a lorry crashed headlong into his car... he was killed on the spot. When the Belgian journalist Colette Braeckman interviewed President Habyarimana soon afterwards, the president replied with a jovial and cynical smile, 'In your country, there are also plenty of car accidents every weekend'" (21).

8. A report on human rights in Rwanda compiled by the association called "Association Rwandaise pour la Défense des Droits de la Personne et des Libertés Publiques ADL" (Rwandan Association for the Defense of Human Rights and Individual Freedom), created in September 1991 by independent university professors, lawyers, and civil servants, noted about the round-up that followed the October 1, 1990 Rwandan Patriotic Front (RPF):

> October 1, 1990: the "invincible" RPF (refugees in Uganda) cross the border again. It is the beginning of a dirty war. One observes multiple consecutive episodes: Zairian military aid to President Habyarimana; French military aid; Belgian diplomatic and military intervention; meetings in Dar-es-Salaam; the Nsélé accord (broken the next day). Very quickly, however, Tutsi inside Rwanda were designated as enemies or collaborators, and gathered (10 thousand suspects) in conditions described in the press. (A subsequent count, carried out by humanitarian associations, however, has shown that those prisoners comprised a majority of Hutu—61%--from the South; the current regime often confuses them with Tutsi. It seems there is only one Hutu authenticity, the one in the north, the President's region). (12) (My translation)

9. The "cellule" (cell) was the basic administrative unit during the Habyarimana regime. It was headed by a "responsable de cellule" (cell head) supervising five other members of the cell executive committee (called in French "membres du comité de cellule").

10. Roughly the equivalents of a county executive and a deputy-governor.

11. It was an international commission that investigated human rights violations in Rwanda since October 1, 1990 up to January 21, 1993. It comprised human rights monitors and experts from Africa, Europe, the USA, and Canada. They came from four different human rights organizations: Fédération Internationale des Droits de l'Homme--FLDH based in Paris, Africa Watch (New York, Washington, London), Union Interafricaine des Droits de l'Homme et des Peuples--UJDH (Ouagadougou), and Centre International des Droits de la Personne et du Développment Démocratique- (Montreal).

12. *Kangura*, No. 40, March 1993, 17-18. Quoted by Jean-Pierre Chrétien et al., *Rwanda: Les médias du génocide* (Paris: Editions Karthala, 1995), 155-156. (My translation)

13. *Kangura*, No. 26, December 1993, cover.

14.. Quoted by Jean-Pierre Chrétien et al., *Rwanda: Les médias du génocide* (Paris: Editions Karthala, 1995), 353. (My translation)

15. *Kangura*, No. 21, August 1991, 6-7. Quoted in *Rwanda: Les médias du génocide*, 103. (My translation)

16. Alison Des Forges, *Leave None to Tell the Story: Genocide in Rwanda* (New York, Washington, London, Brussels, Paris: Human Rights Watch/Fédération Internationale des Ligues des Droits de l'Homme, 1999), 65.

17. Roger Mucchielli, *Psychologie de la publicité et de la propagande; connaissance du problème, applications pratiques* (Paris: Entreprise Moderne de l'Edition, 1970).

18. *Leave None to Tell the Story*, 66.

19. See a fictional account of the event in Aimable Twagilimana, *Manifold Annihilation* (A Novel) (New York and Orlando: Rivercross Publishing Inc., 1996), 98-101.

20. Quoted in *Leave None to Tell the Story*, 76

21. Ibid., 66.

22. *Rwanda: Les médias du génocide*, 1995), 168. The authors of this book note that the timing and content of *Kangura Magazine* suggest that it was created to export agitation to neighboring Burundi. The glorification and encouragement of the Hutu (then relatively underground) armed opposition PALIPEHUTU were obvious to readers. Also, several cartoons in both publications showed Pierre Buyoya, president of Burundi, receiving 'democracy' medicine from no other than Hassan Ngeze.

23. *Kangura Magazine*, No.5, January/February 1992, 18. Quoted in *Rwanda: les médias du génocide*, 169. (My translation)

24. Quoted *in Leave None to Tell the Story*, 80

25. In a preemptive move to deny the RPF one of its justifications for invading Rwanda, Habyarimana quickly accepted one of the recommendations of the national commission on political reform, that is, to allow multiparty democracy.

26. As pointed out earlier, before the other parties were allowed to function, everybody was automatically an MRND member, even children and the elderly. Although many people shifted to other parties in 1991, many still kept their MRND membership to be safe. Probably because of confusion, uncer-

tainty, or lack of political maturity, people carried membership cards of several parties.

27. For a detailed and well-informed discussion of the role played by different parties and the multiparty experiment prior to the 1994 genocide, see Gérard Prunier, *The Rwanda Crisis: History of a Genocide*, Chapters 3-5.

28. It was a common joke in 1992 that to become a member of CDR, one had to pass a crucial test: one's noses had to be flat and big enough to allow one's fist to enter them! It seemed that was the way to tell the "Hutu purs et durs" (unsullied and tough Hutu) (of the north and northwest) from the sullied ones (of the south).

29. Each political party had its flag, and members wore hats bearing their party's logo.

30. After the "cellule" (cell), the "secteur" (sector) was the next administrative unit, headed by an elected councilor.

31. Janvier Afrika disclosed this information from his prison cell in Kigali Central prison in January 1993. He was interned, he said, because he had betrayed the "death squad." He was interviewed by members of an international investigation commission composed of four human rights groups: Africa Watch, Fédération Internationale des Droit de l'Homme, Union Interafricaine des Droits de l'Homme et des Peuples, and Centre International des Droits de la Personne et du Développement Démocratique.

32. *Rapport de la Commission Internationale d'Enquête sur les Violations des Droits de l'Homme au Rwanda depuis le 1er Octobre 1990 (7-21 janvier 1993)*, published in March 1993 by Africa Watch, Fédération Internationale des Droit de l'Homme, Union Interafricaine des Droits de l'Homme et des Peuples, and Centre International des Droits de la Personne et du Développement Démocratique, 33 (my translation).

33. *Africa Watch* (volume 5, No.7, 7-8.

34. For a complete listing of newspapers and their ideological affiliations, see J. P. Chrétien et al., *Rwanda: Les médias du génocide* (Paris: Editions Karthala, 1995), 383-386.

35. André Sibomana, *Hope for Rwanda: Conversations with Laure Guilbert and Hervé Deguine* (London: Pluto Press, 1997), 49-50. A catholic priest, André Sibomana was at the time of this statement the editor of the most respected newspaper *Kinyamateka* and the Vice-President of a human rights organization Association pour la Défense des Droits Publics et des Libertés Individuelles (ADL) (created in 1991), of which I was a member from late 1991 to July 1992.

Chapter Five: From Region to Nation: Ordinary Rwandans and the 1994 Genocide

1. *Leave None to Tell the Story: Genocide in Rwanda*, written by Alison Des Forges (New York, Washington, London, Brussels, Paris: Human Rights Watch and International Federation of Human Rights, 1999), 143-172.

2. Ibid., 150-151.

3. Ibid., 155.

4. Ibid., 162.

5. Ibid.. 170.

6. Already in 1991, several months after the RPF successfully attacked Ruhengeri and liberated the prisoners from its infamous prison, the local government started the practice of drawing lists of people to eliminate. Since many Tutsi were already in prison, had been killed, or had fled the region, the different lists were topped by Hutu southerners who were members of the political opposition, especially MDR, which was the most important challenge to MRND's full control of Gisenyi and Ruhengeri. In early 1992, I personally saw one such list, topped by one Dr. Semabinga, a physician at the Ruhengeri hospital. He hailed from the central prefecture of Gitarama and was the chief MDR representative in the city of Ruhengeri. The list comprised the who's who of southern educated men working in Ruhengeri. We southerners regularly received threats of extermination. In March 1992, roadblocks manned by local men were erected in several places along the highway crossing the town of Ruhengeri. One such roadblock was about one hundred yards from the University residence in a neighborhood called "Yaoundé." Any vehicle that bore license plates from prefectures other than Gisenyi and Ruhengeri was stopped and emptied of its content. Some drivers were beaten up. Particularly targeted were the large trucks transporting beer cases and potatoes to the southern regions. A bottle of beer that normally cost one hundred Rwandan francs cost fifteen Rwandan francs at those roadblocks for a least one day. The immigration officer and the secret service representatives in the town of Ruhengeri hailed respectively from Butare and Gikongoro. Despite their official importance, they were dragged from their cars and beaten up by the mobs at the roadblocks. The prefect of Ruhengeri, a member of the Akazu (little house), refused to intervene to rescue them. They escaped, but their beating sent a clear message to the rest of us southerners living in Ruhengeri.

7. February 1994 publication.

8. Quoted in G. Prunier, *The Rwanda Crisis: History of a Genocide* (New York: Columbia University Press, 1995), 222.

9. Quoted in G. Prunier, 223.

10. For a discussion of who might be responsible for the shooting of the plane, see, among other writings, Gérard Prunier, *The Rwanda Crisis*, 213-229; *Leave None to Tell the Story*, 181-192; Filip Reyntjens, Rwanda: *trois jours qui ont fait basculer l'histoire* (Bruxelles: Institut Africain, 1996).

11. *Leave None to Tell the Story*, 104; Prunier, 167; Filip Reyntjens, Rwanda: *Trois jours qui ont fait basculer l'histoire* (ParisL L'Harmattn, 1996), 11-92.

12. Colonel BEMS Théoneste Bagosora, "L'assassinat du Président Habyarimana ou l'ultime opération du Tutsi pour sa reconquête du pouvoir par la force au Rwanda" Yaoundé, Cameroun, October 30, 1995, 7.

13. *Les médias du génocide*, 136.

14. Bagosora, "L'assassinat du Président Habyarimana" 12-13, as quoted *in Leave None to Tell the Story*, 105.

15. As quoted in *Time International*
<http:/www.time.com/time/international/1996/960610/rwanda.html>
16. Ibid.
17. *Leave None to Tell the Story*, 104.
18. Bruce D. Jones, *Peacemaking in Rwanda: The Dynamics of Failure* (Boulder and London: Lynne Rienner Publishers), 38.
19. *Time International*, <http://www.insite.fr/intedit/2000dec/rwanda10.html>
20. Ibid.
21. For an informed and detailed account of the involvement of these different groups, see *Leave None to Tell the Story*, 180-262.
22. Ibid., 231.
23. This was the expression that one was likely to read or hear in international news outlets as the genocide was taking place.
24. See, for example, Mamdani, *When Victims Become Killers*.
25. See Josias Semujanga, *Récits fondateurs du drame rwandais: discours social, idéologies et stéréotypes,* (Paris: L'Harmattan, 1998).
26. Daniel Goldhagen, *Hitler's Willing Executioners* (New York: A. Knopf, 1996), 416.
27. Ibid., 392.
28. For example, see Robert R. Shandley, ed. *Unwilling Germans? The Goldhagen Debate* (Minneapolis and London: University of Minnesota Press, 1998), 55-73.
29. Christopher R. Browning, "Ordinary Men or Ordinary Germans" in Robert R. Shandley, ed., 59.
30. Daniel Goldhagen, *Hitler's Willing Executioners*, 106.
31. Christopher Browning, 63.
32. Ibid., 64.
33. Ibid.. 65.
34. Ibid., 63-64.
35. See for example, William L. Shirer, *The Rise and Fall of Adolf Hitler.*
36. Daniel Goldhagen, *Hitler's Willing Executioners*, 383-384.
37. Christopher R. Browning, 65.
38. Ibid., 66.
39. Primo Levi, "The Gray Zone" *The Drowned and the Saved* (New York: Vintage International Edition, 1989), 36-37.
40. Ibid.
41. Ibid.. 42.
42. Ibid., 43.
43. Ibid., 44.
44. Ibid.., 46.
45. Ibid., 44.
46. Ibid.
47. Ibid.. 45.
48. Ibid., 47.
49. Ibid., 48.
50. Ibid., 48.

51. Ibid.

52. Ibid., 53.

53. Ibid., 55.

54. Ibid., 62.

55. Ibid., 63.

56. Ibid.

57. Josias Semujanga, *Récits fondateurs du drame rwandais: discours social, idéologies et stéréotypes* (Paris: l'Harmattan, 1998).

58. Josias Semujanga borrows the terms "seuil d'acceptabilité" from Marc Angenot, *Ce que l'on dit des juifs en 1898. Antisemitisme et discours social* (Paris: Presses Universitaires de Vincennes, 1989).

59. In May 1999, the Secretary-General of the United Nations appointed a special inquiry team comprising Ingvar Carlsson (former Prime Minister of Sweden), Han Sung-Joo (former Foreign Minister of the Republic of Korea) and retired Lieutenant-General Rufus M. Kupolati (of Nigeria) whose mandate was to establish "the facts related to the response of the United nations to the genocide in Rwanda, covering the period of October 1993 to July 1994, and to make recommendations to the Secretary-General on this subject" (Report of the Independent Inquiry, 15 December 1999, 2). The report established that "the international community did not prevent the genocide, nor did it stop the killing once the genocide had begun. (...) The failure of the United Nations to prevent, and subsequently, to stop the genocide in Rwanda was a failure of the United Nations system as a whole. The fundamental failure was the lack of resources and political commitment devoted to developments in Rwanda and to the United Nations presence there" (Report of the Independent Inquiry, 15 December 1999, 1).

60. Josias Semujanga, *Récits fondateurs du drame rwandais: discours social, idéologies et stéréotypes* (Paris: l'Harmattan, 1998), 13.

61. Ibid., 13 (my translation).

62. Christopher C. Taylor, *Sacrifice as Terror : The Rwandan Genocide of 1994* (Oxford and New York : Berg, 1999), 159.

63. The enormity of this change was unacceptable for the military and the administration, overwhelmingly dominated by people from Gisenyi and Ruhengeri, which had disproportionately benefited from the regime since 1973. It should be noted that in the absence of a developed private sector, the administration is the main source of capital production, distribution, and consumption. The political economy of the Rwandan situation rarely figures in the analysis of the causes of genocide, along with regionalism, which was more alarming than ethnic considerations between 1973 and 1990.

64. Josias Semujanga, 15. (My translation)

65. Semujanga's argument assumes normal conditions of communication. The period between 1990 and 1994 was exactly the opposite: massacres in different parts of the country, terror, intimidation, and relentless propaganda against the Tutsi and the Hutu of the political opposition produced a different situation of communication whereby the sender of the message did not act on a premise of shared values but was interested in coercing consent.

66. Ibid, 48.

67. International Panel of Eminent Personalities (IPEP), Special Report on Rwanda, July 2000.
http://www.oua-oua.org/Document/ipep/report/rwanda-e/EN-14-CH.htm.>
68. *Rwanda: Death, Despair, and Defiance*. African Rights report. Revised 1995 Edition (London: 1995), 56.
69. Ibid., 115.
70. Ibid.
71. Ibid.
72. Ibid., 115.
73. *Leave None to Tell the Story*, 509.
74. Docteur Catherine Bonnet, "Le viol des femmes survivantes du génocide au Rwanda." *Rwanda: génocide du XXè siècle,* 17-29.
75. See, for example, Aimable Twagilimana, *Manifold Annihilation* (a novel) (New York and Orlando: Rivercross Publishing, 1996), 135-136.
76. Human Rights Watch/FIDH, *Shattered Lives*, 24.
77. Human Rights Watch/FIDH, *Leave None to Tell the Story: Genocide in Rwanda*, written by Alison Des Forges, 215.
78. Catherine Bonnet, "le viol des femmes survivants du génocide au Rwanda." *Rwanda: génocide du XXè siècle*, 22.
79. Ibid.
80.Tzvetan Todorov, *Facing the Extreme: Moral Life in the Concentration Camp*. Trans. Arthur Denner and Abigail Pollak (New York: Metropolitan books, 1996), 121.
81. Ibid., 121-140.
82. Ibid., 119.
83. Ibid., 122-123.
84. Ibid., 122.
85. Quoted in Todorov, 124.
86. Ibid., 125.
87. Quoted by Todorov, 127: "Theodor Eicke, the great inspiration behind the camp and one of their most aggressive promoters, echoed an idea that Lenin had already formulated in the wake of the October Revolution, 'The obligation to destroy an internal enemy of the State,' Eicke said, 'is in no way different from the obligation to kill your adversary on the battlefield.'" Todorov himself is quoting Rudolf Hoss, *Le commandant d'Auschwitz parle* (The Auschwitz Commander Speaks) (Paris, Maspero, 1979), 101.
88. Todorov, 127.
89. Herman Rauschning, *Hitler Speaks: The Voice of Destruction* (New York: Putnam, 1940), quoted by Todorov, 158.
90. Todorov, 128
91. Ibid.
92. Ibid., 129.
93. Ibid.
94 *Leave None to Tell the Story*, 61; for a complete discussion of the earlier period of the war, see Africa Watch, "Rwanda: Talking Peace and Waging War, Human Rights since the October 1990 Invasion" *A Human Rights Watch Report*, Vol. 4, issue no. 3, February 27, 1992, 20-21.

95. Quoted in *Leave None to Tell the Story*. 62.
96. Ibid.
97. Quoted in G. Prunier, *The Rwanda Crisis*, 77.
98. Ibid., 85
99. *African Rights*, 85.
100. Ibid., 1003.
101. Ibid., 1031-1035.
102. In 1995 I spoke with a genocide survivor from the southern province of Butare (Mugusa commune) whose survival, he said, was the result of Hutu and Tutsi neighbors fighting the Interahamwe together towards the end of April 1994 before their resolve was eventually broken. He eventually crossed the Akanyaru swamps into Burundi and later sought refuge in Canada. See also, *Leave None to Tell the Story*, 496-497. *African Rights*, 1001, 1031-1035.

Conclusion: Remembering the Rwandan Genocide

1. Dominick LaCapra, *History and Memory after Auschwitz* (Ithaca, NY: Cornell University Press), 8.
2. Address by Helmut Kohl, Chancellor of the Federal Republic of Germany, during the Ceremony Marking the 40th Anniversary of the Liberation of the Concentration Camps at the Site of the Former Bergen-Belsen Concentration Camp, April 21, 1985." *Bitburg in Moral and Political Perspective*. Ed. Geoffrey H. Hartman (Bloomington, IN: Indiana University Press, 1986), 244.
3. Ibid.
4. Ibid.
5. "Speech by Richard von Weizsäcker, President of the Federal Republic of Germany, in the Bundestag, during the Ceremony of Commemorating the 40th Anniversary of the End of the War in Europe and of National Socialist Tyranny." *Bitburg in Moral and Political Perspective*, 269.
6. Address by Helmut Kohl, Chancellor of the Federal Republic of Germany, during the Ceremony Marking the 40th Anniversary of the Liberation of the Concentration Camps at the Site of the Former Bergen-Belsen Concentration Camp, April 21, 1985." *Bitburg in Moral and Political Perspective*, 247.
7. Ibid., 249
8. Ibid.
9. Jeffrey Herf, *Divided Memory: The Nazi Past in the Two Germanys* (Cambridge, MA and London: Harvard University Press, 1997).
10. Henry Rousso, *The Vichy Syndrome: History and Memory in France since 1944*. Trans. Arthur Goldhammer (Cambridge, MA and London: Harvard University Press, 1991). This is a translation of the second, revised edition of *Le Syndrome de Vichy: De 1944 à nos jours* (Paris: Editions du Seuil, 1990 [1987]).
11. Ibid., 6
12. Ibid.
13. Ibid.
14. Ibid., 7

15. Ibid., 9
16. Ibid.
17. Ibid., 9-10
18. Henry Rousso, June 22, 1999 addressing a National Endowment for the Humanities Summer Institute in Paris. The topic of the institute was "History, Memory, and Dictatorship: The Legacy of World War II in France, Germany, and Italy" (Paris and Caen, June 21-July 29, 1999). Directors: Richard Joe Golsan and Nathan Bracher of Texas A & M University.
19. Georges Poulet, *Studies in Human Time*, trans. Elliott Coleman (Baltimore: Johns Hopkins University Press, 1956), 36.
20. Lynn Higgins, *New Novel, New Wave, New Politics: Representation of History in Postwar France* (Lincoln, NE and London: University of Nebraska Press, 1996), 27.
21. Henry Rousso, presentation to the NEH Summer Institute, June 22, 1999 in Paris. See also, Maurice Halbwachs, *La mémoire collective*.
22. Henry Rousso, *The Vichy Syndrome*, 10.
23. Ibid.
24. NEH communication, Paris, 6/23/99.
25. NEH communication, Paris, 6/23/99. Rousso argued that de Gaulle's purpose was not to unify ideologically all the resistance groups but to put them under his control.
26. NEH communication, Paris, 6/23/99.
27. Pierre Nora, Preface to the English Language Edition of his *Rethinking the French Past of Memory*. Trans. Arthur Goldhammer (New York: Columbia University Press, 1996), xvii.
28. "Remarks of Elie Wiesel at Ceremony for Jewish Heritage Week and Presentation of Congressional Gold Medal, White House, April 19, 1985." *Bitburg in Moral and Political Perspective*, 241.
29. Ibid.
30. Ibid.
31. Ibid., 242.
32. Ibid.
33. Ibid., 243.
34. Ibid.
35. Ibid.
36. Jean-Philippe Schreiber, "le génocide, la mémoire et l'histoire." Raymond Verdier, Emmanuel Decaux, & Jean-Pierre Chrétien, eds. *Rwanda: un génocide du XXè siècle* (Paris: l'Harmattan, 1995), 165-182.
37. Ibid., 170.
38. Ibid., 176.
39. *Les livres du souvenir, mémoriaux juifs de Pologne* (Paris: Gallimard-Julliard,1983), 15.

Bibliography

Adelman, Howard & Astri Suhreke, eds. *The Path of a Genocide: The Rwandan Crisis from Uganda to Zaire.* New Brunswick (USA) and London (UK): Transaction Publishers, 1999.

ADL. *Rapport sur les Droits de l'Homme au Rwanda--Septembre 1991-Septembre 1992.* Kigali: Pallotti-Press, 1992.

Andreopoulos, George L., ed. *Genocide: Conceptual and Historical Dimensions.* Philadelphia: University of Pennsylvania Press, 1994.

Bauer, Yehuda. *The Holocaust in Historical Perspective.* Seattle: University of Washington Press, 1978.

Bledsoe, Robert L. & Boleslaw A. Boczek. *The International Law Dictionary.* Santa Barbara, CA & Oxford, England: ABC-Clio, Inc., 1987.

Braeckman, Colette. *Human Rights Watch: Qui a armé le Rwanda? Chronique d'une tragédie annoncée.* Bruxelles: GRIP, 1994.

---. *Rwanda: Histoire d'un génocide.* Paris: Fayard, 1994.

Braeckman, Colette, et al. *Kabila prend le pouvoir: les premices d'une Chute : la campagne victorieuse de l'ADFL—le Congo d'aujourd'hui.* Bruxelles: GRIP, 1998.

Browning, Christopher R. *The Path to Genocide: Essays on Launching the Final Solution.* Cambridge and New York: Cambridge University Press, 1992.

Bücher, Michel. *Rwanda: mémoire d'un génocide.* Paris: le cherche midi éditeur, 1996.

Cairns, Edmund. *A Safer Future: Reducing the Human Cost of War.* Oxfam, 1997.

Carr, Rosamond Halsey. *Land of a Thousand Hills: My Life in Rwanda.* Harmondsworth: Viking Penguin, 1999.

Césaire, Aimé. "Discourse on Colonialism." *Colonial Discourse and Postcolonial Theory: A Reader.* Ed. Williams Patrick and Laura Chrisman, eds. New York: Columbia University Press, 1994.172-180.

Chalk, Frank & Kurt Jonassohn. *The History and Sociology of Genocide: Analyses and Case Studies.* New Haven & London: Yale University Press, 1990.

Chrétien, Jean-Pierre. *Le défi de l'ethnisme--Rwanda et Burundi : 1990-1996.* Paris : Karthala, 1997.

Chrétien, Jean-Pierre, et al. *Rwanda: les médias du génocide.* Paris: Editions Karthala, 1995.

Cohen, Ronald. ed. *From Tribe to Nation in Africa--Studies in Incorporation Processes.* Scranton, PA: Chandler Publishing Company, 1970.

Dawidowicz, Lucy S. *The Holocaust and the Historians.* Cambridge: Harvard University Press, 1981.

Des Forges, Alison. *Leave None to Tell the Story: Genocide in Rwanda.* New York and Paris: Human Rights Watch & International Federation of Human Rights, 1999.

Destexhe, Alain. *Rwanda and Genocide in the Twentieth Century.* Trans. Alison Marschner. New York: New York University Press, 1995.

De Tocqueville, Alexis. *The Old Regime and the French Revolution.* Garden City: Doubleday Anchor Books, 1955.

Du Toit, Brian M. ed. *Ethnicity in Modern Africa.* Boulder, Colorado: Westview Press, 1978.

Eley, Geoff, ed. *The "Goldhagen Effect": History, Memory, Nazism—Facing the German Past.* Ann Arbor: The University of Michigan Press, 2000.

Fentres, James, and Chris Wickham. *Social Memory.* Oxford: Blackwell, 1992.

Fontette, François. *Le racisme. Que Sais-Je?* Paris: Presses universtaires de France, 1985.

Forbes, H. D. *Ethnic Conflict : Commerce, Culture, and the Contact Hypothesis.* New Haven & London: Yale University Press, 1997.

Freeman, Charles. *Crisis in Rwanda.* Austin, TX: Raintree Steck-Vaugh Publishers, 1999.

Friedlander, Saul. *Memory, History and the Extermination of the Jews of Europe*. Bloomington and Indianapolis: Indiana University Press, 1993.

Gamst, Frederick C. & Edward Norbeck. eds. *Ideas of Culture, Sources and Uses*. New York: Holt, Rinehart & Winston, 1976.

Gellately, Robert. *Backing Hitler: Consent and Coercion in Nazi Germany*. Oxford: Oxford University Press, 2001.

Gillis, John, ed. *Commemorations: The Politics of National Identity*. Princeton: Princeton University Press, 1994.

Goldhagen, Daniel J. *Hitler's Willing Executioners: Ordinary Germans and the Holocaust*. New York: Alfred A. Knopf, 1996.

Gourevitch, Philip. *We Wish to Inform You that Tomorrow We Will Be Killed with our Families. Stories from Rwanda*. New York: Farrar   Strauss and Giroux, 1998.

Grosser, Alfred. *Le Crime et la Mémoire*. Paris: Flammarion, 1989.

Hartman, Geoffrey H., ed. *Bitburg in Moral and Political Perspective*. Bloomington: Indiana University Press, 1986.

Horowitz, Donald L. *Ethnic Groups in Conflict*. Berkeley, Los Angeles, London: University of California Press, 1985.

Huntington, Samuel P. *The Clash of Civilizations and the Remaking of World Order*. New York: Simon & Schuster, 1996.

Huxley, Julian & A.C. Haddon. *We Europeans: A Survey of "Racial" Problems*. London: Penguin Books Ltd., 1939.

Isaacs, H.R. *Idols of the Tribe*. New York: Harper & Row, 1975.

Johnson, Eric A. *Nazi Terror: the Gestapo, Jews, and Ordinary Germans*. New York: Basic Books, 1999.

Jones, Bruce D. *Peacemaking in Rwanda: The Dynamics of Failure*. Boulder and London: Lynne Rienner Publishers, 2001.

Kagame, Alexis. "La poésie du Rwanda" *Compte-rendu des travaux du séminaire d'anthropologie sociale*. Astrida: IRSAC, 1952.

Kajeguhakwa, Valens. *Rwanda : De la Terre de Paix à la Terre de Sang. Et Après*. Paris : Editions Remi Perrin, 2001.

Kammen, Michael. *Mystic Chords of Memory: The Transformation of Tradition in American Culture*. New York: A. Knopf, 1991.

Kamukama, Dixon. *Rwanda Conflict: Its Roots and Regional Implications*. 2nd edition. Kampala: Fountain Publishers, 1997.

Keane, Fergal. *Season of Blood: A Rwanda Journey*. Harmondsworth: Viking Penguin, 1995.

Kellas, James G. *The Politics of Nationalism and Ethnicity*. New York: St. Martin's Press, 1991.

Kuperman, Alan J. *The Limits of Humanitarian Intervention: Genocide in Rwanda*. Washington, D.C.: Brookings Institution Press, 2001.

LaCapra, Dominick. *History and Memory after Auschwitz*. Ithaca, NY: Cornell University Press, 1998.

Landesman, Peter. "A Woman's Work" *The New York Times*, September 15, 2002.
<http://www.nytimes.com/2002/09/15/magazine/15RWANDA.html>

Langer, Lawrence L. *Holocaust Testimonies: The Ruins of Memory*. New Haven and London: Yale University Press, 1991.

Lemarchand, René. *Burundi: Ethnic Conflict and Genocide*. New York: Woodrow Wilson Center Press and Cambridge University Press, 1995.

---. *Rwanda and Burundi*. New York, Washington, and London: Praeger Publishers, 1970.

Levi, Primo. *The Drowned and the Saved*. Trans. Raymond Rosenthal. New York: Summit Books, 1985.

---. *The Reawakening*. Trans. Stuart Woolf. New York: Collier-McMillan, 1965.

---. "Afterword." Trans. Ruth Feldman. *The Reawakening*. Trans. Stuart Woolf, 195-217.

Levinson, David, ed. *Ethnic Relations: A Cross-Cultural Encyclopedia of the Human Experience (series)*. Santa Barbara, Denver, & Oxford: ABC-CLIO, 1994.

Mamdani, Mahmood. *When Victims Become Killers: Colonialism, Nativism, and the Genocide in Rwanda*. Princeton, NJ: Princeton University Press, 2001.

Markusen, Eric & David Kopf. *The Holocaust and Strategic Bombing: Genocide and Total War in the 20th Century*. Boulder: Westview Press, 1995.

Marrus, Michael R. *The Holocaust in History*. New York: Meridian, 1987.

Massey, Irving. *Identity and Community: Reflections on English, Yiddish, and French Literature in Canada*. Detroit: Wayne State University Press, 1994.

Mayo, James M. *War Memorials as Political Landscape in the American Experience*. New York: Praeger, 1988.

McCullum, Hugh. *The Angels Have Left Us: The Rwandan Tragedy and the Churches*. Geneva: World Council of Churches, 1995.

Making Peace. Teaching about Conflict and Reconciliation. Oxfam, 1997 [a resource pack]

Malinowski, Bronislaw. *Magic, Science and Religion and Other Essays*.

New York: Doubleday Anchor Books, 1954.

Maquet, Jacques. "Societal and Cultural Incorporation in Rwanda." Ronald Cohen (1970), 201-216.

Maquet, Jacques. *The Premise of Inequality*. London/New York: Oxford University Press, 1961.

Mecklenburg, Adolphys Frederick. *In the Heart of Africa*. London: Cassell, 1910.

Melvern, Linda R. *A People Betrayed: The Role of the West in Rwanda's Genocide*. London and New York: Zed Books, 2000.

Meyer, Hans. *Die Barundi*. Leipzig: Otto Spamer, 1916.

Milton, Sybil. *In Fitting Memory: The Art and Politics of Holocaust Memorials*. Detroit: Wayne State University, 1991.

---. *Collective Remembering*. Newbury Park and London: Sage Publication, 1990.

Myrdal, Gunnar. *An American Dilemma--The Negro Problem and Modern Democracy*. New York: Harper & Brothers, 1944.

Nadel, Siefried F. *The Nuba: an Anthropological Study of the Hill Tribes in Kordofan*. London: Oxford University Press, 1947.

Nagel, Olzak. "The Ethnic Revolution: Emergence of Ethnic Nationalism." *Ethnic Canada*, ed. Leo Driedger. Toronto: Copp Clark Pitman, 1987, 28-43.

Newbury, Catherine. *The Cohesion of Oppression: Clientship and Ethnicity in Rwanda, 1860-1960*. New York: Columbia University Press, 1988.

Nkundabagenzi, Fidèle, ed. *Rwanda Politique*. Bruxelles: CRISP, 1961.

Nora, Pierre. "Between Memory and History: les lieux de mémoire." Trans. Marc Rondebuch. *Representations* 26 (1989): 13-25.

Nyankazi, Edward L. *Genocide: Rwanda and Burundi*. Rochester, VT: Achenkman Books, Inc., 1998.

Perugia, Pierre del. *Les derniers rois mages*. Paris: Phoebus, 1978.

Prunier, Gérard. *The Rwanda Crisis: History of a Genocide*. New York: Columbia University Press, 1995.

Olzak, Suzan & Joane Nagel. eds. *Competitive Ethnic Relations*. Orlando: Academic Press, 1986.

Pollis, Adamantia and Peter Schwab, eds. *Human Rights: New Perspectives, New Realities*. Boulder and London: Lynne Rienner Publishers, 2000.

Pomeray, J. K. *Rwanda. (Series: Places and Peoples of the World]*. New York: Chelsea House Publishers, 1988.

Rapport de la Commission Internationale d'Enquete sur les Violations des Droits de l'Homme au Rwanda depuis Octobre 1990. Africa

Watch et al., Mars 1993.

Report of the Independent Inquiry into the Actions of the United Nations During the 1994 Genocide in Rwanda. UN, 15 Dec. 1999. (Ingvar Carlsson, Hang Sung-Joo, and Rufus M. Kupolati).

Reyntjens, Filip. *Rwanda: trois jours qui ont fait basculer l'histoire.* Paris: L'Harmattan, 1995.

---. *L'Afrique des Grands Lacs en Crise, Rwanda-Burundi 1990-1994.* Paris: Karthala, 1994.

Rwanda, Death, Despair and Defiance, compiled and published by African Rights, London. Second edition. 1995.

Rieff, David. "Problematizing Evil." *The New Republic,* May 21, 2001, 42-47. Review of Mahmood Mamdani, *When Victims Become Killers: Colonialism, Nativism, and the Genocide in Rwanda.*

Santer, Eric L. *Stranded Objects: Mourning and Memory and Film in Postwar Germany.* Ithaca, New York: Cornell University Press, 1990.

Schama, Simon. *Landscape and Memory.* New York: A. Knopf, 1995.

Schwarz, Daniel R. *Imagining the Holocaust.* New York: St Martin's Press, 1999.

Semujanga, Josias. *Récits fondateurs du drame rwandais: Discours social,   idéologies et stéréotypes.* Paris: L'Harmattan, 1998.

Shandley, Robert, ed. *Unwilling Germans? The Goldhagen Debate.* Minneapolis and London: University of Minnesota Press, 1998.

Shattered Lives: Sexual Violence During the Rwandan Genocide and its Aftermath. New York, Washington, London, and Brussels: Human Rights Watch/Africa and International Federation of Human Rights Leagues, 1996.

Shirer, William L. *The Rise and Fall of Adolf Hitler.* New York: Random House, 1961.

Smith, Pierre. *Le récit populaire au Rwanda.* Paris : Armand Colin, 1975.

Speke, John. *Journal of the Discovery of the Source of the Nile.* London: 1863.

Taylor, Christopher C. *Sacrifice as Terror: The Rwandan Genocide of 1994.* Oxford and New York: Berg, 1999.

The Norton Anthology of African American Literature, ed. Henry Louis Gates and Nellie Y. McKay. New York: W. W. Norton & Co., 1997.

Tocqueville, Alexis de. *The Old Regime and the French Revolution.* Trans. Stuart Gilbert. New York: Doubleday, 1955.

Todorov, Tzvetan. *Facing the Extreme: Moral Life in the Concentration*

Camp. Trans. Arthur Denner and Abigail Pollak. New York: Metropolitan Books, 1996.

Totten, Samuel & William S. Parsons & Israel W. Charny. *Century of Genocide: Eyewitness Accounts and Critical Views.* New York & London: Garland, 1997.

Twagilimana, Aimable. *Manifold Annihilation (A Novel)*. New York & Orlando: Rivercross, 1996.

---. *In Their Own Voices: Teenage Refugees from Rwanda Speak Out.* New York: Rosen Publishing Group, 1997.

---. *Race and Gender in the Making of an African American Literary Tradition*. New York & London: Garland, 1997.

---. *The Heritage Library of African People: Hutu and Tutsi*. New York: Rosen Publishing Group, 1998.

U.S. Committee for Refugees. *Transition in Burundi--the Context for Homecoming*. Washington, D.C.: American Council for Nationalities Services, September 1993.

Uvin, Peter. *Aiding Violence: The Development Enterprise in Rwanda*. West Hartford, CT: Kumarian press, 1998.

Vassal-Adams, Guy. *Rwanda: An Agenda for International action*. Oxfam Insight, 1994.

Verdier, Raymond, Emmanuel Decaux, and Jean-Pierre Chrétien, eds. *Rwanda: un génocide du XXè siècle.* Paris: L'Harmattan, 1995.

Vershave, François-Xavier. *Complicité de genocide? La politique de la France au Rwanda.* Paris XIII: Editions la Découverte, 1994.

Waller, David. *Rwanda: Which Way Now?* Second edition. Oxfam, 1996.

Walter, Paul A.F. *Race and Culture Relations*. New York: McGraw-Hill Book Co., 1952.

Warner, M. Lloyd & Leo Srole. *The Social System of American Ethnic Groups*. New Haven: Yale University Press, 1965.

Wiesel, Elie. *Night*. Trans. Stella Rodway. New York: Bantam Books, 1982. [Initially published in French in Paris by Les Editions de Minuit, 1958]

Wiesel, Elie, et al.. *Dimensions of the Holocaust : Lectures at Northwestern University*. Evanston, Il: Northwestern University Press, 1977.

Willame, Jean-Claude. *Aux sources de l'hécatombe rwandaise*. Paris: L'Harmattan, 1995.

Williams Patrick and Laura Chrisman, eds. *Colonial Discourse and Postcolonial Theory: A Reader*. New York: Columbia University Press, 1994.

Wood, William B. "Geographic Aspects of Genocide: A Comparison of

Bosnia and Rwanda." *Transactions of the Institute of British Geographers*, New Series, Volume 26, Number 1, 2001. 57-75.

Young, James E. *Writing and Rewriting the Holocaust: Narrative and the Consequences of Interpretation*. Bloomington and Indianapolis: Indiana University Press, 1988.

---. *Holocaust Memorials and Meaning: The Texture of Memory*. New Haven: Yale University Press, 1993.

Index